ESP 系列精品教材(第一辑)

Practice of International Trade

国际贸易实务

主 编 阮绩智

副主编 管春林 李克莉

ZHEJIANG UNIVERSITY PRESS
浙江大学出版社

图书在版编目（CIP）数据

国际贸易实务/阮绩智主编．—杭州：浙江大学出版社，2008.1(2013.7 重印)
（ESP 系列精品教材）
ISBN 978-7-308-05745-5

Ⅰ.国… Ⅱ.阮… Ⅲ.国际贸易－贸易实务－高等学校－教材 Ⅳ.F740.4

中国版本图书馆 CIP 数据核字（2007）第 204500 号

国际贸易实务
阮绩智 主编

责任编辑 杜玲玲
封面设计 俞亚彤
出版发行 浙江大学出版社
（杭州市天目山路 148 号 邮政编码 310007）
（网址：http://www.zjupress.com）
排　　版 杭州中大图文设计有限公司
印　　刷 富阳市育才印刷有限公司
开　　本 787mm×960mm 1/16
印　　张 19.75
字　　数 376 千
版 印 次 2008 年 1 月第 1 版 2013 年 7 月第 3 次印刷
书　　号 ISBN 978-7-308-05745-5
定　　价 30.00 元

浙江大学出版社发行部联系方式：0571－88925591；http://zjdxcbs.tmall.com

ESP系列精品教材(第一辑)

序

专门用途英语(ESP)教学作为一种特殊的外语教学模式,大概肇始于16世纪欧洲宗教改革时代,至今已有数百年历史。当时的英国政府对来自欧洲大陆的受宗教迫害的移民进行商务英语教育,以帮助其尽快适应市场经济相对发达的英国生活。从此,以探索英语在各行业中使用的特殊性和规律性的教学与研究便有了开端。20世纪50年代始,高科技的迅猛发展使科技英语教育在西方盛行。而在我国,对英语专业学生系统开设专门用途英语类课程的历史还相对较短。在我国,近十几年外贸经济的迅猛发展对英语教学较早地提出了改革的需求。从20世纪90年代中期开始,为应对地方社会经济建设对应用型外语人才的需要,许多大学系统地开设了专门用途类课程,专门用途英语教材也作为重点建设教材推出,这些都有力地促进了英语教学的改革。如今,专门用途英语教学已成为外语人才培养中广为采用的教学模式。以探索行业英语特殊性和规律性的专门用途英语课程成为各个层面外语教学的必选课程,并在涉外人才培养中起到了非常重要的作用。

专门用途英语类课程融知识性和实践性为一体,拓宽了传统的英语专业人才培养模式。在知识领域,这类课程以英语为工具,涉及多种学科领域,融多家之说,炼自身之长,使学生能在学好英语的同时,了解多种学科知识,为其实现学科交叉、获得国际视野创造条件。在实践层面,这类课程突破传统外语教学以培养人文素质为目的的局限,通过仿真甚至真实的场景,为学生提供英语在各个行业中使用的特殊形态和内在规律。

在专门用途英语课程的建设上,国内仍处在探索阶段。这表现在教材方面,有的是以语言训练为核心,有的是以相关专业的基础知识介绍为核心。可以这样理解,专门英语教材的特殊性就在于它应当是以相关专业知识为载体的语言教学材料,其教学目的是帮助学生掌握英语在各行各业中使用时所产生的特殊的功能语体及其规律,进而增强在各行各业中运用英语进行交际的能力。

这套"ESP系列精品教材"就是本着这一思路编写的。本丛书是多所高校一直在专门用途英语教学方面孜孜研究的诸位教师的经验与智慧的结晶,其编写理念、体例及内容均经过大家多次商讨。希望读者能提出宝贵意见,以使本丛书臻于完美。

总主编

2006年1月20日

前言

经济全球化和中国加入世界贸易组织这个国际经贸大家庭给我们带来巨大的发展机遇和严峻挑战。逼人的形势不仅要求我国企业在国际经营活动中必须遵守国际商务规则和惯例，同时对国际商务从业人员和在校学生的专业知识和外语素质提出了更高的要求。为了适应新形势的需要，近年来，许多高等院校都开设了商务英语专业(方向)或在英语专业课程中开设商务英语课程，旨在把国际商务专业知识与英语技能相结合，培养既通英语又懂商务的复合型、实用型人才。《国际贸易实务》(英文)一书正是基于此需求而编写的，目的是让学生在国际商务英语的语境中系统学习、掌握国际贸易实务的基本知识，学习英语在该语境中的特殊语体，增强其直接使用英语从事国际贸易的能力。

《国际贸易实务》是一门主要研究国际商品交换的基本知识、基本规则和具体操作技术的学科,也是一门具有国际商务活动特点的实践性很强的综合性、应用性课程。对于国贸和商务英语专业学生，该课程是骨干支撑课程。通过该课程的学习，掌握国际贸易基础知识，了解国际贸易业务的基本操作环节和有关的国际贸易惯例和法规，从而具备从事国际贸易业务的基本能力。同时，培养学生从事国内国际经营的兴趣及市场意识，拓展知识，开阔视野，启发思维，并为后续商务英语课的学习打好基础。

本书编者长期从事商务英语教学，具有丰富的国际贸易理论、实践及外语教学经验，使本书更具有实用性、针对性和可读性。与其他同类教材相比，本书的主要特点是:

1. 突出以读者为本的基本编写理念，注重知识性、实用性、针对性、实践性相结合，体现“简明、新颖、实用”的原则。

2. 强调专业基础，重视语言运用。本书各章精心设计了形式多样、素材广泛的练习题。其中既有对原文知识的理解练习，如选择和判断题，也包括词汇如关键术语和词语的强化练习，还有讨论题和案例分析等。通过练习检查、复习和巩固所学的内容。更重要的是，课文为学习者提供了大量实用的专用语言输入和模仿，也为学习者提供了语言实践机会，从而提高英语语言交际能力。

3. 本书由长期从事大学商务英语教学及具有丰富国际贸易实践经验的教师编写，课程内容和语言方面都经过精选和斟酌，并充分考虑到教学对象、学生需求、学习时数等诸多教与学的因素，力求快捷高效、重点突出、学以致用。

4. 本书涉及国际贸易最新知识，采用现代商务英语编写，语言地道，通俗易懂。同时对关键术语和词语附有详尽的中文注释，帮助学习者更好地理解和掌握国际贸易专业知识。

本书可供高校国际贸易、国际商务、英语等专业高年级学生作为复合型专业英语教材使用，也可用作全国国际商务英语等级考试、外销员等专业人员职业资格考试的备考用书。同时对于国际贸易从业者和有一定英语基础并有志从事国际贸易工作的人员也是一本颇具实用性和参考性的指导书。

编者结合自己多年的教学经验为本书编写了配套的教学课件和练习答案。如有需要者请联系浙江大学出版社发行科，或电邮至 dll@zju.edu.cn。

在编写过程中，编者参考并借鉴了国内外近年来出版的许多有关书籍和资料，以及国际商会、世贸组织、国际著名公司等网站和其他商业网站，获益良多，在此表示衷心的谢忱！

本书由阮绩智策划、拟订大纲并负责全书的总纂。参加本书编写的还有管春林、陶正桔、李克莉、李勇、陈冀、张彦和汪瑾。由于编者知识面及水平有限，错误疏漏之处在所难免，恳请各位专家、同仁和广大读者不吝赐教，以便今后进一步修改完善。

编　者

2007 年 11 月于杭州

CONTENTS 目 录

CHAPTER

1 Introduction to International Trade ·················1 国际贸易导论

1.1 What Is International Trade? /2
1.2 Why International Trade? /3
1.3 Benefits of International Trade /4
1.4 Barriers to International Trade /4
1.5 Basic International Trade Theories /7
1.6 International Organizations in International Trade /12
1.7 Laws and Regulations Governing International Trade /14
1.8 Vocabulary Check /17
1.9 Notes and Key Terms /17
1.10 Follow-up Practice /20

2 Business Negotiation and Conclusion of the Contract ·················25 交易磋商与合同订立

2.1 Form and Contents of Business Negotiation /26
2.2 General Procedures of Business Negotiation /28
2.3 Conclusion of the Contract /32
2.4 Form and Contents of the Contract 33
2.5 Vocabulary Check 35
2.6 Notes and Key Terms 36
2.7 Follow-up Practice 37

3 Quality and Quantity of Goods……………………41
商品的品质与数量

3.1 Name of Commodity /42
3.2 Quality of Goods /43
3.3 Quality Clause of the Contract /46
3.4 Quantity of Goods /47
3.5 Quantity Clause of the Contract /50
3.6 Vocabulary Check /51
3.7 Notes and Key Terms /52
3.8 Follow-up Practice /54

4 Packing and Marking……………………………59
包装与标志

4.1 Functions of Packing /60
4.2 Types of Packing /63
4.3 Product Code /66
4.4 Neutral Packing /67
4.5 Marking of Goods /67
4.6 Packing Clause of the Contract /72
4.7 Vocabulary Check /74
4.8 Notes and Key Terms /74
4.9 Follow-up Practice /76

5 International Trade Terms…………………………81
国际贸易术语

5.1 International Trade Terms /82
5.2 Introduction to Incoterms 2000 /82
5.3 Use of Incoterms /83
5.4 The Structure of Incoterms 2000 /84
5.5 Modes of Transport of Incoterms /85
5.6 Notes on Incoterms /86
5.7 The Most Frequently Used Trade Terms /88
5.8 Vocabulary Check /98
5.9 Notes and Key Terms /98
5.10 Follow-up Practice /100

6 International Cargo Transport······105

国际货物运输

6.1 Modes of Transport /106
6.2 General Considerations on Cargo Transport /114
6.3 Major Transport Documents /115
6.4 Clause of Shipment /118
6.5 Vocabulary Check /120
6.6 Notes and Key Terms /120
6.7 Follow-up Practice /123

7 Cargo Transport Insurance······127

货物运输保险

7.1 Fundamental Principles of Cargo Insurance /128
7.2 Risks and Losses in Cargo Transport /130
7.3 Ocean Marine Insurance under C.I.C. /134
7.4 Insurance of Land, Air and Parcel Post Transport /137
7.5 Insurance Practice of International Trade /138
7.6 Vocabulary Check /142
7.7 Notes and Key Terms /143
7.8 Follow-up Practice /145

8 International Payments······149

国际支付

8.1 Payment Amount /150
8.2 Payment Currency /150
8.3 Payment Instruments /152
8.4 Payment Methods /157
8.5 Vocabulary Check /171
8.6 Notes and Key Terms /172
8.7 Follow-up Practice /175

9 Inspection, Claims, Force Majeure and Arbitration ……181 检验、索赔、不可抗力和仲裁

9.1 Commodity Inspection /182
9.2 Claims /185
9.3 Force Majeure /187
9.4 Arbitration /189
9.5 Vocabulary Check /192
9.6 Notes and Key Terms /192
9.7 Follow-up Practice /195

10 Performance of the Contract ……199 进出口合同的履行

10.1 Export Procedures /200
10.2 Import Procedures /210
10.3 Major Import and Export Documents /216
10.4 Vocabulary Check /221
10.5 Notes and Key Terms /222
10.6 Follow-up Practice /223

Appendix I ……227 附录
United Nations Convention on Contracts for the International Sale of Goods
Appendix II ……254
INCOTERMS 2000: ICC Official Rules for the Interpretation of Trade Terms (Excerpts)
Appendix III ……279
Uniform Customs and Practice for Documentary Credits
ICC Publication No. 600 Effective July 1, 2007
References ……304 参考文献

Chapter One

Introduction to International Trade

Learning Objectives

At the end of this chapter, you should be able to understand:

- the concept of and reasons for international trade
- barriers to international trade
- basic international trade theories
- international organizations involved in international trade
- laws and regulations governing international trade

The world has a long, rich history of international trade among nations that can be traced back to the earliest civilizations. It is recognized that trade can be tied directly to an improved quality of life for the citizens of all the partners. If you walk into a supermarket and are able to buy Swiss watches, Brazilian coffee and a bottle of French wine, you are experiencing the effects of international trade. Today, the practice of trade among nations is growing by leaps and bounds. There is hardly a person on earth who has not been influenced in some way by the growing trade among nations.

1.1 What Is International Trade?

Foreign trade refers to the activities of exchanging of goods or service between a country or region and other countries or regions. Viewed from the international sphere, the exchanges of goods and services across international boundaries or territories are worldwide trade transactions, which is also known as international trade or world trade. In most countries, it represents a significant share of GDP. While international trade has been present throughout much of history, its economic, social, and political importance has been on the rise in recent centuries. Industrialization, advanced transportation, globalization, multinational corporations, and outsourcing are all having a major impact. Increasing international trade is the primary meaning of "globalization".

International trade activities include wide range of things. In addition to the traditional form of international trade, it also includes economic and technological cooperation. The traditional form of international trade is composed of the import and export of commodities and can be understood as the import and export of tangible commodities or products because their movements across national borders are visible to observe, thus being called "visible trade". Exporting and importing visible goods makes up the crucial proportion of international economy and is the major source of international revenue and expenditure for most countries.

Broadly speaking, imports also include the so-called invisible imports. That is, the trades of a country include the labor related to transport, insurance, loans, travel, technology and other aspects from other countries. Merchandise export refers to all trade businesses of a country-selling a part of its production and processing of products to another country. In broad terms, exports also include the invisible exports.

In addition to the traditional forms of international trade, the increasing development of international economic cooperation and economic ties between countries are an advanced form. It has greatly enriched and expanded the international trade content and scope of activities.

1.2 Why International Trade?

Why do countries trade? Shouldn't a strong country such as the United States produce all of the computers, television sets, automobiles, cameras, and VCRs it wants rather than import such products from Japan? Why do the Japanese and other countries buy wheat, corn, chemical products, aircraft, manufactured goods, and informational services from such countries as the United States?

Because countries have different natural, human, and capital resources and different ways of combining these resources, they are not equally efficient at producing the goods and services that their residents demand. The decision to produce any product or service has an opportunity cost, which is the amount of another product or service that might otherwise have been produced. Given a choice of producing one product or another, it is more efficient to produce the product with the lower opportunity cost, using the increased production of that product to trade for the product with the higher opportunity cost.

When a country can produce more of a product with the same resources that another country can, it is said to have an absolute advantage in the production of that product. If the second country has an absolute advantage in producing a product that the first country wants, both will be better off if they specialize and trade.

But trade is usually beneficial to both countries even if one has an absolute advantage in the production of both goods that are to be traded. Given any two products, a nation has a comparative advantage in the product with the lower opportunity cost. The terms of trade must be such that both countries lower the opportunity costs of the goods they are getting from the trade.

Why do countries have different opportunity costs? They have different endowments of productive resources—warmer climates and longer growing seasons; more plentiful natural resources such as oil, iron ore, and water; more highly educated and skilled workers; and larger quantities of more sophisticated machinery.

International trade is not static. It has been increasing both in amount and in significance. New supplies of natural resources can be discovered and developed while existing supplies are better managed. Human resources can be improved through better educational programs. Capital resources can be acquired to make the better trained workers even more productive. The increase in international trade should result in more efficient use of the world's scarce resources, and in higher standards of living.

1.3 Benefits of International Trade

There are a number of benefits of international trade. The main benefits can be summarized as follows:

(1) **Goods or Services at a Lower Price**

Countries trade with each other because there is a comparative advantage in cost. So through international trade, countries can buy certain goods or services of the same quality at lower prices. This is the gains from trade. As what the theory of free trade said, trade is beneficial to all the participants. Furthermore, competition in the world market would tend to make prices even lower.

(2) **Goods or Services of Greater Variety**

As is known to all, no nation can produce all the commodities or services that it needs by itself. So international trade provides every country a chance to obtain a wider variety of products for their consumers by trading with each other, and thus help to improve the living standards of the people.

(3) **Promotion of Economic Growth**

International trade can greatly expand the market, which enables the suppliers to take advantage of economies of scale. And the fast development of economies of scale nowadays promotes the economic growth. Therefore, international trade has become more and more important. It helps create jobs that have both economic and political significance. For economies that are highly dependent on international trade, it is crucial for them to keep international trade growing to ensure the development of the economies.

1.4 Barriers to International Trade

It is generally assumed, as the famous economist David Ricardo stated in the nineteenth century, that the free flow of international trade benefits all who participate. In actual practice, however, the world has never had a completely free trading system. This is because every individual country puts controls on trade for the following reasons:

(1) To make up for a deficit on the balance of payment. Such a deficit occurs when the total payments leaving a country are greater than money in receipt entering from abroad. The country then tries to limit imports and increase exports.

(2) To guarantee national security. Countries sometimes restrict exports of critical raw materials, high technology, or equipment when such export might harm its own welfare.

(3) To protect their national industries. Every industry has an infant period. The infant industries need to be shielded from foreign competition during their start-up periods. So a country usually imposes duties on imports of similar foreign goods in order to protect their own national industries against the competition of foreign goods.

Trade barriers can be divided into tariff barrier and non-tariff barriers.

1.4.1 Tariff Barriers

Tariff barriers are the most common form of trade barriers. Tariff barriers restrain foreign goods by means of customs duties, import surcharge and import variable duties. A tariff is a tax levied by the foreign government on goods imported into that country (or import duty). The tariff increases the price at which the goods are sold in the importing country and therefore makes them less competitive with locally produced goods. In this way, the tariff results in the comparative disadvantage of the importing commodities, and thus automatically controls the quantity of a certain imports. Tariffs can be of two types: revenue tariff and protective tariff. A revenue tariff aims to raise money for the government. These tariffs are usually low. A protective tariff is designed to discourage foreign business from shipping certain goods into the country. The basic reason for a protective tariff is to keep out goods that will undersell products made in the home country. For this reason, the protective tariffs are often very high, thereby forcing the foreign business to raise its price to cover the tariff, which makes it easy for domestic firms to compete with these imported goods.

1.4.2 Non-tariff Barriers

Although tariffs have been lowered substantially by international agreements, countries continue to use other devices to limit imports or to increase exports named non-tariff barriers. Non-tariff barriers (NTBs) as defined by the General Agreement on Tariffs and Trade (GATT) allow an importing country to introduce measures which are necessary to protect human, animal or plant life or health. These include quotas, voluntary export restrains, export subsidies and a variety of other regulations and restrictions covering international trade.

(1) **Quota**

A quota is the most important non-tariff trade barrier. It is a direct quantitative restriction on the amount of a commodity allowed to be imported or exported. Historically, the GATT has prohibited import quotas except on agricultural products, as emergency measures, or when a country has short-run balance of payments problems. Countries have circumvented this regulation most notably for textiles, footwear, and automobiles by negotiating (imposing) "voluntary export restraint agreements". Under quotas, if future domestic demand is known, business can subtract the quota and have a reasonable idea of their future production levels. And if domestic demand declined (as it has for autos, textiles, textiles, and footwear), a fixed quota will take up a large percent of the depressed domestic market.

(2) **VERs**

VERs (voluntary export restrains) refer to the case where an importing country induces another nation to reduce its exports of a commodity "voluntarily", under the threat of higher all-round trade restrictions, when these exports threaten an entire domestic industry. Voluntary export restraints have been negotiated since the 1950s by the United States, the European Union, and other industrial nations to curtail exports of textiles, steel, electronic products, automobiles, and other products from Japan, Korea, and other nations. VERs are a kind of export restrictions. They take unjustified export control measures in the name of national security.

(3) **Anti-dumping**

Anti-dumping is a kind of trade remedies; the premise of such practice is that the country must show that its domestic industry has suffered "material" injury by dumped or subsidized imports. Although products at these artificially low prices provide consumers in the importing country with a "good buy", such competition is thought to be "unfair" to domestic producers.

(4) **Export Subsidies**

Export subsidies are direct payments or the granting of tax relief and subsidized loans to the nation's exporters or potential exporters and or low-interest loans to foreign buyers so as to stimulate the nation's exports. As such, export subsidies can be regarded as a form of dumping. Although export subsidies are illegal by international agreement, many nations provide them in disguised and not-so-disguised forms.

(5) **Technical Barriers to Trade**

Technical barriers to trade (TBT) refer to unjustified technical regulations and standards applied to imported products as well as complicated certification and conformity assessment procedure. These include safety regulations for automobile and electrical equipment, health regulations for the hygienic origin and contents. And it also refers to the restrictions resulted from laws requiring governments to buy from domestic suppliers (the so-called government procurement policies). For example, under the "Buy American Act" passed in 1933, U.S. government agencies gave a price advantage of up to 12 percent (50 percent for defense contracts) to domestic United States in order to protect its national industry.

(6) **International Cartels**

An international cartel is an organization of suppliers of a commodity located in different nations (or a group of governments) that agree to restrain output and exports of the commodity in order to maximize the total profits of the organization. The power of international cartels cannot easily be countered because they are not abided by any jurisdiction of any nation. One of the most famous international cartels is OPEC (Organization of Petroleum Exporting Countries), which restricts the production and exports of oil and succeeded in quadrupling the price of crude oil between 1973 and 1974.

1.5 Basic International Trade Theories

1.5.1 Mercantilism

Mercantilism is an economic policy prevailing in Europe during the 16th, 17th, and 18th centuries, under which governmental control was exercised over industry and trade in accordance with the theory that national strength is increased by a preponderance of exports over imports. Mercantilism was characterized not so much by a consistent or formal doctrine as by a set of generally held beliefs. These beliefs included the ideas that exports to foreign countries are preferable both to trade within a country and to imports; that the wealth of a nation depends primarily on the possession of gold and silver; and that governmental interference in the national economy is justified if it tends to implement the attainment of these objectives. The mercantilist approach in economic policy first developed during the growth of national states; efforts were directed toward the elimination of the internal trade barriers that characterized the Middle Ages, when a cargo of commodities might be subject to a toll or tariff at every city and river crossing. Industries were encouraged and assisted in their growth because they provided a source of taxes to support the large armies and other appurtenances of national government. Exploitation of colonies was considered a legitimate method of providing the parent countries with precious metals and with the raw materials on which export industries depended.

Mercantilism, by its very success in stimulating industry and developing colonial areas, soon gave rise to powerful anti-mercantilist pressures. The use of colonies as supply depots for the home economies, and the exclusion of colonies from trade with other nations produced such reactions as the American Revolution, in which the colonists asserted their desire for freedom to seek economic advantage wherever it could be found. At the same time, European industries, which had developed under the mercantile system, became strong enough to operate both without mercantilist protection and in spite of mercantilist limitations. Accordingly, a philosophy of free trade began to take root. Economists asserted that government regulation is justified only to the extent necessary to ensure free markets, because the national advantage represents the sum total of individual advantages, and national well-being is best served by allowing all individuals complete freedom to pursue their economic interests. This viewpoint received its most important expression in The Wealth of Nations (1776) by the Scottish economist Adam Smith.

The free-trade system, which prevailed during the 19th century, began to be curtailed sharply at the beginning of the 20th century in what has been called a revival of elements of mercantilist philosophy, or neo-mercantilism. High protective tariffs were reintroduced, and for political and strategic reasons, great emphasis was put on national self-sufficiency as opposed to national interdependence and a free flow of trade.

1.5.2 Classical Trade Theories

After Mercantilism, the classical trade theories became prevailed in 19th century. Its representatives are Adam Smith's Absolute Advantage Theory and David Ricardo's Comparative Advantage Theory. These are two different ways to describe technology differences. And sometimes these two conceptions can be quite confusing. It is quite common to see misapplications of the principle of comparative advantage. This misconception often leads to erroneous implications such as a fear that technology advances in other countries will cause our country to lose its comparative advantage in everything. As will be shown, this is essentially impossible.

1.5.2.1 The Principle of Absolute Advantage

According to Adam Smith, trade between two nations is based on absolute advantage. When one nation is more efficient than (or has an absolute advantage over) another in the production of one commodity but is less efficient than (or has an absolute disadvantage with respect to) the other nation in producing a second commodity, then both nations can gain by each specializing in the production of the commodity of its absolute advantage and exchanging part of its output with the other nation for the commodity of its absolute disadvantage. By this process, resources are utilized in the most efficient way and the output of both commodities will rise. This increase in the output of both commodities measures the gains from specialization in production available to be divided between the two nations through trade.

A country has an absolute advantage over its trading partners if it is able to produce more of a good or service with the same amount of resources or the same amount of a good or service with fewer resources. In the case of Zambia, the country has an absolute advantage over many countries in the production of copper. This occurs because of the existence of reserves of copper ore or bauxite. We can see that in terms of the production of goods, there are obvious gains from specialization and trade, if Zambia produces copper and exports it to those countries that specialize in the production of other goods or services.

The Theory of Absolute Advantage

Adam Smith

Each country should specialize in the production and export of that good which produces most efficiently, that is, with the fewest labor-hours.

1.5.2.2 The Principle of Comparative Advantage

David Ricardo (1772—1823), in his theory of comparative costs, suggested that countries specialize and trade in goods and services in which they have a comparative advantage. It is easy to see that if countries have an absolute advantage there are advantages to trade. However, what happens if one country has an absolute advantage over its trading partners in the production of a number of goods? Specialization and trade can still result in there being welfare gains made from trade.

A country has a comparative advantage in the production of a good or service that it produces at a lower opportunity cost than its trading partners. Some countries have an absolute advantage in the production of many goods relative to their trading partners. Some have an absolute disadvantage. They are inefficient in producing anything, relative to their trading partners. The theory of comparative costs argues that, put simply, it is better for a country that is inefficient at producing a good or service to specialize in the production of that good it is least inefficient at, compared with producing other goods.

The production possibilities curve (PP curve) can be used to illustrate the principles of absolute and comparative advantage.

Country A has an absolute advantage in the production of both maize and wheat. At all points its PP curve lies to the right of that of Country B. So country B has an absolute disadvantage. Due to abundance of raw materials or more productively efficient production techniques, Country A is able to produce more wheat and more maize than Country B. Perhaps common sense tells us that Country A should produce both goods and export surpluses and Country B neither. However, when comparative advantage is considered a different story emerges.

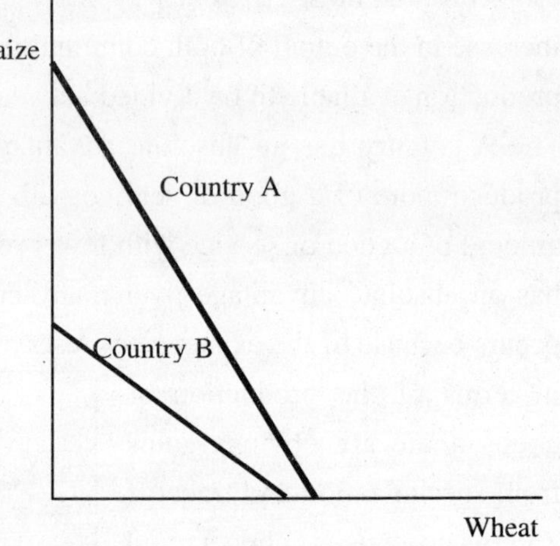

Consider the opportunity cost of Country A producing one more unit of maize. Half a unit of wheat has been foregone. When country B produces one more unit of maize two units of wheat are foregone. Economics is concerned with the allocation of scarce resources. Fewer resources are foregone if Country A concentrates its resources in the production of maize.

The Theory of Comparative Advantage

David Ricardo

Even if one country was most efficient in the production of two products, it must be relatively more efficient in the production of one good. It should then specialize in the production and export of that good in exchange for the importation of the other good.

Now consider the opportunity cost of Country B producing one more unit of wheat. Two units of maize have been foregone. When

Country B produces one more unit of wheat, only half a unit of maize is foregone. Fewer resources are foregone if Country B specializes in the production of wheat.

In the above case Country A should produce maize and Country B wheat. The surpluses produce should then be traded.

1.5.3 New Trade Theories

Great changes have taken place in international trade, and changes are also beginning to occur in the frontier of the research in international trade theories, which would mark the first major shift since the 1970s-1980s when then-prevailing "traditional" trade theory gave way to the "New Trade Theory" advocated by Paul Krugman and Elhanan Helpman. It includes the previous shift from theories grounded in comparative advantage in terms of differences in endowment of production factors and sector-specific input requirements under perfect competition to those that explain intra-industry trade accompanied by product differentiation under monopolistic competition. In comparison, "New Trade Theory", which is emerging in the latest shift, is characterized by the focus on intra-industry heterogeneity (differences observable even among firms belonging to the same sector). Whereas the earlier two lines of trade theory (traditional and "New") have a commonality in that they depend on the "industry" as a unit of analysis, the New Trade Theory, led by Marc J. Melitz and Pol Antras, examines firm-level variations. These pioneering scholars modeled a situation in which a limited number of global firms (those engaged in export, overseas production, and/or offshore outsourcing) and domestic firms (those not directly engaged in any such global activities) coexist within a single industry accompanied by considerable productivity gaps. It is hoped that full-scale empirical studies will be undertaken to test new theoretical predictions based on actual statistical data.

New Trade Theory is based, ultimately, on four innovations that have in recent years modified the reigning neoclassical economics:

(1) An appreciation of market imperfections.

(2) The new industrial economics of strategic behavior.

(3) New Growth Theory, a fresh approach to the question of economic growth.

(4) A changing appreciation of the political context.

New Trade Theory has damaged old theories concerning dynamic gains from free trade in two ways:

First, because conventional trade theory must rely upon general ideas of how economies function, New Trade Theory has exposed the dubious assumptions that it makes in this area. It relies on primitive, simplistic, and outdated economic ideas that are no longer taken seriously in other parts of the discipline.

Second, because anything that conventional trade theory says happens must happen by means of a specific mechanism, it has investigated what these mechanisms must be and has discovered that many do not pan out in detail, no matter how plausible they seem when described casually or in the abstract.

1.6 International Organizations in International Trade

International trade is the trade across the borders of countries which have many differences in terms of political system, law, culture, history, economic level and so on. Different nations have their own policies to do international trade. Unfortunately, the policies of different nations differ from one other. In order to promote international trade, international organizations like the WTO emerged. They focus on trade and transnational business transactions and provide useful resources. Listed below are some of the major international organizations involved in trade and related issues.

1.6.1 GATT and WTO

The General Agreement on Tariffs and Trade (GATT), which was signed in 1947, is a multilateral agreement regulating trade among about 150 countries. According to its preamble, the purpose of the GATT is the "substantial reduction of tariffs and other trade barriers and the elimination of preferences, on a reciprocal and mutually advantageous basis."

There have been eight rounds of negotiations addressing various trade issues. The most recent, the Uruguay Round, addressed issues such as tariffs, services, and the trade related aspects of intellectual property and investment measures.

The Uruguay Round, which was completed on December 15, 1993 after seven years of negotiations, resulted in an agreement among 117 countries to reduce trade barriers and to create more comprehensive and enforceable world trade rules. The agreement coming out of this round, the Final Act Embodying the Results of the Uruguay Round of Multilateral Trade Negotiations, was signed in April 1994. The Uruguay Round agreement was approved and implemented by the U.S. Congress in December 1994, and went into effect on January 1, 1995.

This agreement also created the World Trade Organization (WTO), which came into being on January 1, 1995. The WTO implements the agreement, provides a forum for negotiating additional reductions of trade barriers and for settling policy disputes, and enforces trade rules. Until the establishment of the WTO, GATT functioned de facto as an organization, conducting rounds of talks addressing various trade issues and resolving international trade disputes. Since the end of the Uruguay Round, there have been negotiations on topics such as telecommunications services, information technology products, and financial services.

The WTO functions as the principal international body concerned with multilateral negotiations on the reduction of trade barriers and other measures that distort competition. The WTO also serves as a platform for countries to raise their concerns regarding the trade policies of their trading partners. The basic aim of the WTO is to liberalize world trade and place it on a secure basis, thereby contributing to economic growth and development.

1.6.2 International Chamber of Commerce (ICC)

For most of this century, the International Chamber of Commerce (ICC) has been the world's leading organization in the field of international commercial dispute resolution. Established in 1923 as the arbitration body of ICC, the International Court of Arbitration has pioneered international commercial arbitration as it is known today. The Court took the lead in securing the worldwide acceptance of arbitration as the most effective way of resolving international commercial disputes.

The dispute resolution mechanisms developed by ICC have been conceived specifically for business disputes in an international context. ICC has always led the way in providing international business with alternatives to court litigation. The ICC's Rules of Arbitration, which provide a means for settling disputes in a final and binding manner, are the best known of the services ICC affords international business for the resolution of commercial disputes anywhere in the world.

1.6.3 World Bank

The International Bank for Reconstruction and Development (IBRD), commonly referred to as the World Bank, is an intergovernmental financial institution located in

Washington, D.C. Its objectives are to help raise productivity and incomes and reduce poverty in developing countries. It was established in December 1945 on the basis of a plan developed at the Bretton Woods Conference of 1944. The Bank loans financial resources to credit worthy developing countries. It raises most of its funds by selling bonds in the world's major capital markets. Its bonds have, over the years, earned a quality rating enjoyed only by sound governments and leading corporations. Projects supported by the World Bank normally receive high priority within recipient governments and are usually well planned and supervised. The World Bank earns a profit, which is plowed back into its capital.

1.6.4 International Monetary Fund (IMF)

International Monetary Fund (IMF) is an international financial institution proposed at the 1944 Bretton Woods Conference and established in 1946. IMF seeks to stabilize the international monetary system as a sound basis for the orderly expansion of international trade. Specifically, among other things, the Fund monitors exchange rate policies of member countries, lends them foreign exchange resources to support their adjustment policies when they experience balance of payments difficulties, and provides financial assistance through a special "compensatory financing facility" when they experience temporary shortfalls in commodity export earnings.

1.7 Laws and Regulations Governing International Trade

International trade historically has been subject to numerous domestic legal systems, mainly by virtue of the rules of private international law. The disputes arising out of international sales contracts at times may have been settled at times by different laws. This diversity of the various legal systems applied has hindered the evolution of a strong, distinct, and uniform modern legal systems. Such legal diversity creates legal uncertainty and imposes additional transactional costs on the contracting parties.

Therefore, in order to regulate as well as safeguard international trade, unified laws and regulations were badly needed in international trade, and those basic international trade-related laws and regulations came into being in such circumstances.

Foreign trade operators should know the legal systems in the international sphere and should act in strict accordance with such laws. The basic international trade-related laws and regulations are the *United Nations Convention on Contracts for the International Sale of Goods* (CISG), *UCP* and *INCOTERMS.*

1.7.1 CISG

In 1980, the United Nations Convention for the International Sale of Goods (CISG) came into being as an attempt to create a uniform commercial sales law by regulating the rights and obligations of buyers and sellers in international transactions for the sale of goods. The evidence shows that the CISG is now used by more than two-thirds of the world.

The benefits of a uniform law for the international sale of goods are indeed many and substantial, and not merely of a pecuniary nature. A uniform law would provide parties with greater certainty as to their potential rights and obligations. This is to be compared with the results brought about by the amorphous principles of private international law and the possible application of an unfamiliar system of foreign domestic law.

Another advantage of a uniform law for the international sale of goods is that it would serve to simplify international sales transactions and thus, as envisaged in the Preamble, "contribute to the removal of legal barriers in international trade and promote the development of international trade." The CISG seeks to achieve such uniformity. Whether or not the uniform law is successful will largely depend on two things: first, whether domestic tribunals interpret its provisions in a uniform manner, and second, whether those same tribunals adopt a uniform approach to the filling of gaps in the law.

The unification or harmonization of international commercial law is generally desirable because it can act as a "total conflict avoidance device", which, from a trader's point of view, is far better than conflict solution devices, such as the choice of law clauses. Textual uniformity is, however, a necessary but insufficient step toward achieving substantive legal uniformity, because the formulation and enactment of a uniform legal text provide no guarantee of its subsequent uniform application in practice. The main question regarding the success or failure of the Convention as truly uniform sales law relates to the proper interpretation and uniform application of its provisions as the international sales law of contracts governed by it. Several commentaries have evaluated the CISG from this perspective, and the authors have disagreed on how successful the CISG will be in reaching this unifying goal.

1.7.2 UCP

UCP, short for the Uniform Customs and Practice for Documentary Credits, are rules that apply to any documentary credit (including, to the extent to which they may be applicable, any standby letter of credit) when the text of the credit expressly indicates that it is subject to these rules. They are binding on all parties, unless otherwise expressly stipulated in the credit.

On July 1, 2007, the Uniform Customs and Practice for Documentary Credits (UCP) changed for the first time in over 12 years. The new rules (UCP600) replace UCP500 as the new Uniform Customs and Practice for Documentary Credits published by the International Chamber of Commerce. The objective of this change is to clarify the rules, reduce discrepancies and disputes, and encourage renewed usage of letters of credit. Significant revisions include a change in the amount of time banks are allowed to examine documents, revised rules for bills of lading and multimodal transport, and a provision for documents that are lost in the mail.

1.7.3 INCOTERMS

To improve this aspect of international trade, the International Chamber of Commerce in Paris developed INCOTERMS, a set of uniform rules for the interpretation of international commercial terms defining the costs, risks, and obligations of buyers and sellers in international transactions. First published in 1936, these rules have been periodically revised to account for changing modes of transport and document delivery. The current version is Incoterms 2000.

As international rules that are accepted by governments, legal authorities and practitioners worldwide for the interpretation of the most commonly used terms in international trade, Incoterms either reduce or remove altogether most uncertainties arising from differing interpretations of such terms in different countries.

The scope of Incoterms is limited to matters relating to the rights and obligations of the parties to the contract of sale with respect to the delivery of goods sold, but excluding “intangibles” like computer software.

1.8 Vocabulary Check

accede to 同意；加入
amorphous 无定形的；无组织的
allocation 分配，安置
anti-dumping 反倾销的
appurtenance 附件；附属物
bilateral 双边的
balance of payment 收支平衡
bauxite 矾土；铁铝氧石
capital intensive 资本密集的
copper ore 铜矿
curtail *v.* 缩减；减少(经费)
deficit 赤字；逆差
dynamic gain 动态增益
empirical 经验主义的
envisage *v.* 设想；想象
economies of scale 规模经济
endowment *n.* 捐赠；捐款
enactment *n.* 制定(条例)
formulation *n.* 用公式表示；规划
heterogeneity 异质性；不均匀性
impairment *n.* 损害；损伤
import surcharge 进口附加税
import variable duties 差价税
infant industry 新生工业
intermediaries 中间人，中间商
intra-industry 产业内贸易
invisible trade 无形贸易
labor-intensive 劳动力密集型的
monopolistic competition 垄断性竞争
outsourcing 外部采办；外购
pan out 成功；淘选
preponderance 优势；占优势
product differentiation 产品差异化
promulgate *v.* 公布；发布
prevail *v.* 流行；占优势
preamble 序言
quota 配额
reigning 统治的；起支配作用的
revenue (土地、财产等的)收入；收益
subsidy *n.* 补贴
tangible 有形的；可触摸的
tribunal 法庭
tariff 关税；关税表
visible trade 有形贸易

1. 9 Notes and Key Terms

1) **trade barrier:** 实践中较为常见的贸易壁垒主要体现在以下几个方面：违反承诺的关税措施；缺乏规则依据的进口管理限制(包括通关限制、国内税费、进口禁令、进口许可等)；缺乏科学依据的技术法规、产品标准、合格评定程序、卫生与植物卫生措施；不合理的反倾销、反补贴、保障措施等贸易救济措施；政府采购中违反有关规则限制进口产品的做法；出口限制；补贴；服务贸易

准入和经营限制；不合理的与贸易有关的知识产权措施；其他贸易壁垒等。

2) **technical barrier to trade (TBT)**：技术性贸易壁垒，是指一国以维护国家安全、保护人类的安全和健康、动物和植物的生命及健康、保护环境、防止欺诈行为、保证产品质量为目的或以贸易保护为目的，在对进口商品进行管理时，通过对进口商品提出特殊的，甚至是苛刻的技术性要求，采取包括颁布技术法规和标准、实施合格评定程序等在内的技术性措施而设置的贸易保护主义壁垒，是国际贸易中非关税壁垒的一项重要措施，也是非关税壁垒中最为隐蔽、最难对付的一种贸易保护主义壁垒。

3) **VERs (voluntary export restrains):** 自动出口限制，又称自动出口配额(voluntary export quotas)，是指出口国家或地区在进口国的要求或压力下，“自动”规定某一时期内(一般为三年)，某些商品对该国的出口限制，在限定的配额内自行控制出口，超过配额即禁止出口。

4) **cartel:** 卡特尔，垄断集团，通常是指竞争者之间限制竞争的协议、共谋做法或者安排，包括固定价格、操纵投标、建立出口限制或配额、分享或分割市场等行为。由来自两个以上国家的企业参与的卡特尔称为国际卡特尔(international cartel)。

5) **mercantilism:** 重商主义，是封建主义解体之后16－17世纪西欧资本原始积累时期的一种经济理论或经济体系，反映资本原始积累时期商业资产阶级利益的经济理论和政策体系。15－18世纪中在欧洲流行，后为古典经济学取代。认为一国积累的金银越多，就越富强。主张国家干预经济生活，禁止金银输出，增加金银输入。该名称最初是由亚当·斯密在《国民财富的性质和原因的研究》一书中提出来的。

6) **absolute advantage:** 绝对优势。如果一个国家用一单位资源生产的某种产品比另一个国家多，那么，这个国家在这种产品的生产上与另一国相比就具有绝对优势。

7) **Adam Smith:** 亚当·斯密(1723－1790)，18世纪英国著名经济学家。在经济思想史上，斯密被尊为古典经济学派的创始人。1776年，斯密出版了一部奠定古典政治经济学理论体系的著作《国民财富的性质和原因的研究》(简称《国富论》(*The Wealth of Nations*)。斯密的思想对国际贸易乃至整个经济学的发展都产生了重大影响。

8) **David Ricardo:** 大卫·李嘉图(1772－1823)，是英国产业革命高潮时期的资产阶级经济学家，古典政治经济学的集大成者。1817年，他在其代表作《政治经济学及赋税原理》中提出了以“比较成本学说”为核心的国际贸易理论，极大地发展了亚当·斯密的经济思想，使古典政治经济学达到了最高峰。

9) **New Trade Theory:** 由于传统的贸易理论无法解释发达国家之间的贸易以及

产业内贸易，因此一些早期的经济学家就开始从技术、需求、收入等不同的角度来探讨战后国际贸易发生的原因，比较典型的有技术差距理论、产品生命周期理论、收入与偏好相似理论等。但是这些理论都只是从某个角度来说明国际贸易中的现象，不能概括全部或大部分国际贸易中出现的新现象，并且各种理论都是建立在各自特殊的假定条件下，相互之间并不能建立起有机的联系，一个统一的一般理论没有建立起来，这些理论与传统贸易理论相脱节，既没有推翻传统贸易理论，也没有与传统贸易理论融为一体。因此，一些经济学家试图建立一个完整的理论体系，这一理论体系后来被称之为新贸易理论(New Trade Theory)。新贸易理论的主要代表人物有狄克西特(A Dixit)、斯蒂格利茨(J Stiglitz)、保罗·克鲁格曼(Paul R Krugman)、詹姆斯·布兰德(J Brander)、赫尔普曼(E Helpman)、格罗斯曼(G Grossman)、兰卡斯特(Lancaster)、斯宾塞(B Spencer)等。在习惯上，人们经常把狄克西特-斯蒂格利茨模型称为新贸易理论的开端。

10) **New Growth Theory**：新增长理论，是 20 世纪 80 年代初期麻省理工学院的保罗·罗默(Paul Romer)提出的，又称内生增长理论(Endogenous Growth Theory)。该理论比较好地解释了发达国家和不发达国家的发展水平为什么没有出现如古典增长理论所推论的那样收敛，而是差距越来越大的经济现象。新增长理论认为，发达国家的教育、R&D 以及人力资本的投入具有规模报酬递增效应，而发展中国家在这方面的投入却严重不足。

11) **International Monetary Fund (IMF)**：国际货币基金组织。该组织 1945 年成立，它是一个政府间的、合作性的货币和金融机构，目的是为了促进国际间的货币合作与汇率的稳定，鼓励经济发展，促进高度就业，同时提供国际收支的融通。

12) **ICC**：国际商会(The International Chamber of Commerce)，成立于 1919 年，发展至今已拥有来自 130 多个国家的成员公司和协会，是全球惟一的代表所有企业的权威代言机构。国际商会以贸易作为促进和平、繁荣的强大力量，推行一种开放的国际贸易、投资体系和市场经济。由于国际商会的成员公司和协会本身从事于国际商业活动，因此它所制定用以规范国际商业合作的规章，如：《托收统一规则》、《跟单信用证统一惯例》、《2000 国际贸易术语解释通则》等被广泛地应用于国际贸易中，并成为国际贸易不可缺少的一部分。国际商会属下的国际仲裁法庭是全球最高的仲裁机构，它为解决国际贸易争议起着重大的作用。

13) **United Nations Convention on Contracts for the International Sale of Goods (CISG):**《联合国国际货物销售合同公约》。联合国大会于 1980 年 4 月 11 日在维也纳通过了该公约。目前，该公约的缔约国已近 60 个国家，包括世界

上最主要的贸易大国，如美国、德国、法国、意大利、荷兰、加拿大、澳大利亚等。该公约是迄今为止有关国际货物买卖合同的一项最为重要的国际条约。我国是公约的原始缔约国，公约自 1988 年 1 月 1 日开始对我国生效。

14) **Uniform Customs and Practice for Commercial Documentary Credits:**《跟单信用证统一惯例》。该惯例对跟单信用证当事人的权利和义务，有关业务和术语作了统一的解释，成为信用证业务的行为准则。随着国际贸易的发展，新的运输方式和通讯方式的出现，以及使用《统一惯例》过程中暴露的问题，国际商会多次对其进行了修订，最新的版本为《跟单信用证统一惯例》国际商会第 600 号出版物(简称"UCP600")(the Uniform Customs and Practice for Documentary Credits, ICC Publication No. 600)，于 2007 年 7 月 1 日起实施，并代替之前的"UCP500"。相比之下，UCP600 更全面地反映了近年来国际银行业、运输业和保险业出现的变化，并体现了一定的前瞻性；在结构上借鉴了 ISP98 的模式，改掉了 UCP500 分类不科学、次序排列不足、语言繁杂欠精练等欠缺；虽然 UCP600(共 39 条)比 UCP500 减少了 10 条，但却比 UCP500 更加准确、清晰，更加易读易掌握，极大地丰富和影响了今后跟单信用证业务的实务操作和审核单据的标准。

15) **Incoterms:** 国际贸易术语解释通则(International Rules for the Interpretation of Trade Terms)，简称"通则"，也有人认为是 International Commercial Terms 的英文缩写，其宗旨是为国际贸易中最普遍使用的贸易术语提供一套解释的国际规则，以避免因各国不同解释而出现的不确定性，或至少在相当程度上减少这种不确定性。在国际贸易中合同双方当事人之间互不了解对方国家的贸易习惯的情况时常出现，这就会引起误解、争议和诉讼，从而浪费时间和费用。为了解决这些问题，国际商会(ICC)于 1936 年首次公布了一套解释贸易术语的国际规则，名为 INCOTERMS 1936，后来经过 1953、1967、1976、1980 和 1990 年五次修改和补充，INCOTERMS 2000 是在 INCOTERMS 1990 的基础上经过修订而产生的，该通则包含了 13 种贸易术语。按照其国际代码的第一个字母的不同，这 13 种术语被分为四个组，分别称作 E 组、F 组、C 组和 D 组。

1.10 Follow-up Practice

1.10.1 Review and Discussion Questions

1) What is international trade?

2) What benefits does international trade bring to us?

3) What's the difference between international trade and domestic trade?

4) Why do many countries impose restrictions on trade?
5) What is a tariff? How is it classified?
6) Could you explain the theory of absolute advantage and the theory of comparative advantage?
7) What is the comparative advantage of China? Do you think the theory of comparative advantage is still workable in China?
8) Could you name some of the organizations involved in the international trade and explain them?
9) Give two examples of the most frequently used laws and regulations in the international trade?

1.10.2 Give the Chinese equivalents to the following English terms and match their definitions given below.

a. comparative advantage ____________ b. mercantilism ____________
c. tariff ____________ d. UCP600 ____________
e. quota ____________ f. invisible trade ____________
g. Incoterms ____________ h. opportunity cost ____________
i. dumping ____________ j. CISG ____________

1) ________ is a duty or fee levied on goods being imported into a country.
2) ________ a doctrine that holds that exports are good for a country, whereas imports are harmful.
3) ________ is the ability to produce a good at a lower cost, relative to other goods, compared to another country.
4) ________ is a quantitative restriction that is expressed in terms of either physical quantity or value.
5) ________ is the official ICC rules for the interpretation of trade terms.
6) ________ is a practical and comprehensive set of 39 rules that address the major issues in documentary credit usage.
7) ________ involves the exchange of services between nations.
8) ________ is the practice of selling products in a foreign country at lower prices than those charged in the producing country
9) ________ refers to the cost of using a resource in one enterprise when it could be used in alternative enterprises or investment opportunities measured by the return that could be obtained from using the resources in the alternative in investment.

10) ________ is a uniform commercial sales law by regulating the rights and obligations of buyers and sellers in international transactions for the sale of goods.

1.10.3 Choose the right answer from each of the following.

1) When a country can produce something more economically than another country, it has ________.

A. comparative advantage B. absolute advantage

C. comparative disadvantage D. absolute disadvantage

2) If a country can produce something with a lower opportunity cost than another country, it has ________.

A. absolute disadvantage B. absolute advantage

C. comparative advantage D. comparative disadvantage

3) Which of the following sentence is NOT true?

A. Trade is beneficial to all the participants.

B. As long as a country has comparative advantage in something, it can gain in the international trade.

C. If a country has absolute disadvantage in everything, it can gain nothing in the international trade.

D. Even if a country has no absolute advantage in everything, it still can gain in international trade.

4) If you are a farmer in France exporting wheat, one day the government urges you to raise your exporting price, by compensating you a big sum of money for your loss of exporting quantity. This belongs to ________.

A. tariff B. subsidy

C. quota D. anti-dumping

5) Which of the following barriers doesn't belong to the non-tariff barrier?

A. Revenue tariff. B. VERs.

C. Anti-dumping. D. TBT.

6) Which of the following statements of WTO is NOT true?

A. WTO and GATT are the current existing two big international trade agencies.

B. WTO came after GATT in 1995.

C. WTO helps to solve the international trade disputes between countries.

D. WTO is short for World Trade Organization.

7) If China's government regulates that every piece of clothes for exporting should add 1 RMB to the customs, this belongs to ________.

A. VERs
B. exporting tariff
C. quota
D. importing tariff

8) Which of the following business belongs to the invisible trade?
A. Exporting cars.
B. Importing steels.
C. Exporting mobile phones.
D. Technology license.

9) Which of the following is considered as international trade?
A. Selling garments to Hong Kong.
B. Traveling to Japan.
C. Buying a camera in Japan and tanking it back to China.
D. Exporting bikes to Japan.

10) ________ is defined as unjustified technical regulations and standards applied to imported products as well as complicated certification and conformity assessment procedure.
A. Quota
B. VERs
C. Tariff
D. TBT

1.10.4 Decide whether the following statements are true or false.

1) David Ricardo said that the real basis for trade between countries is absolute advantage. (   )
2) The comparative advantage theory states that international trade can be beneficial to all the participants. (   )
3) When nations export more than they import, they have a favorable balance of trade. (   )
4) Trade barriers are good ways to protect the domestic trade industry as well as the international trade. (   )
5) GATT is now replaced by WTO as the main origination in the international trade. (   )
6) Visible trade involves the exchange of services between nations, while invisible trade involves the import and export of goods. (   )
7) According to the absolute advantage theory, a country should focus on the production of those goods in which it has an absolute advantage and acquire or purchase from abroad those goods which it cannot produce at home cheaply or efficiently. (   )
8) UCP600 is the rules that replaced UCP500 on July 1, 2007 as the new Uniform Customs and Practice for Documentary Credits published by WTO. (   )

9) According to the mercantilist theory, international trade is a zero sum game，i.e. that the benefit which one country gains from international trade means a corresponding detriment to another country. ( )

10) If a country has no absolute advantage in producing everything, it can gain no profit in the international trade. ( )

1.10.5 Case Study

Look at the table below: the United Kingdom now has an absolute disadvantage in the production of both wheat and cloth with respect to the United States.

Table: Comparative Advantage

	US	UK
Wheat (bushels/man-hour)	6	1
Cloth (yards/man-hour)	4	2

Explain how international trade benefits both countries.

An example of VERs: the United States negotiated in 1981 to impose the voluntary restraint on Japanese automobile exports to the United States. The United States also negotiated voluntary export restraints with major steel suppliers in 1982 that limited imports to about 20 percent of the U.S. steel market.

Now please discuss what the reasons are for the United States to do so, and what the consequences will be to other countries.

1. http://www. wto.org 世界贸易组织网站
2. http://www.iccwbo.org 国际商会网站
3. http://www.mofcom.gov.cn 中国商务部网站

2

Chapter Two

Business Negotiation and Conclusion of the Contract

Learning Objectives

At the end of this chapter, you should be able to understand:

- the form and contents of business negotiation
- the basic procedures of business negotiation
- the relevant legal rules on business negotiation
- the main contents of the contract
- how to interpret clauses in the contract

The procedure of a transaction for the international sale of goods, whether it is import or export, generally includes the three stages: preparation before business negotiation, business negotiation and the conclusion and the implementation of a sales contract. Among them business negotiation, which has direct influence on the conclusion and implementation of a contract, plays a basic part in the conclusion of a sales contract. Business negotiation is conducted for the purpose of reaching an agreement or concluding a sales contract, and is a process of discussing the relevant terms and conditions of a transaction between the buyer and the seller, and it determines the success or failure of a transaction and the contract quality. Therefore it has a great bearing on the economic interests of the parties concerned.

2.1 Form and Contents of Business Negotiation

Business negotiation can be conducted either by writing or verbally. In the latter case, traders talk about the terms and conditions of a transaction with each other in person or by telephone. The foreign businessman may call on the domestic trader upon invitation, or the exporter will pay a visit to an overseas importer on his own account. Business negotiations are also held at international fairs where businessmen all over the world can negotiate with one another over export and import trade. Through verbal negotiations trading transactions between Chinese and foreign businessmen are concluded in large amounts at trade fairs like the China Import and Export Fair in Guangzhou and East China Fair in Shanghai.

Written communication for international transactions used to be done by letter, cable and telex. With the rapid development of modern communication technology and the application of computer networks, nowadays most businesses use fax, e-mail, and even MSN for their business negotiation.

Whichever way of communication is used, in practice, letter-writing plays a major role and that's why a prosperous trader always has a great deal of correspondence to deal with. However, sometimes both types, communications in writing and in spoken words, are used interchangeably in one single transaction, as the case may be.

Business negotiation in international trade is the process by which the seller and the buyer negotiate about the trade terms of a transaction with the intent of reaching an agreement about the sales of goods. The trade terms are made up of five items as follows:

(1) the subject matter of the contract (the name, quality, quantity, and packing of the goods);

(2) the price of the goods;

(3) the liabilities of the seller (including the time, place, and method of the delivery of the goods, the varieties and number of copies of the required documents, etc.);

(4) the liabilities of the buyer (including the time, place, method and the currency for payment of the goods, the date by which his assigned carrier should have reached the port of shipment in case the deal is done under FOB, etc.);

(5) the methods to prevent the occurrence of disputes and methods to settle disputes in case there is any (including commodity inspection, claims, arbitration, etc.).

The above trade terms of a sales contract can be classifies as major terms and conditions (or specific terms) and general terms and conditions:

Major terms and conditions	General terms and conditions
Name of commodity	Inspection
Quality	Claim
Quantity	Arbitration
Packing	Force majeure
Price	
Shipment	
Payment	

The seller and the buyer pay most attention to the major terms and conditions of the transaction for they will vary a lot from transaction to transaction. The general terms and conditions, on the other hand, are relatively fixed in each transaction. They are usually first discussed before the formal business negotiation takes place except the trade terms like quality, quantity, price, time of shipment, and payment, and sometimes, even some of these terms are previously discussed and included in the general terms and conditions. If the seller and buyer have built up long standing trade relations, they will tend to employ the same general terms and conditions in all transactions to save time and money. However, if the seller and the buyer are negotiating their first transaction, it is necessary to talk carefully about both the major terms and conditions and general terms and conditions.

2.2 General Procedures of Business Negotiation

To reach an agreement of the various terms and conditions mentioned above in the international business negotiation, generally, needs going through five links, namely, **enquiry**, **offer**, **counter-offer**, **acceptance** and **conclusion of a sales contract**.

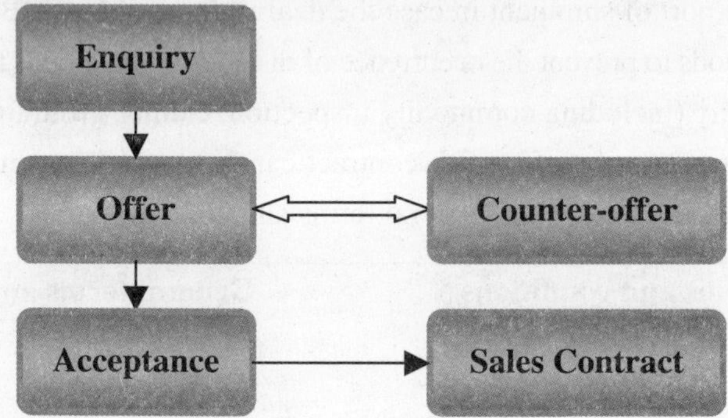

The flow chart of contract negotiation

Of course, it is not necessary to have all the five links taken for every transaction. Among them, offer and acceptance are the two indispensable links which are required for the formation of a sales contract.

2.2.1 Enquiry

Business negotiations in international trade usually start with an enquiry by an overseas buyer to a seller, inquiring for sales information. Nevertheless, at some times, a seller can also initiate the negotiation by making an enquiry to a foreign buyer, including his intention of selling certain goods to the latter. It is worthy of note that whoever makes an enquiry is not liable for the buying or the selling, and, the opposite party, at the same time, can make no reply at all. But, according to the commercial practice the receiver of an enquiry will respond without delay in the usual form of a quotation, an offer, or a bid.

An enquiry can be made not only to one party alone but also to several clients. In this way the enquirer can make a comparison between the terms of sales stated in the different replies and thus trade beneficially with the one who has quoted or offered the best terms.

The following is a letter of enquiry from a buyer:

> Dear Sirs,
>
> We are interested in buying large quantities of steel screws in all size. We would be obliged if you would give us a quotation per kilogram CIF London.
>
> It would also be appreciated if you could forward samples and your price list to us.
>
> We used to purchase these products from other sources. We may now prefer to buy from your company because we understand that you are able to supply larger quantities at more attractive prices. In addition, we have confidence in the quality of your products.
>
> We look forward to hearing from you by return.
>
> Yours faithfully,
> Peter Brown

2.2.2 Offer

According to the *United Nations Convention on Contracts for the International Sale of Goods* (*CISG*), an offer is a proposal for concluding a contract addressed to one or more specific persons if it is sufficiently definite and indicates the intention of the offeror to be bound in case of acceptance.

An offer is normally made in response to an enquiry. But it is not always so. If the seller makes an offer, it is called a "selling offer"; if a buyer makes an offer, it is called a "buying offer".

There are two kinds of offer: a firm offer or offer with engagement and a non-firm offer or offer without engagement. The former has legal effect and is binding on the offeror within its validity. The latter has no legal effect. It should be noted that according to *CISG* there is no such term as a non-firm offer.

A firm offer must satisfy the following requisite conditions:

(1) It must be sent to one or more specific persons.

(2) The contents of the offer must be definite, that is, the conditions given must be complete, clear and final. A firm offer should include at least three specific conditions: the name, the quantity, the price of the commodity.

(3) It must indicate that once it has been unconditionally accepted by the offered within its validity, the offer is binding on both parties.

(4) It takes effect only after the offer reaches the offeree. It is always necessary to state the specific time zone when specifying the time of arrival.

The following is a firm offer from an exporter to an importer:

Dear Sirs,

In response to your enquiry of 20 May, we wish to inform you that we have airmailed you, under separate cover, one catalogue and two sample books for our printed shirting. We hope they will reach you in due course and will help you in making your selection.

In order to start a concrete transaction between us, we take pleasure in making you a special offer. This offer is firm subject to the receipt of your reply at the end of this month.

1. Art. No.	81000 Printed Shirting
2. Design No.	72435-2A
3. Specifications:	30×36 72×60 35/6″ ×42 yds
4. Quantity:	18,000 yds
5. Packing:	In bales or in wooden cases, at seller's option
6. Price:	USD … per yard CIF Hamburg
7. Shipment:	To be made in two equal monthly installments, beginning from July
8. Payment:	By confirmed, irrevocable L/C payable by draft at sight to be opened 30 days before the time of shipment.

We trust the above will be acceptable to you and await with keen interest your trial order.

Yours faithfully,

2.2.3 Counter-offer

A counter-offer is a proposal made by an offeree who does not fully accept the offer made by the offeror and makes modification or alteration to the offer. A counter-offer, in fact, is a rejection of the offer and constitutes a new offer. According to the stipulations of *CISG*, a reply to an offer which purports to be an acceptance but contains additions, limitations or other modifications is a rejection of the offer and constitutes a counter-offer. However, a reply to an offer which purports to be an acceptance but contains additional or different terms which do not materially alter the terms of the offer constitutes an acceptance, unless the offeror, without undue delay, objects orally to the discrepancy or dispatches a notice to that effect. If he does not object, the terms of the contract are the terms of the offer with the modifications contained in the acceptance. Additional or different terms relating, among other things, to the price, payment, quality and quantity of the goods, place and time of delivery, extent of one party' s liability to the other or the settlement of disputes are considered to alter the terms of the offer materially.

The following is a counter-offer made by a buyer:

Dear Sirs,

Thank you for your letter about the offer for the bicycles. Although we appreciate the quality of your bicycles, we regret to say that their price is too high to be acceptable. Referring to the Sales Confirmation No. 89SP-754, you will find that we ordered 1,000 bicycles with the same brand as per the terms and conditions stipulated in that Sales Confirmation, but the price was 10% lower than your present price. Since we placed the last order, price for raw materials has decreased considerably. Retailing price for your bicycles here has also been reduced by 5%. Accepting your present price will mean great loss to us, let alone profit. We would like to place repeat orders with you if you could reduce your price at least by 2%. Otherwise, we have to shift to the other suppliers for our similar request.

We hope you take our suggestion into serious consideration and give us your reply as soon as possible.

Yours truly,

2.2.4 Acceptance

In business law, an acceptance is the assent to the terms of an offer or counter-offer required before a contract can be valid. It means that the buyer and the seller have come to an agreement on the sale. It is binding on both parties.

A legally valid acceptance must meet the following requirements:

(1) The acceptance must be made by the offeree.

(2) The acceptance must be shown either by words or actions or in written form.

(3) The acceptance must reach the offeror within the time of validity of the offer.

(4) The acceptance must be unconditional. It should be an unreserved assent to all the terms designated in the offer. In principle, if additions, modifications or limitations to the offer are made, it will be a counter-offer and not an acceptance.

2.3 Conclusion of the Contract

A contract is an agreement that creates an obligation, that is binding, legally enforceable agreement between two or more competent parties. It generally consists of an exchange of promises—an offer and an acceptance—resulting in an obligation to perform some particular act. In order to be valid, a contract must have the genuine assent of the parties to it, that is, it must involve both offer and acceptance.

In international trade a sales contract is a legal document made by and entered into between a seller and a buyer on the basis of their offer and acceptance. In the contract the right and obligation of both the parties are definitely stipulated. The contract is binding on them all. In the course of business negotiation, when an offer with engagement or a counter-offer of this kind is accepted, the transaction is completed and a contractual relationship between the offeror and the offeree is concluded. According to *CISG,* "A contract of sale need not be concluded in or evidenced by writing and is not subject to any other requirement as to form. It may be proved by any means, including witnesses." This means a written contract endorsed by both parties of the transaction is not a required condition for the formation of a contract. However, in keeping with the regular practice in international trade, a written contract or confirmation is usually signed to bind both the seller and the buyer. It is important because:

(1) Endorsed by both parties to the sale, the written contract is evidence that the

two parties have come to an agreement. According to *CISG,* a contract is not restricted to the written form, but according to Chinese commercial law, only the written form of contract can be considered a legal contract.

(2) The written contract is sometimes a necessary condition for the formation of a contract. In business negotiation, when one or two parties declare beforehand that the agreement must be in the form of written contract, the written contract becomes a precondition for the formation of the contract.

(3) The written contract forms the basis upon which the parties concerned perform the contract. In international trade practice, to perform a contract will go through many procedures and involve many parties. Without a written contract, a verbal offer is always impossible to be executed.

2.4 Form and Contents of the Contract

In international trade, a contract can take the form of either a sales contract or a sales confirmation. The former contains not only the main terms of the transaction such as the name of commodities, specifications, quantity, packing, marking, price, shipment, port of shipment and port of destination, and payment, it also provides such clauses as claims, force majeure, arbitration covering the rights and liabilities of the parties and the dispute settlement; while the latter, a contract in a simplified form, only contains some main terms. A contract document can be worked out either by the seller or the buyer. When it is drafted by the seller, it is called a sales contract. When it is drafted by the buyer, it is called a purchase contract. The same is true with a confirmation. When it is drafted by the seller, it is called a sales confirmation. When it is drafted by the buyer, it is called a purchase confirmation. Legally, both the sales contract (or the purchase contract) and the sales confirmation (or the purchase confirmation) are equally binding on the parties concerned. It goes without saying that both the parties will best benefit from the sales or the purchase contract if disputes occur because the contract has provided in detail the relative terms and the ways of how to handle and settle the disputes. It is, then, appropriate to transactions of large amount and huge quantity. If the amount is not large or the business is done by means of agency arrangement or exclusive sales agreement, the sales or the purchase confirmation is often used.

Sample Sales Contract

Sales Contract

Contract No: Date:

Signed at:

Sellers: Address:

Postal Code: Tel: Fax:

Buyers: Address:

Postal Code: Tel: Fax:

The seller agrees to sell and the buyer agrees to buy the under-mentioned goods on the terms and conditions stated below:

1. Article No.:
2. Description & Specification:
3. Quantity:
4. Unit Price:
5. Total Amount:

   With _____% more or less both in amount and quantity allowed at the sellers option.
6. Country of Origin and Manufacturer:
7. Packing:
8. Shipping Marks:
9. Time of Shipment:
10. Port of Loading:
11. Port of Destination:
12. Insurance：To be effected by buyers for 110% of full invoice value covering _____ up to _____ only.
13. Payment:

    By confirmed, irrevocable, transferable and divisible L/C to be available by sight draft to reach the sellers before ___/___/_____ and to remain valid for negotiation in China until 15 days after the aforesaid time of shipment. The L/C must specify that transshipment and partial shipments are allowed.
14. Documents:
15. Terms of Shipment:
16. Quality/Quantity Discrepancy and Claim:
17. Force Majeure:

Either party shall not be held responsible for failure or delay to perform all or any part of this agreement due to flood, fire, earthquake, draught, war or any other events which could not be predicted, controlled, avoided or overcome by the relative party. However, the party affected by the event of Force Majeure shall inform the other party of its occurrence in writing as soon as possible and thereafter send a certificate of the event issued by the relevant authorities to the other party within 15 days after its occurrence.

18. Arbitration:

All disputes arising from the execution of this agreement shall be settled through friendly consultations. In case no settlement can be reached, the case in dispute shall then be submitted to the Foreign Trade Arbitration Commission of the China Council for the Promotion of International Trade for Arbitration in accordance with its Provisional Rules of Procedure. The decision made by this commission shall be regarded as final and binding upon both parties. Arbitration fees shall be borne by the losing party, unless otherwise awarded.

19. Remark:

Sellers: Buyers:

Signature: Signature:

2.5 Vocabulary Check

arbitration 仲裁
binding 有约束力的
business negotiation 商务磋商/洽谈
commodity inspection 商品检验
consultation 协商
discrepancy 差异
dispute 争议
economic interests 经济利益
endorse 背书；赞同
enforceable agreement 可实施的协议
force majeure 不可抗力
implementation of a sales contract 履行合同
in due course 及时
liability 责任；义务
occurrence 事件；发生
partial shipments 分运
printed shirting 印花细布
relevant authorities 有关当局
subject matter 标的物
transaction 交易
transshipment 转运
under separate cover 另邮

2.6 Notes and Key Terms

1) **major terms and conditions:** 主要交易条件，包括货物的品名、品质、数量、包装、价格、交货和支付条件等内容，买卖双方欲达成交易、订立合同，必须至少就这七项交易条件进行磋商并取得一致意见(特殊情况可以例外)。

2) **general terms and conditions:** 一般交易条件，指由出口商为出售或进口商为购买货物而拟订的对每笔交易都适用的一套共性的交易条件。我国出口企业所拟订的一般交易条件包括的内容有：(1) 有关预防和处理争议的条件；(2) 有关主要交易条件的补充说明；(3) 个别的主要交易条件。使用方式：一般交易条件大都印在进口商或出口商自行设计和印刷的销售合同或购货合同格式的背面或格式正面的下部。只有在实际交易前，事先得到对方对由我方提出的一般交易条件的确认，才能对双方日后订立的合同具有约束力。在磋商具体交易时，买卖双方完全可以根据交易的具体需要，提出与一般交易条件不同的条件。

3) **offer：**发盘，报价或报盘，是买方或卖方向对方提出各项交易条件，并愿意按这些条件达成交易、订立合同的一种肯定的表示。在发盘有效期内，一经对方接受，合同就告成立。发盘的主要内容应包括商品名称、品质、数量、包装、价格、交货日期和方式以及支付方式等。发盘还有实盘(firm offer 或 offer with engagement)和虚盘(non-firm offer或offer without engagement)之分。实盘指从发盘的内容上可以判断发盘人有肯定订立合同的意图。此发盘一经接受，发盘人就不得更改或撤销其内容，否则将承担法律责任。实盘具有内容明确(clear)、完整(complete)和无保留(final)三个特点。虚盘则指从发盘的内容上可以看出发盘人有某种保留并无肯定的订立合同的意图。此发盘对发盘人来说，无任何法律上的约束力，其特点是不明确或主要交易条件不完整或有保留条件。

4) **counter-offer:** 还盘，也称还价，是由受盘人在接受发盘人的一些条款的情况下向发盘人发盘。像发盘一样，还盘也有两种，一种是实盘，一种是虚盘。实际上还盘是受盘人以发盘人的地位所提出的新发盘。还盘后原发盘失效。还盘过程可以多次也可以没有，即一次发盘就接受。

5) **acceptance：**接受，是指受盘人在发盘的有效期内无条件地同意发盘人在发盘中所提出的交易条件，并同意按此条件订立合同的一种表示。发盘一经受盘人接受，交易即告达成，合同即告成立。构成一项法律上有效的接受，必须具备以下四个条件：(1) 接受必须是特定的合法的受盘人做出；(2) 接受必须是无条件地同意发盘所提出的交易条件；(3) 接受必须在发盘有效期内送达发盘人；(4) 必须以一定的方式明确表示出来。表示方法可以是口头的、书面的，也可以按对方的习惯表示。

6) **a sales contract**：销售合同，内容全面，对双方的权利和义务均有明确的规定，包括主要条款(品名、质量、规格、数量、包装、单价、装运港和目的港、交货期、支付方式)和一般条款(保险、商检、争议索赔、仲裁和不可抗力等)，可分为销售合同和购货合同(a purchase contract)。

7) **a sales confirmation**：销售确认书，是销售合同的简化形式，一般只包括交易的主要条件和部分一般条件，分为销售确认书和购货确认书(a purchase confirmation)。

2.7. Follow-up Practice

2.7.1 Review and Discussion Questions

1) Before business negotiations what preparations do you think the seller should make?
2) How many stages does a business negotiation usually undergo? Which are indispensable stages for the formation of a sales contract? Why?
3) What do the seller and buyer negotiate in international trade negotiation?
4) Why should there be general terms and conditions?
5) What is a firm offer and what is non-firm offer?
6) Can you tell briefly the requisite conditions that a firm offer must satisfy?
7) What does an acceptance mean?
8) Why is a written contract so important?

2.7.2 Complete the following sentences with appropriate terms or words.

1) ________ is the process in which the seller and the buyer discuss about ________ in order to reach an agreement about the sales of goods.
2) International business negotiation, generally, needs going through five stages or links: ________, ________, ________, ________, and ________.
3) ________ is a proposal of terms and conditions presented in a potential contract by one party, called the ________, to another party, called the ________.
4) An offer can be made either by ________ or by ________. The former is customarily called "________".
5) Offers with phrases such as "subject to our final confirmation", "subject to prior sale", or "subject to the goods being unsold" can be taken as ________.

6) A firm offer should be ________, ________ and ________ in its wording.
7) A reply to an offer which purports to be an acceptance but contains additions, limitations or other modifications is a ________ of the offer and constitutes a ________.
8) A reply to an offer which purports to be an acceptance but contains additional or different terms which do not materially alter the terms of the offer constitutes ________, unless ________, without undue delay, objects orally to the discrepancy or dispatches a notice to that effect.
9) In international trade, written contracts can take two forms: ________ and ________. ________ is appropriate to transactions of large amount and huge quantity.
10) According to different regulations and laws, the conclusion of a contract depends on the procedure of making ________ by one party and making ________ by the other, and signing a contract in writing is not ________ for the formation of a contract.

2.7.3 Decide whether the following statements are true or false.

1) An offer without engagement is made when a seller promises to sell goods at a stated price within a stated period of time. (   )
2) According to the UN Convention on Contracts for the International Sale of Goods, an offer should be regarded as a definite offer unless it expressly indicates all the details relating to the transaction, including the validity for acceptance and the phrases to indicate the finality. (   )
3) In international trade, the effective formation of a sales contract must go through five links, namely, enquiry, offer, counter-offer, acceptance and conclusion of a sales contract. (   )
4) According to the UN Convention on Contracts for the International Sale of Goods, a sale contract need not be concluded in or evidenced by writing and is not subject to any other requirement as to form. It may be proved by any means, including witnesses. (   )
5) It is a widely accepted rule in international trade that silence and inactivity on the part of offeree constitute acceptance. (   )
6) When accepting an offer, there should be no conditions of acceptance or any material modification, addition or restriction in the acceptance. Otherwise such an offer would be regarded as a rejection of the offer and constitutes a counter-offer. (   )

7) According to international trade convention, under no circumstance can an offer be revoked once it is made by the offerer. ( )

8) An offer containing such phrases as "subject to our final confirmation", "subject to prior sale" can only be taken as an offer without engagement and can be revoked even after it has been accepted by the offeree. ( )

9) When a counter-offer has been rejected by the offeror, the offeree can still accept the original offer before the time of validity of the original offer expires. ( )

10) Legally, there is no difference between the sales contract (or the purchase contract) and the sales confirmation (or the purchase confirmation). Both are equally binding on the parties. ( )

2.7.4 Case Study

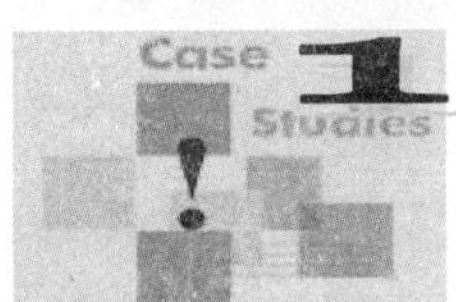

A Chinese international trade company made an offer for an agricultural product to an American company. In addition to all the essential terms and conditions, the packing condition "Packing in sound bags" was also indicated in the offer. Within the time of validity of the offer, the American company gave a reply: "Refer to your fax first accepted, packing in new bags." After receipt of the reply, the Chinese company started to prepare the goods. A few days later, when the price of the agricultural product plummeted in the international market, the American company claimed in its fax: "The contract is invalid because you have not confirmed our alteration to the offer." But the Chinese company insisted that the contract was valid. A dispute was thus aroused. What do you think the case should be settled? Please give your reasons.

On July 16, 2006 a Chinese company (Company A) received an offer from a French company (Company B) reading: "We take pleasure in making you an offer subject to your reply reaching us before July 20 for 500 metric tons of tin plates US$ 545 M/T CFR China Port, payment by sight L/C, which must reach us one month before the time of shipment in August." Company A replied on July 17 as follows: "We can accept an offer US$ 540 M/T CFR China Port for 500 M/T of tin plates. Any dispute arising from the execution of the contract shall be settled by arbitration in China." Company B replied on the same day as follows: "As the market is firm, we can't reduce the price but accept your arbitration condition. Pls reply asap." As the price for tin plates was advancing this time, Company A replied on July 19 as follows: "We accept your offer dated July 16. The relevant L/C has been issued by Bank of China. We are looking forward to your confirmation." But Company B did not confirm and instead returned the L/C. Can you tell whether the contract is formed or not in this case and why? What mistakes did Company A make?

Web Links

1. http://www.cnexp.net 中国出口精英网
2. http://www.China-Customs.com 海关综合信息资讯网
3. http://www.iccwbo.org 国际商会

Chapter Three

Quality and Quantity of Goods

Learning Objectives

At the end of this chapter, you should be able to understand:

- the importance of the name of goods of the contract
- the different methods expressing the quality of goods
- the quality latitude and quality tolerance clauses
- units of measurement and weights and the calculation of weight
- how to stipulate the quantity clause of the contract

In international trade, the sellers and buyers are located in different countries. Generally, after sales contracts have been concluded, the sellers then prepare and deliver goods. Therefore, in business negotiation, the buyers are usually unable to see the actual goods delivered until they arrive at the port of destination. They only ascertain the subject matter of the transaction by means of some necessary descriptions of goods which they order. The description of goods generally consists of the name and quality of goods. Each commodity has its specific name expressed by a certain quality.

It is evident that a business transaction cannot be completed without caring for the quantity of the goods sold or bought. In international trade, quantity is another key factor that affects a transaction and it is also a basis on which the sellers prepare goods and the buyers make payment. Quantity constructs an indispensable part of an effective contract.

3.1 Name of Commodity

The name of commodity is an indispensable part of the contract, and it is a main component of the description of the commodity which provides a basis for the seller to deliver the goods and for the buyer to take the delivery. It concerns the rights and obligations of the parties to the contract. If the goods delivered do not conform to the agreed name of commodity, the buyer is entitled to claim against the seller for compensation, reject the goods or even cancel the contract. Therefore, it is of great importance to specify the name of commodity clearly in the contract. When setting the clause of the name of commodity, the following points should be considered:

(1) **Be clear and specific**

It is required by laws that each commodity of a transaction should be legal and uncontroversial. Meantime, there are different ways of naming commodities. Therefore, the name of commodity in the contract should be clear, specific and free from ambiguous expressions so as to avoid trouble in the execution of the contract. For example, the word "shirt" is not a good name of commodity for there are different kinds of shirts, and even shirts for men (men's shirts) and shirts for women (women's shirt). Sometimes a name will be too general for the name of commodity designation such as "garment".

(2) **Be practical and realistic**

The name of commodity stipulated in the contract must be in conformity with the goods that the seller is able to produce or supply and the buyer requires. Exaggerated or unnecessary descriptions should not be used.

(3) **Try to adopt a name of commodity which is widely accepted internationally**

Sometimes a commodity has different names in different areas. To avoid misunderstanding, both the seller and the buyer shall agree on the name. When naming new products or translating product names, try to use the names customarily accepted in the world.

(4) **Select appropriate names of commodities to facilitate importing and reduce customs duties and freight charges**

In international trade, sometimes a certain commodity has different names, and tariff rates and freight rates may be different for the same commodity with different names. Besides, there may be some import and export restrictions in such a case. Therefore, choosing an appropriate name as the name of commodity in the contract can be beneficial to both the exporter and the importer.

3.2 Quality of Goods

3.2.1 The Definition of Quality of Goods

Quality of goods refers to the intrinsic attributes and the outside form or shape of the goods. The former includes chemical composition, physical and mechanical performance, biological features and the like; the latter includes modeling, structure, color and luster, and taste of a commodity. In another sense, a certain kind of goods possesses both natural and social attributes. From a narrow point of view, it possesses natural attributes, while from a broad point of view it also includes its social attributes, that is, how it meets the subjective requirements and different tastes of its customers.

3.2.2 Methods Expressing Quality of Goods

In international trade, international transactions cover a wide range of commodities and their features differ from one another. There are also a number of methods to express the quality of goods which can be divided into two categories as shown in the table below:

<table>
<tr><th></th><th colspan="2">Mode of Transaction</th><th>Method Expressing Quality</th></tr>
<tr><td rowspan="3">Sale by actual quality</td><td colspan="2">Sale by inspection</td><td>Inspect the goods</td></tr>
<tr><td rowspan="2">Sale by sample</td><td>Sale by seller's sample</td><td>Seller's sample</td></tr>
<tr><td>Sale by buyer's sample</td><td>Buyer's sample</td></tr>
<tr><td rowspan="4">Sale by description</td><td colspan="2">Sale by specification, grade or standard</td><td>Specification, grade or standard</td></tr>
<tr><td colspan="2">Sale by brand name/ trade mark</td><td>Brand name / trade mark</td></tr>
<tr><td colspan="2">Sale by description</td><td>Instructions, drawings, etc.</td></tr>
<tr><td colspan="2">Sale by name of origin</td><td>Name / place of origin</td></tr>
</table>

3.2.2.1 Sale by Actual Quality

➢Sale by inspection

Sale by inspection is concluded with the spot inspection by the buyers or their agents and the quality is determined thereof. This method is of special necessity for particular goods such as ornaments, jewels, paintings, artworks, etc.

In many cases, the buyer may be advised to arrange for inspection of the goods before or at the time they are handed over by the seller for carriage (pre-shipment inspection or PSI). Unless the contract stipulates otherwise, the buyer would have to pay the cost for such inspection that is arranged in his own interest. However, if the inspection has been made in order to enable the seller to comply with any mandatory rules applicable to the export of the goods in his own country the seller would have to pay for that inspection.

➢Sale by sample

A sample is a small quantity of a product, often taken out from a whole lot or specially designed and processed. It is usually given to encourage prospective customers to buy the product or set aside as the quality standard of the whole consignment. Such products as garments, arts and crafts, light industrial products and agricultural native produce are generally sold by sample. If the goods are sold by sample, the goods to be delivered must be in full conformity with the sample.

Samples are usually provided by the seller (sale by seller's sample), but sometimes, the buyer may provide samples (sale by buyer's sample). In the case of sale by seller's sample, the seller should keep a **duplicate sample or keep sample** of the **original sample** or **type sample.** The duplicate sample can serve as proof of quality if a dispute about the quality of goods occurs. In the case of sale by buyer's sample, the seller usually first duplicate the sample and then send the duplicate to the buyer for confirmation. This sample is called a **return sample or counter sample or confirming sample**.

Whether the sample is provided by the seller or the buyer, as long as it is confirmed by the two parties, it shall become the basis of quality on which delivery is made in the execution of the contract. In some cases the quality of the goods delivered will by no means be the exact same as shown in the sample. Samples of such goods as timber, coal, some mineral products, and natural products cannot really represent the exact quality of goods to be delivered. Just for this reason, the terms and conditions of the contract about quality should be flexible, like "quality to be about equal to the sample", "quality to be similar to the sample", otherwise, the exporter might be involved in trouble.

3.2.2.2 Sale by Description

In international trade, most commodities are suitable for sale by description which can be subdivided into the following kinds shown in the table below:

	Example
Specification	Chinese Groundnut 2007 Crop, F.A.Q. Moisture (max.) 13% Admixture (max.) 5% Oil content (min.) 44%
Grade	Fresh Hen Eggs: Shell light brown and clean, even in size Grade AA: 60—65 g per egg Grade A: 55—60 g per egg Grade B: 50—55 g per egg Grade C: 45—50 g per egg
Standard	Tetracycline Hydrochloride Tablets (Sugar Coated), 250 mg, B.P. (British Pharmacopoeia) 1973
Brand name / trade mark	Maling Brand Canned Pork Luncheon Meat Haier Air Conditioner
Description and illustration	Quality & technical data to be strictly in conformity with the description submitted by the seller
Place of origin	Yantai Apples Xinjiang Raisins China Northeast Rice

3.3 Quality Clause of the Contract

3.3.1 Basic Contents

The quality clause is one of the main conditions of the contract. Both parties to the contract must agree upon the details covering the quality of the contracted commodity. Generally the name of commodity and specific quality should be indicated explicitly in the quality clause. However, as there are many ways to indicate the quality of commodities, the contents of the quality clause are also various. In the case of a contract for sale by sample, it is necessary to indicate the number of the sample and the date of dispatch. In the case of a contract for sale by description, it should be stipulated clearly the name of goods, specification, grade, standard, brand, trademark or place of origin. When it is a contract for sale by description, the name and number of illustration, drawing and the like should be also indicated in the contract.

3.3.2 Quality Latitude and Quality Tolerance

In international trade, the quality clause of goods in the contract is the cornerstone and basis of goods delivery. According to international trade laws and practices, the seller must deliver goods which are of the quality and description required by the contract. In case the quality of goods delivered does not correspond with the stipulation of the contract, the buyer will be entitled to lodge a claim against the seller or even cancel the contract. However, as certain commodities may be affected by some factors like natural losses in production, production capacity, and characteristics of commodities, the quality of delivered goods cannot be in full conformity with the stipulation of the contract. Therefore, when laying down the quality clause in the contact, it is necessary to add some flexible conditions, leaving enough room for deviation.

3.3.2.1 Quality Latitude

Quality latitude means that the seller and buyer agree that the quality of the delivered goods can vary with an agreed range. Three ways are commonly used in stating to quality latitude as shown in the table below:

Ways of Stating Quality Latitude	Example
➢Flexible Range	Printed Shirting (width) 41″ —42″ Plank (thickness) 3″ —5″
➢Maximum & Minimum	White Kidney Bean, 2007 Crop, F.A.Q. Moisture (max.): 17% Admixture (max.): 1% Imperfect Grains (max.): 3%
➢Allowed Deviation	Grey Duck Feather Down Content 90%, Allowing 1% More or Less

3.3.2.2 Quality Tolerance

Quality tolerance means an allowed deviation in quality stipulated by an international organization and recognized internationally. In the production of industrial products, sometimes it is unavoidable that there is a very slight difference between the product quality and the specification of the quality. For example, a clock or watch is allowed to gain or lose a certain amount of time within a day.

3.4 Quantity of Goods

3.4.1 The Definition of Quantity of Goods

Quantity of goods refers to the weight, number, length, volume, area, capacity, etc. which are indicated by different measuring units. Goods in the contract for the international sale of goods are not only shown by a certain quality, but also a certain quantity. The quantity clause is the foundation for the seller to make delivery and the buyer to take delivery. The quantity of goods is one of the key conditions for the conclusion of the contract and another key factor that affects a transaction.

3.4.2 Units of Measurement and Weights

Different countries use different systems on measurements and weights. In international trade, three systems of measurement are commonly used: the Metric System, the British System and the US System. In addition, there is the International System of Units (SI), an international decimal system of weights and measures derived from and extending the metric system of units, which has been used by more and more countries.

3.4.2.1 Units of Measurement

The following table shows some common units of measurement used in international trade:

Measurement	Used for the goods below	Common Measurement Units
Weight	general natural products and some industrial finished products, such as wool, cotton, grain, mineral products, etc.	kilogram, gram, ton, metric ton, pound, ounce, long ton, short ton, etc.
Length	textiles, metal cord, etc.	meter, centimeter, foot , mile, yard, inch, etc.
Number	consumer goods, light industrial products, machinery products, native produce & animal by-products, etc.	piece, pair, set, dozen, gross, ream, roll, unit, head, etc. case, carton, bundle, barrel, bag, bottle, etc. (used as package units)
Area	textiles, building materials, animal by-products, plastic products, etc.	square meter, square inch, square foot, square yard, etc.
Volume	timber, natural gas, chemical gases, etc.	cubic yard, cubic meter, cubic foot, cubic inch, etc.
Capacity	liquid products, agricultural products, petroleum, etc.	litre, pint, gallon, bushel, etc.

3.4.2.2 Weights

Generally speaking, quantity can be calculated according to the above six aspects: weight, length, number, area, volume and capacity. In international transactions of goods, the quantity of a large number of goods, such as ores, salt, wool and oil, is measured by weight. The following methods are commonly used to calculate weight.

➢**By gross weight**

Gross weight refers to the actual weight of the commodity and the tare, i.e. the package weight. In international trade, some commodities with low value are sold by "gross for net", i.e. they are priced by gross weight instead of by net weight, because the price difference between the goods and the package used is not big, or the package is difficult to weigh separately.

➢By net weight

Net weight refers to the weight of the goods excluding the tare. However, in a few countries, it is defined as including the weight of the immediate container.

There are four ways to calculate tare:

1) By actual tare or real tare: The actual weight of the package.

2) By average tare: The package weight so reckoned on the basis of an average tare of a part of the commodities.

3) By customary tare: Certain standard packages have a generally recognized weight, which is used as the customary tare to denote the weight of such packages.

4) By computed tare: The tare previously agreed upon by the seller and the buyer.

If the contract does not state whether the goods are to be calculated by gross weight or net weight, they are customarily calculated by net weight.

➢By conditioned weight

Conditioned weight means the weight derived from the process with which the moisture content of the commodity is removed and standardized moisture content added by scientific means. Conditioned weight is usually applicable to such goods as raw silk and wool, which are of high economic value and with unsteady moisture content.

The formula of calculating conditioned weight is given as follows:

$$\textbf{Conditioned weight} = \frac{\text{actual weight} \times (1+ \text{standard regaining rate of water})}{1 + \text{actual regaining rate of water}}$$

➢By theoretical weight

Commodities with regular specifications and regular size, such as galvanized iron and steel plate are often subject to the use of theoretical weight. So long as the specifications and the size of such commodities are the same, their theoretical weight is construed by the number of the sheets put together.

➢By legal weight

Legal weight (used mainly by Latin American countries) is the weight of the goods plus any immediate wrappings which are sold along with the goods. Such kinds of goods include can, small paper boxes, small bottles, etc.

➢By net net weight

Net net weight of the goods refers to the weight of only the product itself, without any wrapping, packaging, etc., e.g., the weight of a garment, excluding tissues, pins (used in folding), poly-bags, etc. Net net weight is mainly used in the exercise of customs duties.

3.5 Quantity Clause of the Contract

3.5.1 Basic Contents of the Quantity Clause

The quantity clause of a sales contract is the foundation for effecting delivery and taking delivery of the goods. The basic contents of the quantity clause consist of two parts—the quantity to be delivered and the measurement to be used. If the goods are measured by weight, the way of calculating the weight should also be indicated. The contents of the quantity clause can be various depending on the characteristics of goods.

It is the buyer's basic obligation to deliver the goods based on the quantity stipulated in the sales contract. The business laws of certain countries stipulate that the quantity of goods delivered should be identical to that called for in the contract, otherwise the buyer is entitled to claim against the seller, and even reject the goods. According to ***CISG***, the seller must deliver goods which are of the quantity required by the contract. If the seller delivers a quantity of goods greater than that provided for in the contract, the buyer may take delivery or refuse to take delivery of the excess quantity. The buyer also has the right to reject the goods if the quantity delivered is found to be less than that called for in the contract. Therefore due attention should be paid to the quantity terms during business negotiation.

3.5.2 How to Stipulate the Quantity Clause

3.5.2.1 More or Less Clause

It is generally required that the quantity of the transaction in the contract should be clearly stated, and expressions like "about" and "approximately" should not be allowed. However, the weights of some goods are not easy to be accurate. Owing to the influence of natural conditions, limitations of packing or transportation conditions, the actual quantity of the goods tends to be hardly in conformity with that stipulated in the contract. In order to avoid disputes in the fulfillment of the contract, both the seller and the buyer should decide the delivery quantity reasonably and flexibly beforehand by setting a more or less clause (also called a plus or minus clause) in the contract. This is used because quite often the shipment is over-delivered or under-delivered, esp. for trading of bulk goods like agricultural or mineral products. This quantity clause consists of three parts: **the quantity of the deal + the measurement unit + a more or less clause**. e.g.:

Dehydrated Garlic Flakes, 300 M/T with 5% more or less at seller's option

Under the more or less clause, the payment for the over-delivered or under-delivered will be effected according to the contract price or at the market price at the time of shipment.

3.5.2.2 Approximate Quantity

Sometimes an approximate quantity clause can also be used to indicate the tolerance of the actual quantity to be delivered. In such a clause, the words like "about", "circa" and "approximately" are used to define the quantity of goods. UCP600, Article 30 provides that the words "about" or "approximately" used in connection with the amount of the credit or the quantity or the unit price stated in the credit are to be construed as allowing a tolerance not to exceed 10% more or 10% less than the amount, the quantity or the unit price to which they refer. A tolerance not to exceed 5% more or 5% less than the quantity of the goods is allowed, provided the credit does not state the quantity in terms of a stipulated number of packing units or individual items and the total amount of the drawings does not exceed the amount of the credit. However, it should be noted that different countries may interpret these words differently, i.e. these words represent a different amount of quantity allowance in different countries. Therefore, it is advisable not to use this method in international trade practice.

3.6 Vocabulary Check

approximate quantity clause 约量条款

admixture 杂质；混合物

actual tar 实际皮重

average tare 平均皮重

actual quality 实际品质

barrel 桶

British Pharmacopoeia 英国药典

bushel 蒲式耳

computed tare 约定皮重
conditioned weight 公量
customary tare 习惯皮重
customs duties 关税
deviation 误差
down content 含绒量
exaggerated 夸张的
freight charges 运费
gallon 加仑
grey duck feather 灰鸭毛
gross, gr. 罗(=12 打)
head 头
imperfect grains 不完善粒
intrinsic attributes 内在的属性
indispensable 必不可少的
liter 升
long ton, L/T 长吨
mandatory rules 强制性的法规
moisture 水分
metric ton, M/T 公吨
name of origin 原产地名称
oil content 含油量
ounce, oz. 盎司
pair 双
piece, pc. 只
pint 品脱
pound, lb. 磅
ream, rm. 令
rights and obligations 权利和义务
short ton, S/T 短吨
sale by inspection 看货买卖
tetracycline hydrochloride tablets 盐酸四环素片
unit 辆
uncontroversial 无争议的
white kidney bean 白芸豆

3.7 Notes and Key Terms

1) **quality of goods:** 货物的品质，指货物的内在质量和外观形态的综合。前者包括货物的化学成分、物理和机械性能、生物特征等自然属性；后者包括货物的款式、结构、色泽、味觉和嗅觉等。
2) **sale by sample**：凭样品买卖。凡以样品表示商品品质并以此作为交货依据的，称为凭样品买卖。在国际贸易中，根据样品提供者的不同，样品的种类也很多，以下是常见的样品表达方式：
   duplicate sample / keep sample 复样/留样
   original sample / type sample 原样/标准样品
   return sample / counter sample / confirming sample 回样/对等样品/确认样品
   reference sample 参考样品
   representative sample 代表性样品
   sealed sample 封样

color sample 色彩样品
pattern sample 款式样品

3) **F.A.Q.:** 良好平均品质(Fair Average Quality)，在国际市场上买卖农副产品时常见的一种品质标准，我国出口的某些农产品使用F.A.Q.，一般指“大路货”。此外还有 **G.M.Q.** (Good Merchantable Quality, 上好可销品质)，指卖方交货品质只需要保证为上好的，适合于销售即可。这种标准太过笼统，一般只适用于木材或冷冻水产品。因此，国际货物买卖中，一般很少使用G.M.Q.。

4) **sale by standard:** 凭标准买卖。商品的标准一般由标准化组织、政府机关、行业团体、商品交易所等规定并颁布。世界各国都有自己的标准。另外，还有国际标准和国外先进标准。在国际贸易中，对一些已经被广泛接受的标准，一般倾向于按该项标准进行交易。根据标准适用的范围和地域的不同可分为国际标准、国家标准、行业标准和企业标准。我国外贸实践中，除使用国际标准和某些国家的标准外，也有使用我国国家标准。在实际业务中，买方常要求卖方交货质量符合其指定标准，并经其确定。

5) **quality latitude:** 品质机动幅度，指经交易双方商定，允许卖方交货的品质与合同要求的品质略有不同，只要没有超出机动幅度的范围，买方就无权拒收。

6) **quality tolerance**: 品质公差，指国际性工商组织所规定的或各国同行业所公认的产品品质的误差。

7) **the Metric System, the British System and the US System and the International System of Units (SI):** 公制、英制、美制和国际单位制，这四种是当今使用较广泛的度量衡制度。不同的度量衡制度导致同一计量单位所表示的数量有差异。

8) **gross for net:** 以毛作净。净重是指商品本身的重量，除包装物后的商品实际重量。净重是国际贸易中最常见的计重办法。不过有些价值较低的农产品或其他商品，有时也采用“以毛作净”的办法计重，即以毛重当作净重计价。

9) **net net weight:**净净重，又称实物净重，它是法定重量减去直接接触商品的包装重量，即纯商品的重量。

10) **more or less clause**：溢短装条款，指在规定标准交货数量的同时，还要在合同中规定允许多交或少交货物的数量或百分比的条款。合同中溢短装条款的具体伸缩量的掌握一般由卖方决定(at buyer’s option)，但也有可能由买方或船方来决定(at seller’s option 或 at carrier’s/ship’s option)。如在租船运输的情形下，交货机动幅度多由船方掌握。对此，在合同中最好予以明确。

11) **UCP 600, Article 30:** 国际商会跟单信用证统一惯例600号第30条。该条规定：a.“约”或“大约”用于信用证金额或信用证规定的数量或单价时，应解释为允许有关金额或数量或单价有不超过10%的增减幅度；b. 在信用证未以包装单位件数或货物自身件数的方式规定货物数量时，货物数量允许有 5%的增减幅度，只要总支取金额不超过信用证金额；c. 如果信用证规定了货物数量，而该数量已全部发运，及如果信用证规定了单价，而该单价又未降低，或当第 30 条 b 款不适用时，则即使不允许部分装运，也允许支取的金额有 5%的减幅。若信用证规定有特定的增减幅度或使用第 30 条 a 款提到的用语限定数量，则该减幅不适用。

3.8 Follow-up Practice

3.8.1 Review and Discussion Questions

1) What is meant by quality of goods? Why is it considered to be a key factor in international trade?
2) What methods are commonly used to express the quality of goods?
3) What products are generally sold by sample? Why?
4) What should be done in the case of a contract for sale by sample or sale by description?
5) Explain quality latitude and quality tolerance and their functions.
6) How can we ensure quantity in the international sale of goods?
7) How many methods are commonly used to calculate weight?
8) How tare is calculated when weight is measured by net weight?
9) If a contract does not stipulate whether a consignment is to be got by gross weight or net weight, how do we decide the weight of the goods?
10) What is a more or less clause? Why do we need to stipulate this clause in the contract?
11) How is the price determined for the shipment over-delivered or under-delivered?

3.8.2 Give the Chinese equivalents to the following English terms and put them into the sentences given below.

a. sale by actual quality ________	b. counter sample ________
c. sale by description ________	d. more or less clause ________
e. F.A.Q. ________	f. SI ________
g. quality tolerance ________	h. conditioned weight ________
i. computed tare ________	j. the Metric System ________

1) ________ is the tare which is previously agreed upon by the seller and the buyer.
2) ________ is a complete, coherent system of units used for scientific work, in which the fundamental quantities are length, time, electric current, temperature, mass, luminous intensity, and amount of substance.
3) ________ denotes a quantity of a product that is offered not on a particular quality specification but on the basis that is equal to the average quality of the current crop, recent shipment, etc.
4) ________ generally includes sale by inspection and sale by sample. In the case of sale by inspection, the quality is determined by inspection. In the case of sale by sample, the sample is used to determine the quality.
5) The sample made by the seller according to the buyer's sample is called ________.
6) ________ is often used, particularly, in trading of agricultural or mineral products because it is difficult to calculate the weight of these commodities accurately.
7) In the international sale of goods, most commodities are suitable for ________ which can take various forms such as sale by specification and sale by grade.
8) ________ refers to the weight obtained by deducting actual moisture content and adding standardized moisture content.
9) ________ is a decimal system of units based on the meter as a unit length, the kilogram as a unit mass, and the second as a unit time.
10) ________ means that the very slight difference between the quality of goods and the actual specification of the quality is universally recognized and accepted.

3.8.3 Choose the right answer from each of the following.

1) In the quality clause of a sales contract, ________.
   A. to make the obligation clear, more than two ways of expressing quality of goods should be used
   B. for the sake of accuracy, two ways of expressing quality of goods should be used
   C. to avoid disputes over quality, it is not advisable to use two or more than two ways of expressing quality of goods
   D. to avoid disputes over quality, products should be sold by sample
2) ________ can serve as proof of quality if a dispute about the quality of goods occurs.
   A. A duplicate sample　　B. A buyer's sample
   C. A seller's sample　　D. A reference sample

3) In the case of sale by sample, a sample can be ________.

A. only provided by the buyer

B. only provided by the seller

C. either provided by the seller or the buyer

D. only provided by the seller and accepted by the buyer

4) A counter sample is also called ________.

A. a return sample B. a duplicate sample

C. a type sample D. a sealed sample

5) In international trade, most commodities are suitable for sale by description which can be subdivided into ________ kinds.

A. 3 B. 4 C. 5 D. 6

6) F.A.Q. is the abbreviation of ________.

A. Free Average Quality B. Fair Average Quantity

C. Fair Average Quality D. Free Average Quantity

7) Technological instruments are suitable for ________.

A. sale by description B. sale by sample

C. sale by brand name D. sale by name of origin

8) The quality tolerance refers to the allowed ________ from a given standard of size, content, performance, purity, or other measurable characteristics in the specifications of a commodity.

A. difference B. distance C. derivative D. deviation

9) In international trade, the ________ is entitled to reject the goods if their quantity delivered is less than that agreed upon.

A. seller B. buyer C. carrier D. broker

10) The net weight of goods refers to the weight of the goods alone, the ________ is not counted in.

A. tare B. rate C. rare D. tear

11) There are ________ ways to calculate tare.

A. 2 B. 3 C. 4 D. 5

12) Legal weight refers to the weight of the goods plus any ________ packages of the goods.

A. immediate B. outer C. shipping D. transport

13) ________ is usually applicable to such goods as raw silk and wool, which are of high economic value and with unsteady moisture content.

A. Legal weight B. Net weight

C. Theoretical weigh D. Conditioned weight

14) If the contract does not state whether the goods are to be calculated by gross weight or net weight, they are customarily calculated by ________.

A. gross weight B. gross for net

C. net weight D. net net weight

15) According to UCP600, the words "about" or "approximately" in the quantity clause in the L/C are to be construed as allowing a tolerance not to exceed ________ more or less in quantity.

A. 5% B. 10% C. 15% D. 20%

3.8.4 Decide whether the following statements are true or false.

1) The quality clause is a supplementary clause of a sales contract. ( )

2) A certain kind of goods possesses both natural and social attributes. ( )

3) Sometimes a certain commodity has different names, and tariff rates and freight rates may be different for the same commodity with different names. ( )

4) Sale by inspection is usually used for particular goods such as ornaments, jewels, paintings, artworks, etc. ( )

5) In international trade, most commodities are suitable for sale by sample. ( )

6) Sometimes G.M.Q. can substitute for F.A.Q. as the standard of quality. ( )

7) The counter sample sent to the buyer can act as the type sample. ( )

8) The quality tolerance can not be compensated by increase or decrease of the price in proportion to the degree of the tolerance. ( )

9) Units of measures and weight are uniform worldwide. ( )

10) In international trade, the British and American measuring systems are widely used. ( )

11) In international trade, some goods with high value are sold by "gross for net". ( )

12) Goods without regular specifications and size are often subject to the use of theoretical weight. ( )

13) A more or less clause is usually used for trading of bulk goods like agricultural or mineral products. ( )

14) Under the more or less clause, the quantity over-delivered or under-delivered will be paid only at the contract price. ( )

15) It is advisable to use the words like "about" and "approximately" in the quantity clause in the contract in order to be flexible for the seller to make delivery. ( )

3.8.5 Case Study

A Chinese exporter signed a sales contract with a European company to export five metric tons of Chinese dates. Both the contract and the L/C specified that the dates were of Grade 3. When preparing the goods for shipment, the seller found that Grade 3 Chinese dates were out of stock. In order to make delivery in time, the seller shipped the Grade 2 Chinese dates to the buyer and indicated in the commercial invoice that the Grade 2 Chinese dates were priced as per Grade 3. Do you think it is reasonable for the exporter to do so? What kind of risk is there for the seller?

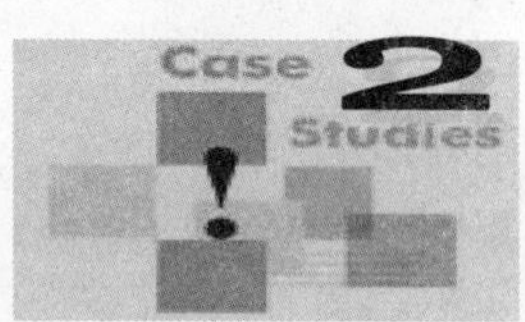

A Chinese company exported 1,000 electric fans to a country in the Middle East. Both the contract and L/C stipulated that partial shipment was not allowed. When the fans were transported to the port for shipment, it was found that 40 fans were damaged and it was impossible to replace the defective fans because of the time for the shipment. The consignor thought that according to UCP500 5% more or less was allowed if the amount didn't exceed the L/C amount and under-delivering 40 fans was still within 5%. In the end, 960 fans were delivered to the importer. When the seller surrendered the shipping documents to the bank for the negotiation of payment, he was rejected by the bank. Was it reasonable for the bank to do so?

1. http://www. cnexp.net 中国出口精英网
2. http://www.cqc.com.cn 中国质量认证中心
3. http://www.trust-trade.com.cn 国际贸易网
4. http://www.iso.org 国际标准化组织网

4 Chapter Four

Packing and Marking

Learning Objectives

At the end of this chapter, you should be able to understand:

- the importance of packing and marking in international trade
- the functions of packing
- the different types of packing and marking and their uses
- how to make shipping marks
- how to draft the packing clause of the contract

Packing is of particular importance in international trade because goods have to travel long distances before reaching their destination—often across oceans or across continents. Accidents, rough weather, unloading and reloading on the way, everything has to be taken into consideration. It is proper packing that can not only serve as a form of protection, but also facilitate loading, unloading and stowage, and prevent pilferage. Furthermore it can promote sales.

In addition, shipping marks, indicative and warning marks play an important role in the identification and proper handling of commodities during transportation and process of loading and unloading.

In international trade, requirements for packing vary according to the differences of the natures and characters of commodities. In most cases, the parties would know beforehand which packaging is required for the safe carriage of the goods to the destination. However, since the seller's obligation to pack the goods may vary according to the type and duration of the transport envisaged, it has been felt necessary to stipulate that the seller is obliged to pack the goods in such a manner as is required for the transport, but only to the extent that the circumstances relating to the transport are made known to him before the sales contract is concluded. According to ***CISG***, the seller should deliver goods which are contained or packaged in the manner required by the contract. The packages should be fit for any particular purpose expressly or impliedly made known to the seller at the time of the conclusion of the contract, except where the circumstances show that the buyer did not rely, or that it was unreasonable for him to rely on the seller's skill and judgment. Except where the parties have agreed otherwise, the goods should be packaged in the manner usual for such goods, or, where there is no such manner, in a manner adequate to preserve and protect the goods.

4.1 Functions of Packing

The functions of packing are divided into primary, secondary and tertiary functions. In contrast with the primary functions, which primarily concern the technical nature of the packing, secondary functions relate to communications. Primary, secondary and tertiary functions are divided into the following sub-functions:

4.1.1 Primary Functions

4.1.1.1 Protective Function

The protective function of packing essentially involves protecting the contents from the environment and vice versa. The inward protective function is intended to ensure full retention of the utility value of the packed goods. The packing is thus intended to protect the goods from loss, damage and theft.

In addition, packing must also reliably be able to withstand the many different static and dynamic forces to which it is subjected during transport, handling and storage operations. The goods frequently also require protection from climatic conditions, such as temperature, humidity, precipitation and solar radiation, which may require "inward packaging measures" in addition to any "outward packing measures".

The outward protection provided by the packing must prevent any environmental degradation by the goods. This requirement is of particular significance in the transport of hazardous materials, with protection of humans being of primary importance. The packing must furthermore as far as possible prevent any contamination, damage or other negative impact upon the environment and other goods.

The inward and outward protective function primarily places demands upon the strength, resistance and leakproof properties of transport packing.

4.1.1.2 Storage Function

The packing materials and packing containers required for producing packages must be stored in many different locations both before the packing of the goods and once the package contents have been used. Packing must thus also fulfill a storage function.

4.1.1.3 Loading and Transport Function

Convenient goods handling entails designing transport packing in such a manner that it may be held, lifted, moved, set down and stowed easily, efficiently and safely. Packing thus has a crucial impact on the efficiency of transport, handling and storage of goods. Packing should therefore be designed to be easily handled and to permit space-saving storage and stowage. The shape and strength of packages should be such that they may not only be stowed side by side leaving virtually no voids but may also be stowed safely one above the other.

The most efficient method of handling general cargo is to make up cargo units. Packing should thus always facilitate the formation of cargo units; package dimensions and the masses to be accommodated should be tailored to the dimensions and load-carrying capacity of standard pallets and containers.

Where handling is to be entirely or partially manual, packages must be easy to pick up and must be of a suitably low mass. Heavy goods must be accommodated in packages which are well suited to mechanical handling. Such items of cargo must be forkliftable and be provided with convenient load-bearing lifting points for the lifting gear, with the points being specially marked where necessary (handling marks).

The loading and transport function places requirements upon the external shape of the package, upon the mass of the goods accommodated inside and upon the convenient use of packaging aids. The strength of the package required for stowing goods on top of each other demonstrates the close relationship between the loading and transport function and the protective function.

4.1.2 Secondary Functions

4.1.2.1 Sales Function

The purpose of the sales function of a package is to enable or promote the sales process and to make it more efficient.

4.1.2.2 Promotional Function

Promotional material placed on the packaging is intended to attract the potential purchaser's attention and to have a positive impact upon the purchasing decision. Promotional material on packaging plays a particularly important role on sales packaging as it is directly addressed to the consumer. This function is of subordinate significance in transport packaging. While product awareness is indeed generated along the transport chain, excessive promotion also increases the risk of theft.

4.1.2.3 Service Function

The various items of information printed on packaging provide the consumer with details about the contents and use of the particular product. Examples are the nutritional details on yogurt pots or dosage information on medicines.

4.1.2.4 Guarantee Function

By supplying an undamaged and unblemished package, the manufacturer guarantees that the details on the packaging correspond to the contents. The packaging is therefore the basis for branded goods, consumer protection and product liability. There are legislative requirements which demand that goods be clearly marked with details indicating their nature, composition, weight, quantity and storage life.

4.1.3 Tertiary Functions

4.1.3.1 Additional Function

The additional function in particular relates to the extent to which the packaging materials or packaging containers may be reused once the package contents have been used. The most significant example is the recycling of paper, paperboard and cardboard packaging as waste paper.

4.1.3.2 Labeling Function

Labels are often required by law and they perform several functions. A label can identify the product or the brand. It might grade the product, describe it, list its content, provide warnings, tell how to use it, such as with cleaners and pesticides, and promote the product using attractive and recognizable graphics.

4.2 Types of Packing

The types of packing of goods are various in international trade. In terms of the functions of packing in the process of circulation, packing can be divided into transport packing and sales packing.

4.2.1 Transport Packing

Transport packing is also referred to as outer packing or big packing and is mainly used for protecting the goods and facilitating loading/unloading, stowage, transport and sorting & counting of the goods.

According to the method of packing, transport packing can also be divided into unit outer packing and assemblage outer packing. Unit outer packing means single piece packing in the course of transportation as shown below:

The Types of Unit Outer Packing

No.	Packing Method		Packing Material	Suitable Goods
1	case	wooden case, carton, plastic case, crate, corrugated box	wood, paper, plastic, iron sheet	cargoes that cannot be pressed, such as glassware, fruits, etc.
2	bag	paper bag, gunny sack, plastic bag	jute, cotton, plastic, paper, etc.	cement, fertilizer, flour, oil cakes, animal feeding products, chemicals, etc.
3	bale, bundle	cotton bale, jute bale	cotton, jute	cargoes that can be pressed, such as cotton, wool, sheepskin, carpet, packaging paper, etc.
4	drum, barrel	wooden cask, iron drums, barrel, hogshead, plastic cask	wood, plastic, metal	liquid, powder, chemicals, paint, etc.

Besides, there are such types as bottle, can, demijohn, cylinder, jar and basket.

Assemblage outer packing means that unit goods are assembled or consolidated into large containers. Containers for this purpose include flexible containers, pallets and large metal containers. Flexible containers are bags made of fiber able to hold powdery commodities, like cement, flint, powder rubber, etc.; pallets are a kind of portable platforms intended for handling, storing, or moving materials and packages; large metal containers are one of the most important inventions of the 20 th century in transportation. The practice of packing in large metal containers, although relatively expensive, has become increasingly popular. Packing goods in such a way facilitates loading and unloading by mechanical handling. It also reduces the risks of water damage, handling damage and pilferage. Today most ports and ships are equipped to handle containers.

When planning transport packing for export, exporters need to keep in mind the following requirements regarding transportation, product and distribution.

(1) **Transportation Requirements**

1) Are the climatic conditions throughout the transportation cycle known?

2) Has the package been constructed to protect its contents against climatic hazards such as weather, humidity, changes of temperature, etc.?

3) Are the handling methods, number of reloadings, equipment used, etc., throughout the transportation cycle known?

4) Has the package been constructed to withstand shocks during transport and strain during storage?

5) Has the package used for the domestic market also been used for export?

6) Can the same export package be used for all export destinations and ways of

transportation?

7) Have all different ways of transportation (sea, air, road, rail) and their technical and economic effects on the construction of the transport packing been studied?

8) Has the effect of palletization and containerization on the construction and economy of the transport packing been studied?

9) Have the standards, laws and regulations affecting transport packing in the target markets been observed?

(2) **Product Requirements**

1) Is the product designed to be easily packed for transport?

2) Are changes in product design possible to adapt it to the transport packing?

3) Does the product need extra protection to keep its properties in the form of:

➢Anti-corrosive agents?

➢Protection against contamination?

➢Shock-absorbing materials?

➢Protection against rodents, insects, mould, etc.?

(3) **Distribution Requirements**

1) What kind of transport packing do your competitors use and why?

2) Is there any particular trend to be observed that will entail changes in the near future?

3) Have the importers'/wholesalers'/retailers' opinions been ascertained on:

➢Quality standards?

➢Packaging sizes and weights?

➢Closure methods, etc.?

4.2.2 Sales Packing

Sales packing is also called inner packing, small packing or immediate packing which is not only adopted as a form of protection to reduce the risks of goods being damaged in transit and prevent pilferage, but also mainly used for the propose of promoting sales. It helps to improve the image of commodities and enables the consumers to easily identify, select, carry and use the commodities. So it has become an important factor directly affecting the sales volume and the price. It is acting as "a silent salesman". Various types of sales packing have been developed to meet the demands of consumers and marketing competitions, including suspensible packing, transparent packing, portable packing, gift packing, etc.

4. 3 Product Code

A product code (bar code) is an encoded set of lines and spaces that can be scanned and interpreted into numbers to identify a product.

There are two main bar codes internationally. One is UPC (Universal Product Code – USA), the other is EAN (European Article Number)

(1) UPC bar codes originate with the only legal source called Gs1. Gs1 is the new name for EAN International and the UCC (Uniform Code Council). UPC bar codes appear as lines (bars) of varying widths representing the series of numbers commonly shown below the bars. Barcode scanners read the bars and convert them back to the 12-digit UPC number that they represent. This number is then looked up within the retailer's inventory system to find the corresponding product name and price that you provided them with when you signed your agreement for them to carry your product.

In short, the UPC bar code is a 12-digit unique code for your product represented by scannable bars. The 12-digit bar code number consists of a number system character, a manufacturer's number, a product number and a check digit. The first six to nine digits of a UPC bar code are referred to as the manufacturing number that always remains constant on all of a company's products. The manufacturing number is followed by a product number that is unique to each product. The last digit in the UPC bar code is known as the check digit.

(2) EAN is an international product marking bar code standard. It is the 13-digit standard for product identification in global trade. EANs are distributed by EAN International, an organization that also establishes the standards and rules for assigning numbers to products and encoding these numbers in readable bar codes, electronic data interchange (EDI), and RFID messages.

China adopted EAN in April, 1991. The bar codes with "690", "691" and "692" mean that the products are made in China.

4.4 Neutral Packing

Neutral packing is the packing that does not show the name and address of the manufacturer, the origin of country, the trademark and brand. Neutral packing is chiefly utilized for breaking through different limitations and political discriminations of importing countries and regions. Also it can be used to break through the tariff and non-tariff barriers of some importing countries or regions, to meet the special demand of the transaction (such as entrepot). Moreover, it helps the manufacturers in the exporting countries to increase the competitiveness of their products and expand the exports. Therefore, using neutral packing is a general practice frequently used in international trade as a means to promote export sales.

4. 5 Marking of Goods

When an order is received from abroad the exporter gets the goods ready for the shipment. It is most important for him to see that they are suitably packed. Associated with packing is the marking of goods.

Correct and complete marking of packages helps to prevent incorrect handling, accidents, incorrect delivery, losses of weight and volume and Customs fines.

Marking must be clear and precise. Its color should stand out clearly from that of the package; it is usually black in color. Alternatively, it may also be applied on adhesive labels. Where possible, black symbols on a white background should be used. Both when the marking is applied directly onto the package and when adhesive labels are used, care must be taken to ensure that marking is applied in a legible and durable manner.

Adequate marking is an indispensable component of the package. If the marking is at variance with the details on the shipping documents, objections may be raised by the Customs authorities. If handling marking is inadequate, those parties whose actions during transport, handling or storage of the cargo have caused damage may be excluded from liability.

4.5.1 Types of Marks

Generally speaking, marks are classified into the following three categories, i.e., shipping mark, indicative mark and warning mark.

4.5.1.1 Shipping Mark

Of the three types of marks, a shipping mark is the most important. It should be discussed and agreed on by both parties of a transaction. Shipping marks are used for the identification of shipment during transit to ensure smooth and prompt delivery. They are not only stenciled on the transport packing of cargoes but also appear on the commercial documents such as invoices, insurance policy or certificate, bills of lading, etc. Previously it was composed of a specific geometric figure, abbreviations or initials of a consignee, the port of destination and the package number. For example:

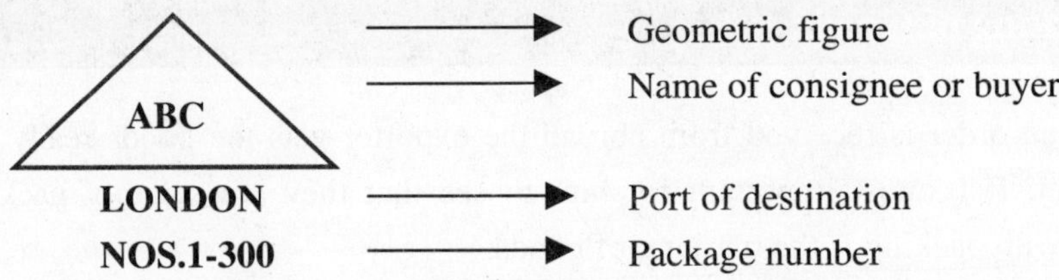

To improve efficiency of cargo handling, to reduce cost and to promote the application of EDI (Electronic Data Interchange), ISO has suggested a standardized form of shipping mark, which has four lines in total with no more than 17 letters in each line and contains no graphs. The standardized shipping marks consist of the following four parts.

1) Abbreviations of consignee or buyer. The abbreviation is used instead of the full name of the customer to reduce the risk of pilferage as potential criminals or receivers cannot easily relate the contents.

2) Reference number. It can be the number of sales confirmation, order, or letter of credit.

3) Port of destination

4) Package number. The shipper should list in the shipping mark the total number of the whole lot of consignment and the number of the individual packages consecutively, so as to convenience the verification of each individual package of the whole patch. For example:

WSG	→	Name of consignee or buyer
S/C NO. 200801108	→	Contract number
HAMBURG	→	Port of destination
NOS. 1–200	→	Package number

Requirements for shipping marks for road, railway and air transport are different from those for ocean transport. For instance, for railway transport, importer's name must be written in full; for air transport, AWB (Air Waybill) number can be used to replace importer's name and reference number.

➢**General requirements for stenciling shipping marks**

1) It is not advisable that shipping marks be designed to be complicated. They should be simple and clear and easy to be identified.

2) The position should be proper, and the color should be durable.

3) No advertising propaganda words and pictures are allowed to be inserted into the marks.

4.5.1.2 Indicative Mark

Indicative marks refer to the symbols or words that indicate the nature of the contents of the package and give instructions to facilitate the smooth handling of the cargo that needs special care. They are mainly used for transport packing of fragile and perishable goods.

In order to unify the symbols and words of indicative marks for transport packing used by different countries, ISO, IATA and RID have made some uniform symbols and indicative words for the member nations to adopt.

Examples of indicative marks

Designation	Symbol	Explanation
Fragile, Handle with care		The symbol should be applied to easily broken cargoes. Cargoes marked with this symbol should be handled carefully and should never be tipped over or slung.
Keep dry		Cargoes bearing this symbol must be protected from excessive humidity and must accordingly be stored under cover. If particularly large or bulky packages cannot be stored in warehouses or sheds, they must be carefully covered with tarpaulins.

(*Continued*)

This way up		The package must always be transported, handled and stored in such a way that the arrows always point upwards. Rolling, swinging, severe tipping or tumbling or other such handling must be avoided. The cargo need not, however, be stored "on top".
Use no hooks		Any other kind of point load should also be avoided with cargoes marked with this symbol. The symbol does not automatically prohibit the use of the plate hooks used for handling bagged cargo.
Center of gravity		This symbol is intended to provide a clear indication of the position of the center of gravity. To be meaningful, this symbol should only be used where the center of gravity is not central. The meaning is unambiguous if the symbol is applied onto two upright surfaces at right angles to each other.
Keep away from heat (solar radiation)		Compliance with the symbol is best achieved if the cargo is kept under the coolest possible conditions. In any event, it must be kept away from additional sources of heat. It may be appropriate to enquire whether prevailing or anticipated temperatures may be harmful. This label should also be used for goods, such as butter and chocolate, which anybody knows should not be exposed to heat, in order to prevent losses.
Protect from heat and radioactive sources		Stowage as for the preceding symbol. The cargo must additionally be protected from radioactivity.
Stacking limitation		The maximum stacking load must be stated as "... kg max.". Since such marking is sensible only on packages with little loading capacity, cargo bearing this symbol should be stowed in the uppermost layer.
Clamp here		Stating that the package may be clamped at the indicated point is logically equivalent to a prohibition of clamping anywhere else.

(Continued)

Temperature limitations		According to regulations, the symbol should either be provided with the suffix "...°C" for a specific temperature or, in the case of a temperature range, with an upper ("...°C max.") and lower ("...°C min.") temperature limit. The corresponding temperatures or temperature limits should also be noted on the consignment note.
Do not use forklift truck here		This symbol should only be applied to the sides where the forklift truck cannot be used. Absence of the symbol on other sides of the package amounts to permission to use forklift trucks on these sides.

4.5.1.3 Warning Mark

When dangerous cargoes are shipped, warning marks, also called dangerous cargo marks, are used to remind the cargo handlers to take necessary safety measures. They are stenciled clearly on outer packages with warning phrases. Sometimes, they are composed of pictures and phrases on the outer packing by the seller as per some dangerous characteristics such as flammable, explosive, poisonous, corrosive, radioactive, etc. The following are some warning marks for packages of dangerous goods.

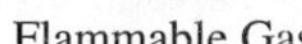

Flammable Gas　Toxic Gas　Radioactive Material　Corrosive

Apart from the above three types of marks, sometimes according to the stipulations of the relevant laws or regulations of the importing countries, or upon the request of the importer, it is the practice of the exporter to supply the subsidiary mark giving the dimensions of the package which may be used for customs clearance or forwarder's assessment of the freight. Moreover, it is preferable for the gross and net weight to be shown on the outer packages. Besides, the place of origin needs to be printed on the outer package. For example:

Gross Weight 120 kgs
Net Weight 100 kgs
Measurement 44×50×60
Made in P. R. China

4.6 Packing Clause of the Contract

4.6.1 Packing Clause

Packing is one of the main conditions and the main component part of the goods description. In international trade practice, the packing clause concerns the interests of the parties to a sales contract. Therefore, in the business negotiation, an agreement on the packing clause should be reached and the packing clause should be explicitly stipulated in the sales contract. The following are some examples of packing clause in the sales contract.

1. To be packed in new strong wooden cases / cartons suitable for long voyage and well protected against dampness, moisture, shock, rust and rough handling. The Seller shall be liable for any damage to the goods due to improper packing and for any damage attributable to inadequate or improper protective measures taken by the Seller. In such case all losses and/or expenses incurred shall be borne by the Seller.

2. Packing must be suitable for ocean shipment and sufficiently strong to withstand rough handling. Bales must be press-packed and hooped with adequate inside waterproof protection and the outer wrapping must comprise good quality canvas. Cases or other outside containers must be externally of the smallest cubic dimension consistent with adequate protection of the goods. Packages must bear full marks and shipping numbers stenciled in good quality stencil ink in large plain characters on two sides and one end of each package. All bales must be marked "use no hooks".

3. Each set packed in one export carton, each 810 cartons transported in one 40 ft container.

4. To be packed in double polythene bags of 20 kgs net, overpacked with a carton.

5. Each package shall be stenciled with gross and net weights, package number, measurement, port of destination, country of origin and the following shipping mark:

99ZHPC-0802
SHANGHAI

4.6.2 General Considerations in Drafting the Packing Clause

(1) The stipulations about packing should be definite. The packing clause should clearly stipulate the packing material, manner of packing, packing specification, packing expenses to be borne, shipping marks and so on. Ambiguous phrases such as "seaworthy packing", "customary packing" or "seller's usual packing" should be avoided.

(2) The party who is to bear the packing expenses should be specified. Generally speaking, the packing expenses are included in the price, and shall be borne by the exporter. If the importer has any special requirements for packing, which is beyond the exporter's ability, the additional charges should be borne by the importer. In case the importer supplies the sales packing or packing material, the packing clause in the contract should specify the time, the way and charges for the importer to supply the packing material, as well as the obligations to be borne in case of the exporter's delay in shipment caused by the importer's delay in supplying the packing material.

(3) According to international trade practice, shipping marks are usually designated by the exporter, and it is not necessary to specify them in the contract. Shipping marks can also be definitely specified at the importer's request. If it is stipulated in the contract that the importer will designate the shipping marks, a deadline for the designated shipping marks should be set, and it should be also indicated that the exporter shall decide the shipping marks if the importer fails to provide the exporter with details of the shipping marks in time.

4.7 Vocabulary Check

assemblage outer packing 集合运输包装
bale 包
bundle 捆
consignee 收货人
consignor 发货人
contamination 污染
container 集装箱
containerization 集装箱化
carton 纸板箱
corrugated carton 瓦楞纸箱
crate 板条箱
cylinder 钢瓶
degradation 恶化；降级
demijohn / carboy 坛
discrimination 歧视
entrepot 储运仓库
fragile goods 易碎货物
flexible container 集装袋
general cargo 普货
gift packing 礼品式包装
gunny / jute bag 麻袋
hazardous materials 危险材料
hogshead 大木桶
indicative mark 指示性标志
iron drum 铁桶
pallet 托盘
palletization 托盘化
pilferage 偷窃
perishable goods 易腐货物
portable packing 便携式包装
retailer 零售商
reference number 参考号
storage 储存
stowage 装载
solar radiation 太阳辐射
suspensible packing 悬挂式包装
transparent packing 透明式包装
unit outer packing 单件运输包装
unblemished 无瑕疵的
warning mark 警告性标志
wholesaler 批发商
wooden cask 木桶

4.8 Notes and Key Terms

1) **In terms of the functions of packing in the process of circulation, packing can be divided into transport packing and sales packing. In addition, according to international trade practices, there is another special mode of packing — neutral packing**：根据包装在流通过程中所起的作用，货物的包装可以分为运输包装和销售包装两大类。另外，按照国际贸易的习惯做法，还有一种特

殊的包装方式，即中性包装。

2) **neutral packing:** 中性包装，是指既不标明生产国别、地名和厂商名称，也不标明商标或品牌的包装，也就是说，在出口商品包装的内外，都没有原产地和出口厂商的标记。中性包装包括无牌中性包装和定牌中性包装两种。前者，是指包装上既无生产国别和厂商名称，又无商标、品牌；后者，是指包装上仅有买方指定的商标或品牌，但无生产国别和厂商名称。采用中性包装，是为了打破某些进口国家与地区的关税和非关税壁垒以及适应交易的特殊需要(如转口销售等)，它是出口国家厂商加强对外竞销和扩大出口的一种手段。

3) **transport packing:** 运输包装。运输包装按其包装方式可分成单件包装(unit outer packing)和集合包装(assemblage outer packing)。单件包装，指货物在运输过程中作为一个计件单位的包装，如箱(case)、包(bale)、桶(drum)、袋(bag)等。集合包装，是在单件包装的基础上，把若干单件组合成一件大包装。以适应港口机械化作业的要求。集合包装能更好地保护商品，提高装卸效率，节省运输费用。常见的集合包装方式有托盘(pallet)、集装袋(flexible container)和集装箱(container)。

4) **sales packing:** 销售包装，又称内包装(inner packing)、小包装(small packing)或直接包装(immediate packing)，指直接接触商品，随着商品进入零售环节和消费者直接见面的包装，实际上是零售包装。它除了保护商品外，还具有美化商品、宣传推广、便于销售和使用等作用。

5) **product code:** 物品条码标志，它是一组粗细间隔不等的平行线及其相应的数字组成的标记。这些线条和空间表示一定的信息，通过光电扫描阅读装置输入相应的计算机网络系统，即可判断出该商品的生产国别或地区、生产厂家、品种规格和售价等一系列有关该产品的信息。国际上通用的条码种类很多，主要有以下两种：一种是美国统一代码委员会编制的 UPC 条码(Universal Product Code)；另一种是由欧洲 12 国成立的欧洲物品编码协会(后改名为国际物品编码协会)编制的 EAN 条码(European Article Number)。目前使用 EAN 物品标识系统的国家(地区)众多，EAN 系统已成为国际公认的物品编码标识系统。中国物品编码中心成立于 1988 年，该中心于 1991 年 4 月代表中国加入国际物品编码协会，并成为正式会员，统一组织、协调、管理我国的条码工作。目前，国际物品编码协会分配给我国的国别号为“690”、“691”和“692”，凡有这些条码的商品，即表示是中国的商品。

6) **RFID:** 射频识别(Radio Frequency Identification)。射频识别技术是利用无线电波对记录媒体进行读写。射频识别的距离可达几十厘米至几米，且根据读写的方式，可以输入数千字节的信息，同时，还具有极高的保密性。射频识别技术适用于物料跟踪、运载工具和货架识别等要求非接触数据采集和交换的场合，在要求频繁改变数据内容的场合尤为适用。射频技术在物品的识别及自动化管理方面也得到了较广泛的应用。

7) **shipping mark:** 运输标志，又称唛头，是一种识别标志。按国际标准化组织(ISO)的建议，包括四项内容：(1) 收货人名称的英文缩写或简称；(2) 参考号，如订单、发票或运单号码；(3) 目的地；(4) 件号。

运输标志在国际贸易中还有其特殊的作用。按《公约》规定，在商品特定化以前，风险不转移到买方承担。而商品特定化最常见的有效方式，是在商品外包装上标明运输标志。此外，国际贸易主要采用的是凭单付款的方式，而主要的出口单据如发票、提单、保险单上，都必须显示出运输标志。商品以集装箱方式运输时，运输标志可被集装箱号码和封口号码取代。

8) **EDI:** 电子数据交换(Electronic Data Interchange)，它是一种利用计算机进行商务处理的新方法。EDI 是将贸易、运输、保险、银行和海关等行业的信息，用一种国际公认的标准格式，通过计算机通信网络，使各有关部门、公司与企业之间进行数据交换与处理，并完成以贸易为中心的全部业务过程。

9) **AWB:** 航空运单(Air Waybill)，是承托运双方缔结的运输合同，也是货物收据，但它不具有物权凭证的性质，不能转让也不凭以提货。收货人提货凭航空公司发出的通知单。

10) **IATA:** 国际航空运输协会(International Air Transport Association)。

11) **RID:** 国际铁路货运会议(Reglement International Dangereux)。

4. 9 Follow-up Practice

4.9.1 Review and Discussion Questions

1) What is the significance of packing in international trade?

2) How is packing of goods classified in international trade? What are some of the major functions of each type of packing?

3) For some commodities, why are indicative and warning marks necessary in international trade?

4) Why are shipping marks important in international cargo transportation? Please describe the standardized form of shipping mark suggested by ISO?

5) What is neutral packing? Why is it used in international trade?

6) What is a product code? Can you describe briefly about UPC and EAN?

7) Why do the exporter and importer need to explicitly stipulate the packing clause in the sales contract?

4.9.2 Choose the right answer from each of the following.

1) ________, usually made of jute, are suitable for transporting such cargoes as cement, fertilizer, flour, oil cakes, animal feeding products, chemicals, etc.

A. Bales　　B. Sacks

C. Cartons　　D. Cases

2) ________ are a kind of portable platforms intended for handling, storing, or moving materials and packages.

A. Flexible containers　　B. Large metal containers

C. Corrugated boxes　　D. Pallets

3) ________ acts as "a silent salesman".

A. Shipping packing　　B. Shipping mark

C. Sales packing　　D. Neutral packing

4) Neutral packing is chiefly used for ________ different limitations and political discriminations of importing countries and regions.

A. opening　　B. setting up

C. setting aside　　D. breaking through

5) ________ is composed of a specific geometric figure, abbreviations of consignee, the port of destination and the package number.

A. A shipping mark　　B. An indicative mark

C. A warning mark　　D. A subsidiary mark

6) ________, also called dangerous cargo marks, are used to remind the cargo handlers to take necessary safety measures.

A. Indicative marks　　B. Warning marks

C. Shipping marks　　D. Subsidiary marks

7) ________ is also called linear code which refers to the electronic identification code attached on the commodities.

A. Tested Code　　B. UCP

C. UPC　　D. ICC

8) ________ should clearly stipulate the packing material, manner of packing, packing specification, packing expenses to be borne, shipping marks and so on.

A. Quality clause　　B. Quantity clause

C. Shipment clause　　D. Packing clause

9) According to international trade practice, shipping marks are usually designated by ________ and it is not necessary to specify them in the contract.

A. the importer B. the exporter

C. the carrier D. the forwarder

10) ________ are mainly used for transport packing of fragile and perishable goods.

A. Warning marks B. Shipping marks

C. Indicative marks D. Subsidiary marks

4.9.3 Decide whether the following statements are true or false.

1) The primary functions of packing primarily concern the technical nature of the packing. ( )

2) Transport packing is not only adopted as a form of protection to reduce the risks of goods being damaged in transit and prevent pilferage, but also used for the propose of promoting sales. ( )

3) UPC and EAN are the two main bar codes used internationally. ( )

4) Neutral packing is a kind of packing which only shows the origin of country and doesn't show the name and address of the manufacturer. ( )

5) Shipping marks are not only stenciled on the transport packing of cargoes but also appear on the commercial documents such as invoices, insurance policy or certificate, bills of lading, etc. ( )

6) Marks are generally classified into shipping mark, indicative mark and warning mark. ( )

7) ISO has suggested a standardized form of shipping mark, which is composed of a specific geometric figure, abbreviations or initials of a consignee, the port of destination and the package number. ( )

8) Requirements for shipping marks for road, railway and air transport are the same as those for ocean transport. ( )

9) Generally speaking, the packing expenses are included in the price, and shall be borne by the exporter. ( )

10) In the international sale of goods, "seaworthy packing", "customary packing" and "seller's usual packing" are commonly used in the packing clause. They are favorable for the seller. ( )

4.9.4 Translate the following indicative and warning phrases into Chinese and match them with the indicative and warning marks below.

No.	English	Chinese	No.	English	Chinese
1	Center of gravity		11	Flammable Gas	
2	Do not use forklift truck here		12	Organic Peroxide	
3	Sling here		13	Oxidizer	
4	Temperature limitations		14	Dangerous When Wet	
5	Clamp here		15	Infectious Substance	
6	No hand truck here		16	Explosive	
7	Use no hooks		17	Corrosive	
8	Keep away from heat		18	Non-Flammable Gas	
9	Stacking limitation		19	Toxic Gas	
10	Don't roll		20	Radioactive II	

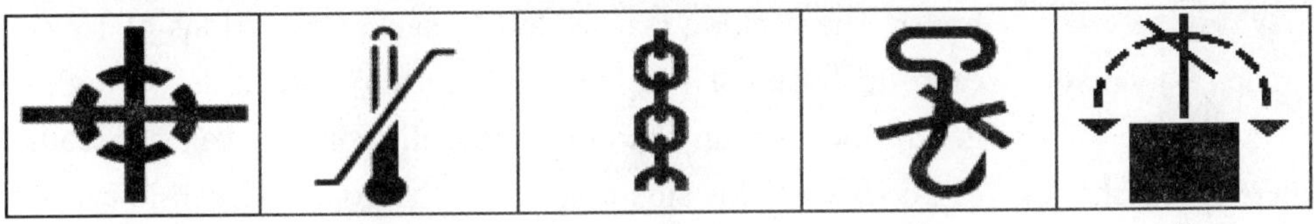

1 2 3 4 5

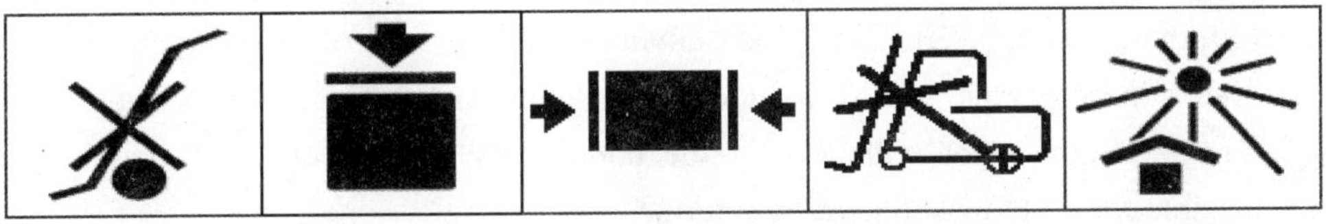

6 7 8 9 10

11 12 13 14 15

16 17 18 19 20

4.9.5 Case Study

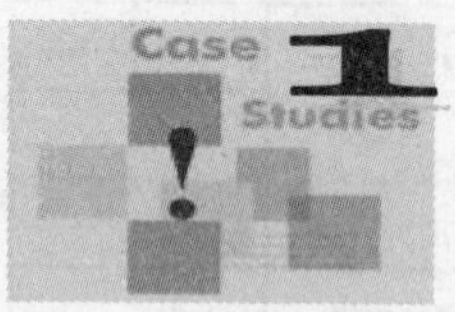

A Chinese importer purchased some flammable liquid chemical raw material from a French exporter. When the shipment arrived at the destination, it was found that there was a slight leakage caused by the defect in a few packages. However, the Chinese importer failed to take any measures to save the loss and prevent the damage from expanding. As a result, the leakage worsened after the warehousing of the goods and led to a self-ignited fire. Afterwards, the Chinese importer lodged a claim against the French exporter for full compensation of the total loss, but was refused.

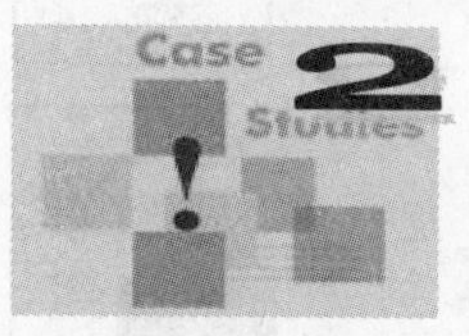

A Chinese company concluded a sales contract with a European buyer. The packing clause stated "packed in cartons of 15 kgs each, 15 boxes of 1 kg each in a carton", When delivering the goods, the company had to employ different packages, because there was a shortage of goods with this small packing. The goods packed in cartons of 15 kgs each, 30 boxes of 0.5 kg each in a carton were delivered. When the goods arrived, the buyer refused to take the delivery on the ground of discrepant packing. But the Chinese company held that the buyer should make the payment because the quantity was consistent with that in the contract. Who do you think should be responsible for it? How should it be settled?

Web Links

1. http://www. cnexp.net 中国出口精英网
2. http://news.pack.net.cn 中国包装网
3. http://www.chinesewto.net/company/hs/hs.asp WTO 中文网
4. http://www.china-gb-bz.com 中国标准标志网
5. http://www.tradehr.com 外贸英才网
6. http://www.biaozhi.net 中国标志网

International Trade Terms

At the end of this chapter, you should be able to understand:

- the importance of trade terms
- the definition of Incoterms
- the most frequently used trade terms
- how to use various trade terms in international trade

In international trade, it is of great importance to determine the responsibilities and obligations of both the seller and buyer. In order to make definite the obligations, risks and costs of the two parties in the transfer of the goods, the buyer and seller, during business negotiation, must adopt a certain trade term, which is a indispensable part of the contract for the international sale of goods, because trade terms are directly related to the prices of commodities. Therefore, it is essential for the people engaged in international trade to understand and master various kinds of trade terms that are in universal use in international trade and relevant international trade practices so that they can choose them to their own advantage.

5. 1 International Trade Terms

Trade terms, also referred to as "price terms" or "delivery terms", stand for specific obligations of the buyer and the seller. Every commercial transaction is based upon a sales contract, and the trade terms used in the contract have the important function of naming the exact point at which the ownership of the merchandise is transferred from the seller to the buyer. The trade terms also define the responsibilities and expenses of both the seller and the buyer. The use of the trade terms greatly simplifies the contract negotiation, and thus saves time and cost. The price of commodity usually refers to the unit price. A complete unit price must comprise four elements, namely a measuring unit, unit price, employed currency and trade term, for example, USD 100 per M/T CIF New York.

Trade terms are key elements of international contracts of sale, since they tell the parties what to do regarding:

➢delivery terms (carriage of the goods from the seller to the buyer and division of costs and risks between the parties);

➢price terms (stipulating what are included in the price the buyer paid to the seller, e.g. cost, freight, insurance, export and import clearance fees, etc.);

➢delivery obligations (what documents should the seller provide, e.g. bill of lading, insurance policy, etc.).

5. 2 Introduction to Incoterms 2000

By the 1920s, commercial traders had developed a set of trade terms to describe their rights and liabilities with regard to the sale and transport of goods. These trade

Standard trade definitions from the International Chamber of Commerce.

terms consisted of short abbreviations for lengthy contract provisions. Unfortunately, there was no uniform interpretation of them in all countries, and therefore misunderstandings often arose in cross-border transactions.

To improve this aspect of international trade, the International Chamber of Commerce (ICC) in Paris developed Incoterms—short for International Commercial Terms, a set of uniform rules for the interpretation of international commercial terms defining the costs, risks, and obligations of buyers and sellers in international transactions. First published in 1936, these rules have been periodically revised to account for changing modes of transport and document delivery. The current version is Incoterms 2000.

Most contracts made after 1 January 2000 will refer to the latest edition of Incoterms, which came into force on that date. The correct reference is to "Incoterms 2000". Unless the parties decide otherwise, earlier versions of Incoterms—like Incoterms 1990—are still binding if incorporated in contracts that are unfulfilled and date from before 1 January 2000.

5.3 Use of Incoterms

Incoterms are not implied into contracts for the sale of goods. If you desire to use Incoterms, you must specifically include them in your contract. Further, your contract should expressly refer to the rules of interpretation as defined in the latest revision of Incoterms, for example, Incoterms 2000, and you should ensure the proper application of the terms by additional contract provisions. Also, Incoterms are not "laws." In case of a dispute, courts and arbitrators will look at: 1) the sales contract, 2) who has possession of the goods, and 3) what payment, if any, has been made.

5.3.1 Incoterms Do...

Incoterms 2000 may be included in a sales contract if the parties desire the following:

(1) To complete a sale of goods.

(2) To indicate each contracting party's costs, risks, and obligations with regard to delivery of the goods as follows:

➢When is the delivery completed?

➢How does a party ensure that the other party has met that standard of conduct?

➢Which party must comply with requisite licenses and government-imposed formalities?

➢What are the mode and terms of carriage?

➢What are the delivery terms and what is required as proof of delivery?

➢When is the risk of loss transferred from the seller to the buyer?

➢How will transport costs be divided between the parties?

➢What notices are the parties required to give to each other regarding the transport and transfer of the goods?

(3) To establish basic terms of transport and delivery in a short format.

5.3.2 Incoterms Do Not...

Incoterms 2000 are not sufficient on their own to express the full intent of the parties. They will not:

➢Apply to contracts for services.

➢Define contractual rights and obligations other than for delivery.

➢Specify details of the transfer, transport, and delivery of the goods.

➢Determine how title to the goods will be transferred.

➢Protect a party from his/her own risk of loss.

➢Cover the goods before or after delivery.

➢Define the remedies for breach of contract.

5.4 The Structure of Incoterms 2000

In 1990, for ease of understanding, the terms were grouped in four basically different categories: namely starting with the term whereby the seller only makes the goods available to the buyer at the seller's own premises (the "E"-term Ex works); followed by the second group whereby the seller is called upon to deliver the goods to a carrier named by the buyer (the "F"-terms FCA, FAS and FOB); continuing with the "C"-terms where the seller has to contract for carriage, but without assuming the risk of loss of or damage to the goods or additional costs due to events occurring after shipment and dispatch (CFR. CIF, CPT and CIP); and, finally, the "D"-terms whereby the seller has to bear all costs and risks needed to bring the goods to the place of destination (DAF, DES, DEQ, DDU and DDP). The following chart sets out this classification of the trade terms.

Incoterms 2000

Group E Departure	EXW	Ex Works Departure (...named place)
Group F Main Carriage Unpaid	FCA	Free Carrier Main carriage unpaid (...named place)
	FAS	Free Alongside Ship (...named port of shipment)
	FOB	Free On Board (...named port of shipment)
Group C Main Carriage Paid	CFR	Cost and Freight Main carriage paid (...named port of destination)
	CIF	Cost. Insurance and Freight (...named port of destination)
	CPT	Carriage Paid To (...named place of destination)
	CIP	Carriage and Insurance Paid To (…named place of destination)
Group D Arrival	DAF	Delivered At Frontier Arrival (...named place)
	DES	Delivered Ex Ship (...named port of destination)
	DEQ	Delivered Ex Quay (...named port of destination)
	DDU	Delivered Duty Unpaid (...named place of destination)
	DDP	Delivered Duty Paid (...named place of destination)

5.5 Modes of Transport of Incoterms

Not all Incoterms are appropriate for all modes of transport. Some terms were designed with sea vessels in mind while others were designed to be applicable to all modes. The following table sets out which terms are appropriate for each mode of transport.

Modes of Transport of Trade Terms

All modes of transport including multimodal transport	EXW	Ex Works (...named place)
	FCA	Free Carrier (...named place)
	CPT	Carriage Paid To (...named place of destination)
	CIP	Carriage and Insurance Paid To (...named place of destination)
	DAF	Delivered at Frontier (...named place)
	DDU	Delivered Duty Unpaid (...named place of destination)
	DDP	Delivered Duty Paid (...named place of destination)
Sea and inland waterway transport	FAS	Free Alongside Ship (...named port of shipment)
	FOB	Free On Board (...named port of shipment)
	CFR	Cost and Freight (...named port of destination)
	CIF	Cost, Insurance and Freight (...named port of destination)
	DES	Delivered Ex Ship (...named port of destination)
	DEQ	Delivered Ex Quay (...named port of destination)

5.6 Notes on Incoterms

(1) Underlying Contract—Incoterms were designed to be used within the context of a written contract for the sale of goods. Incoterms, therefore, refer to the contract of sale, rather than the contract of carriage of the goods. Buyers and sellers should specify that their contract be governed by Incoterms 2000.

(2) EXW and FCA—If you buy Ex Works or Free Carrier you will need to arrange for the contract of carriage. Also, since the shipper will not receive a bill of lading, using a letter of credit requiring a bill of lading will not be possible.

(3) EDI—It is increasingly common for sellers to prepare and transmit documents electronically. Incoterms provides for EDI so long as buyers and sellers agree on their use in the sales contract.

(4) Insurable Interest—Note that in many cases either the buyer or the seller is not obligated to provide insurance. In a number of cases neither party is obligated to provide insurance. However, both the seller and buyer should be aware that they may have insurable interest in the goods and prudence dictates purchase of insurance coverage.

(5) Customs of the Port or Trade—Incoterms are an attempt to standardize trade terms for all nations and all trades. However, different ports and different trades have their own customs and practices. It is best if specific customs and practices are specified in the sales contract.

(6) Precise Point of Delivery—In some cases it may not be possible for the buyer to name the precise point of delivery at contract. However, if the buyer does not do so in a timely manner, it may give the seller the option to make delivery within a range of places that is within the terms of the contract. For example, the original terms of sale may state CFR Port of Rotterdam. The Port of Rotterdam is huge and the buyer may find that a particular point within the port is best and should so state in the sales contract and in the trade term. Also, since the buyer becomes liable for the goods once they arrive, he or she may be responsible for unloading, storage and other charges once the goods have been made available at the place named.

(7) Export and Import Customs Clearance—It is usually desirable that export customs formalities be handled by the seller and import customs formalities be handled by the buyer. However, some trade terms require that the buyer handle export formalities and others require that the seller handle import formalities. In

each case the buyer and seller will have to assume risk from export and import restrictions and prohibitions. In some cases foreign exporters may not be able to obtain import licenses in the country of import. This should be researched before accepting final terms.

(8) Added Wording—It is possible, and in many cases desirable, that the seller and buyer agree to additional wording to an Incoterm. For example, if the seller agrees to DDP terms, agreeing to pay for customs formalities and import duties, but not for VAT (Value Added Taxes) the term "DDP VAT Unpaid" may be used.

(9) Packing—It is the responsibility of the seller to provide packaging unless the goods shipped are customarily shipped in bulk (usually commodities such as oil or grain). In most situations it is best if the buyer and seller agree in the sales contract on the type and extent of packing required. However, it may not be possible to know beforehand the type or duration of transport. As a result, it is the responsibility of the seller to provide for safe and appropriate packaging, but only to the extent that the buyer has made the circumstances of the transport known to the seller beforehand. If the seller is responsible for packing goods in an ocean or air freight container it is also his responsibility to pack the container properly to withstand shipment.

(10) Inspection—These are several issues related to inspections: a) the seller is responsible for costs of inspection to make certain the quantity and quality of the shipment is in conformity with the sales contract, b) pre-shipment inspections as required by the export authority are the responsibility of the party responsible for export formalities, c) import inspections as required by the import authority are the responsibility of the party responsible for import formalities, and d) third-party inspections for independent verification of quality and quantity (if required) are generally the responsibility of the buyer. The buyer may require such an inspection and inspection document as a condition of payment.

(11) Passing of Risks and Costs—The general rule is that risks and costs pass from the seller to the buyer once the buyer has delivered the goods to the point and place named in the trade term.

Passing of risks and costs under Incoterms 2000

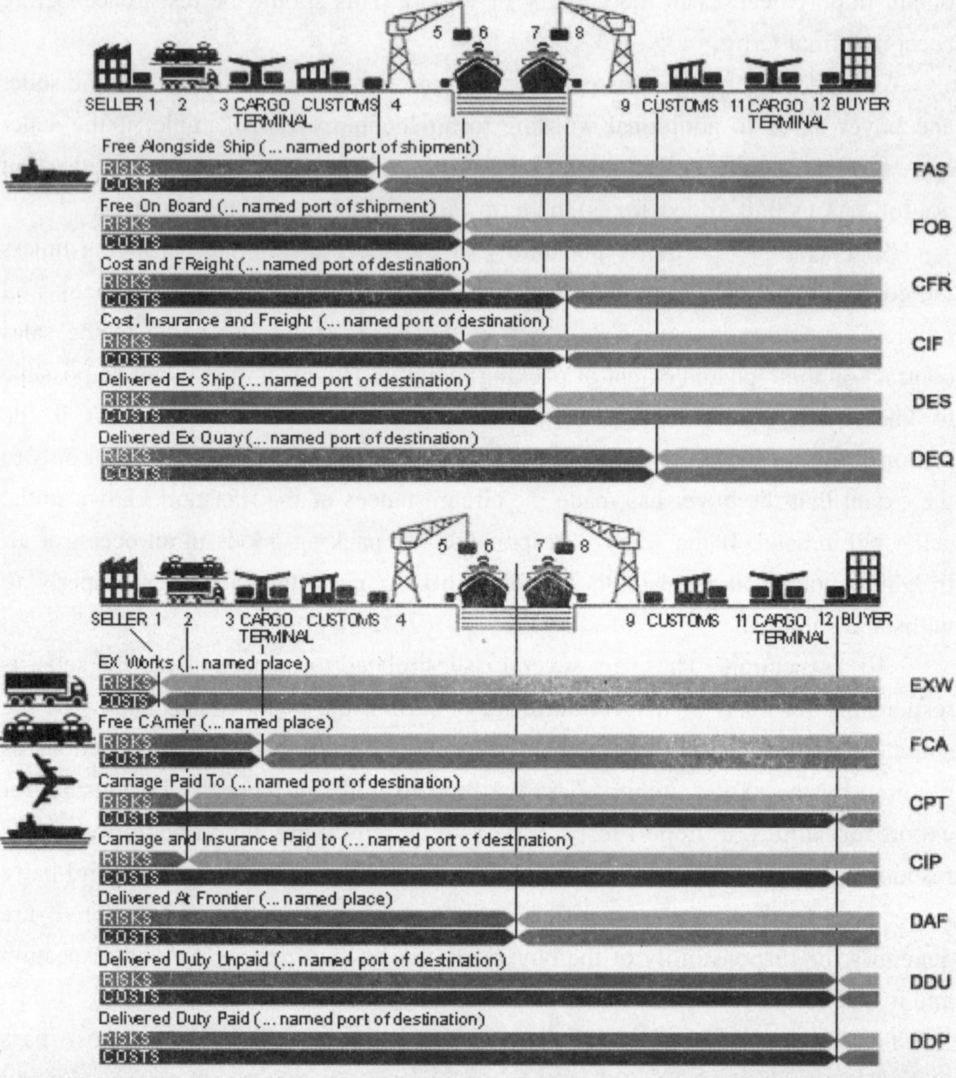

5.7 The Most Frequently Used Trade Terms

FOB, CFR and CIF are the three traditional trade terms that are widely used in international trade. With the development of transportation technology, FCA, CPT and CIP have also developed based on FOB, CFR and CIF. The former three trade terms apply to ocean carriage whereas the latter three can be used for all modes of transport, but are particularly suitable for container transport and all forms of multimodal transport. These terms are universally used in international trade. However, there are no internationally unified interpretations concerning trade terms within the international trade circles. What is stated below is just from Incoterms 2000. Their interpretations are most generally, not compulsorily, accepted by exporters and importers. In addition, there are also "*Warsaw-Oxford Rules 1932*", and "*Revised American Foreign Trade Definitions 1941*", all of which are also often referred to when trade terms are used. Though popular and generally acceptable, these instruments, after all, are not laws or international pacts. They are not binding on all parties except when they have agreed to use whichever of them to interpret the trade terms. In a word, what is stipulated in the sales contract counts for much. The detailed descriptions of the three most frequently used trade terms are given here.

5.7.1 FOB (Free on Board) (...named port of shipment)

This term means that the seller delivers when the goods pass the ship's rail at the named port of shipment. This means that the buyer has to bear all costs and risks of loss of or damage to the goods from that point. The FOB term requires the seller to clear the goods for export. This term can only be used for sea or inland waterway transport. If the parties do not intend to deliver the goods across the ship's rail, the FCA term should be used.

5.7.1.1 The Seller's Obligations

(1) Provision of goods in conformity with the contract

The seller must provide the goods and the commercial invoice, or its equivalent electronic message, in conformity with the contract of sale and any other evidence of conformity which may be required by the contract.

(2) Licenses, authorization and formalities

The seller must obtain at his own risk and expense any export licenses or other official authorization and carry out, where applicable, all customs formalities necessary for the export of the goods.

(3) Delivery

The seller must deliver the goods on the date or within the agreed period at the named port of shipment and in the manner customary at the port on board the vessel nominated by the buyer.

(4) Transfer of risks

The seller must bear all risks of loss of or damage to the goods until such time as they have passed the ship's rail at the named port of shipment.

(5) Division of costs

The seller must pay all costs relating to the goods until such time as they have passed the ship's rail at the named port of shipment; and the costs of customs formalities necessary for export as well as all duties, taxes and other charges payable upon export.

(6) Notice to the buyer

The seller must give the buyer sufficient notice that the goods have been delivered.

(7) Proof of delivery, transport document or equivalent electronic message

The seller must provide the buyer at the seller's expense with the usual proof of delivery.

The seller must render the buyer, at the latter's request, risk and expense, every assistance in obtaining a transport document for the contract of carriage (for example, a negotiable bill of lading, a non-negotiable sea waybill, an inland waterway document, or a multi-modal transport document).

(8) Checking, packaging, marking

The seller must pay the costs of those checking operations which are necessary for the purpose of delivering the goods. The seller must provide at his own expense packaging (unless it is usual for the particular trade to ship the goods of the contract description unpacked) which is required for the transport of the goods, to the extent that the circumstances relating to the transport (for example modalities, destination) are made known to the seller before the contract of sale is concluded. Packaging is to be marked appropriately.

5.7.1.2 The Buyer's Obligations

(1) Payment of the price

The buyer must pay the price as provided in the contract of sale.

(2) Licenses, authorization and formalities

The buyer must obtain at his own risk and expense any import license or other official authorization and carry out all customs formalities for the import of the goods and where necessary, for their transit through any country.

(3) Contracts of carriage and insurance

The buyer must contract at his own expense for the carriage of the goods from the named port of shipment.

(4) Delivery

The buyer must take delivery of the goods when they have been delivered.

(5) Transfer of risks

The buyer must bear all risks of loss or damage to the goods from the time they have passed the ship's rail at the named port of shipment.

(6) Division of costs

The buyer must pay all costs relating to the goods from the time they have passed the ship's rail at the named port of shipment; and any additional costs incurred, either because the vessel nominated by him fails to arrive on time, or is unable to take the goods etc; all duties, taxes and other charges as well as the costs of carrying out customs formalities payable upon import of the goods and for their transit through any country.

(7) Notice to the seller

The buyer must give the seller sufficient notice of the vessel name, loading point and required delivery time.

(8) Inspection of goods

The buyer must pay the costs of any pre-shipment inspection except when such inspection is mandated by the authorities of the country of export.

5.7.1.3 Variations of FOB Term

As the loading of the goods is a continuous process, sometimes it is hard to use the ship's rail as a point to divide responsibilities and costs. To avoid dispute, there are several derived price terms:

(1) FOB Liner Terms

It means that the ship will be responsible for loading and unloading and the seller does not have to pay loading expense.

(2) FOB under Tackle

This term only requires the seller to send and place the goods on the wharf within the reach of the ship's tackle. Loading expenses incurred thereafter will be borne by the buyer.

(3) FOB Stowed

Under this term, the seller loads the goods into the ship's hold and pays the loading expenses including stowing expenses.

(4) FOB Trimmed

The seller pays all the loading expenses including trimming expenses (which actually also includes stowing expense).

5.7.1.4 Special Interpretation of FOB Term by America

Revised American Foreign Trade Definitions 1941 has six interpretations for FOB, among which only the FOB vessel, named port of shipment is close to the interpretation of Incoterms 2000.Therefore, the interpretation of *Revised American Foreign Trade Definitions 1941* for FOB is greatly different from the normal international interpretation:

(1) If a contract is signed with an American or Canadian trader, the word "Vessel" is necessary to go with FOB besides the port's name, for example, "FOB Vessel New York". If it is written as "FOB New York" without the word "Vessel", the seller is only responsible for transporting the goods to any uncertain place inside of the city of New York but not to New York port.

(2) For the transfer of risk, ship's rail is not the division but the seller has to shoulder all the responsibilities until the goods have been safely transferred onto the board.

(3) The buyer should pay for the costs that the seller used to help afford the export documents, export tax and other related costs.

5.7.2 CIF (Cost, Insurance and Freight) (...named port of destination)

This term means that the seller delivers when the goods pass the ship's rail in the port of shipment. The seller must pay the costs and freight necessary to bring the goods to the named port of destination. But the risk of loss or damage to the goods, as well as any additional costs due to events occurring after the time of delivery, are transferred from the seller to the buyer. However, in CIF the seller also has to procure marine insurance against the buyer's risk of loss of or damage to the goods during the carriage. Consequently, the seller contracts for insurance and pays insurance premium. The buyer should note that under the CIF term the seller is required to obtain insurance only on minimum cover. Should the buyer wish to have the protection of greater cover, he would either need to agree as such expressly with the seller or to make his own extra insurance arrangements.

The CIF term requires the seller to clear the goods for export. This term can be used only for sea and inland waterway transport. If the parties do not intend to deliver the goods across the ship's rail, the CIP should be used.

5.7.2.1 The Seller's Obligations

(1) Provision of goods in conformity with the contract

The seller must provide the goods and the commercial invoice, or its equivalent electronic message, in conformity with the contract of sale and any other evidence of conformity which may be required by the contract.

(2) Licenses, authorization and formalities

The seller must obtain at his own risk and expense any export licenses or other official authorization and carry out, where applicable, all customs formalities necessary for the export of the goods.

(3) Contracts of carriage and insurance

A) Contract of carriage

The seller must contract on usual terms at his own expense for the carriage of the goods to the named port of destination by the usual route in a seagoing vessel (or inland waterway vessel as the case may be) of the type normally used for the transport of goods of the contract description.

B) Contract of insurance

The seller must obtain at his own expense cargo insurance as agreed in the contract, such that the buyer, or any other person having an insurable interest in the goods, shall be entitled to claim directly from the insurer and provide the buyer with the insurance policy or other evidence of insurance cover.

The insurance shall be contracted with underwriters or insurance company of good repute and, failing express agreement to the contrary, be in accordance with minimum cover of the Institute Cargo Clause (Institute of London Underwriters) or any similar set of clauses. When required by the buyer, the seller shall provide at the buyer's expense war, strikes, riots and civil commotion risk insurance if procurable. The minimum insurance shall cover the price provided in the contract plus ten per cent and shall be provided in the currency of the contract.

(4) Delivery

The seller must deliver the goods on board the vessel at the port of shipment on the date or within the agreed period.

(5) Transfer of risks

The seller must bear all risks of loss of or damage to the goods until such time as they have passed the ship's rail at the port of shipment.

(6) Division of costs

The seller must pay all costs relating to the goods until such time as they have been delivered, and the freight and all other including the costs of loading the goods on board; and the costs of insurance and any charges for unloading at the agreed port of discharge which were for the seller's account under the contract of carriage; and where applicable, the costs of customs formalities necessary for export as well as all duties, taxes and other charges payable upon export, and for their transit through any country if they were for the seller's account under the contract of carriage.

(7) Notice to the buyer

The seller must give the buyer sufficient notice that the goods have been delivered as well as any other notice required in order to allow the buyer to take measures which are normally necessary to enable him to take the goods.

(8) Proof of delivery, transport document or equivalent electronic message

The seller must, at his own expense, provide the buyer without delay with the usual transport document for the agreed port of destination. This document (for example a negotiable bill of lading, a non-negotiable sea waybill or inland waterway document) must cover the contract goods, be dated within the period agreed for shipment, enable the buyer to claim the goods from the carrier at the port of destination and, unless otherwise agreed, enable the buyer to sell the goods in transit by the transfer of the document to a subsequent buyer (the negotiable bill of lading) or by notification to the carrier. When such a transport document is used in several originals, a full set of originals must be presented to the buyer. Where the seller and the buyer have agreed to communicate electronically, the document referred to in the preceding paragraphs may be replaced by an EDI message.

(9) Checking, packaging, marking

The seller must pay the costs of those checking operations which are necessary for the purpose of delivering the goods. The seller must provide at his own expense packaging (unless it is usual for the particular trade to ship the goods of the contract description unpacked) which is required for the transport of the goods. Packaging is to be marked appropriately.

5.7.2.2 The Buyer's Obligations

(1) Payment of price

The buyer must pay the price as provided in the contract.

(2) Licenses, authorizations and formalities

The buyer must obtain at his own risk and expense any import license or other official authorization and carry out, where applicable, all customs formalities necessary for the import of the goods and for their transit through any country.

(3) Taking delivery

The buyer must accept the delivery of the goods when they have been delivered and receive them from the carrier at the named port of destination.

(4) Transfer of risks

The buyer must bear all risks of loss of or damage to the goods from the time they have passed the ship's rail at the port of shipment.

(5) Division of costs

The buyer must pay all supplementary costs for the goods once they have passed the ship's rail at the port of shipment, including unloading, lighterage and wharfage at the port of destination and all costs relating to import formalities including duties, taxes and other charges including transshipment.

(6) Notice to the seller

The buyer must, whenever he is entitled to determine the time for shipping the goods and/or the port of destination, give the seller sufficient notice thereof.

(7) Proof of delivery, transport document or equivalent electronic message

The buyer must accept the transport document.

(8) Inspection of goods

The buyer must pay all the costs of any pre-shipment inspection except when such inspection is mandated by the authorities of the country of export.

5.7.2.3 Variations of CIF Term

(1) CIF Liner Terms

It denotes that the loading and unloading charges are met by the shipping company or specifically the seller.

(2) CIF Landed

It means that the unloading costs, including lighterage and wharfage are borne by the seller.

(3) CIF Ex-Ship's Hold

It means that the buyer pays for the unloading charges.

5.7.3 CFR (Cost and Freight) (...named port of destination)

This term means that the seller delivers when the goods pass the ship's rail in the port of shipment. The seller must pay the costs and freight necessary to bring the goods to the named port of destination but the risk of loss of or damage to the goods, as well as any additional costs due to events occurring after the time of delivery, are transferred from the seller to the buyer. The CFR term requires the seller to clear the goods for export. This term can be used only for sea and inland waterway transport. If the parties do not intend to deliver the goods across the ship's rail, the CPT term should be used.

5.7.3.1 The Seller's Obligations

(1) Provide the goods and the commercial invoice, or its equivalent electronic message, in conformity with the contract of sale and any other evidence of conformity which may be required by the contract.

(2) Obtain at his own risk and expense any export licenses or other official authorization and carry out, where applicable, all customs formalities necessary for the export of the goods.

(3) Contract on usual terms at his own expense for the carriage of the goods to the named port of destination by the usual route in a seagoing (or inland waterway vessel as the case may be) of the type normally used for the transport of goods of the contract description.

(4) Deliver the goods on board the vessel at the port of shipment on the date or within the agreed period.

(5) Bear all risks of loss of or damage to the goods until such time as they have passed the ship's rail at the port of shipment.

(6) Pay all costs relating to the goods until such time as they have been delivered and the freight and all other costs, including the costs of loading the goods on board and any charges for unloading at the agreed port of discharge which were for the seller's account under the contract of carriage; and, where applicable, the costs of customs formalities necessary for export as well as all duties, taxes and other charges payable upon export, and for their transit through any country if they were for the seller's account under the contract of carriage.

(7) Give the buyer sufficient notice that the goods have been delivered as well as any other notice required in order to allow the buyer to take measures which are normally necessary to enable him to take the goods.

(8) Provide at his own expense the buyer without delay with the usual transport document for the agreed port of destination.

(9) Pay the costs of those checking operations (such as checking quality, measuring, weighing, counting) which are necessary for the purpose of delivering the goods. The

seller must provide at his own expense packaging (unless it is usual for the particular trade to ship the contract description unpacked) which is required for the transport of the goods arranged by him. Packaging is to be marked appropriately.

5.7.3.2 The Buyer's Obligations

(1) Pay the price as provided in the contract of sale.

(2) Obtain at his own risk and expense any import license or other official authorization and carry out, where applicable, all customs formalities for the import of the goods and for their transit through any country.

(3) Accept delivery of the goods when they have been delivered and receive them from the carrier at the named port of destination.

(4) Bear all risks of loss of or damage to the goods from the time they have passed the ship's rail at the port of shipment. The buyer must, should he fail to give notice, bear all risks of loss of or damage to the goods from the agreed date or the expiry date of the period fixed for the shipment provided, however, that the goods have been duly appropriated to the contract, that is to say, clearly set aside or otherwise identified as the contract goods.

(5) Pay all supplementary costs for the goods once they have passed the ship's rail at the port of shipment, including unloading, lighterage and wharfage at the port of destination and all costs relating to import formalities including duties, taxes and other charges including transshipment.

(6) Whenever he is entitled to determine the time for shipping the goods and/or the port of destination, give the seller sufficient notice thereof.

(7) Accept the transport document if it is in conformity with the contract.

(8) Pay the costs of any pre-shipment inspection except when such inspection is mandated by the authorities of the country of export.

5.8 Vocabulary Check

authorization *n.* 授权
bill of lading 提单
breach of contract 违反合同
compulsorily 强制性地
customs clearance 清关
customs formalities 海关手续
document delivery 交单；文件传递
for ease of understanding 为了便于理解
government-imposed formalities 政府强制规定的手续
insurable interest 可保利益
insurance coverage 保险范围
insurance policy 保险单
international pacts 国际公约
interpretation *n.* 解释
license 许可证
modes of transport 运输方式
mandate *n. v.* 命令；托管；强制
multimodal transport 多式联运
named carrier 指定承运人
named place 指定地点
named port of destination 指定目的港
negotiable 可议付的
nominate *v.* 指定
point of delivery 交货点
prudence *n.* 谨慎
requisite licenses 必要的许可证
remedy *n. v.* 补救
transfer of risks 风险转移
standardize *v.* 使标准化
title to the goods 货物所有权
in conformity with 符合；按照
VAT (Value Added Taxes) 增值税
wharf 码头

5.9 Notes and Key Terms

1) **trade terms:** 贸易术语又叫价格术语(price terms)或交货条件(delivery terms)，它是在国际贸易实践中产生的，用以表示商品的价格构成以及商品在交接过程中有关风险、责任和费用划分问题的专门用语。贸易术语通常用简略的文字或英文缩写表示，如 Ex works 或 EXW，即指“工厂交货价”。

2) **merchandise:** 商品，货物。在商务英语中，表示“商品”的词很多，如 commodity, goods。这三个词意思相同，但是仍有一些差别。(1) commodity 是个较正式的经济学名词，如“商品经济”的英文是 commodity economy，在此短语中不用 goods。commodity 有时也用来指小件商品，而不指“商品”这个经济学概念，commodity 可以和 goods 通用，不过，commodity 指“商品”的时候更多，goods 指“货物”的时候更多。如果说丝绸、茶叶是我国的商品，这时最好用 commodity；如果说货源充足、装货等，常用 goods。(2) merchandise 泛指商品，不指一件商品，前面不加 a，也无复数形式；此外，merchandise 还指大商人经营的商品。此外，表示“商品”的词还有 article, ware, item, product 等。

3) **However, both the seller and buyer should be aware that they may have insurable interest in the goods and prudence dictates purchase of insurance coverage:** 然而买卖双方应该明白，他们在货物上有可保利益存在，基于谨慎原则要购买保险。

4) **Warsaw-Oxford Rules 1932**：《1932 年华沙—牛津规则》是国际法协会专门为解释 CIF 合同而制定的。19 世纪中叶，CIF 贸易术语开始在国际贸易中得到广泛采用，然而对使用这一术语时买卖双方各自承担的具体义务并没有统一的规定和解释。对此，国际法协会于 1928 年在波兰首都华沙开会，制定了关于 CIF 合同的统一规则，称之为《1928 年华沙规则》，共包括 22 条。其后，将此规则修订为 21 条，并更名为《1932 年华沙—牛津规则》，沿用至今。这一规则对于 CIF 的性质、买卖双方所承担的风险、责任和费用的划分以及所有权转移的方式等问题都作了比较详细的解释。

5) **Revised American Foreign Trade Definitions 1941**：《1941 年美国对外贸易定义修订本》，它最早由美国 9 个商业团体于 1919 年在纽约制定，原称为《美国出口报价及其缩写条例》(The U.S. Export Quotations and Abbreviations)，后来于 1941 年在美国第 27 届全国对外贸易会议上对该条例作了修订，命名为《1941 年美国对外贸易定义修订本》。解释的贸易术语共有六种，分别为：①Ex (Point of Origin，产地交货)；②FOB (Free on Board，在运输工具上交货)；③FAS (Free Along Side，在运输工具旁边交货)；④C&F (Cost and Freight，成本加运费)；⑤CIF (Cost, Insurance and Freight，成本加保险费、运费)；⑥Ex Dock (Named Port of Importation，目的港码头交货)。

《美国对外贸易定义》主要在北美国家采用。由于它对贸易术语的解释与《2000 年国际贸易术语解释通则》有明显的差异，所以，在同北美国家进行交易时应加以注意。

6) **derived price terms:** 变形价格术语。

在按 FOB 条件成交时，卖方要负责支付货物装上船之前的一切费用。但各国对于“装船”的概念没有统一的解释，有关装船的各项费用由谁负担，各国的惯例或习惯做法也不完全一致。如果采用班轮运输，船方负责装卸，装卸费计入班轮运费之中，自然由负责租船的买方承担；而采用程租船(voyage charter)运输，船方一般不负担装卸费用。这就必须明确装船的各项费用应由谁负担。为了说明装船费用的负担问题，双方往往在 FOB 术语后加列附加条件，这就形成了 FOB 的变形。主要包括以下几种：①FOB Liner Terms (FOB 班轮条件)；②FOB Under Tackle (FOB 吊钩下交货)；③FOB

Stowed (FOB 理舱费在内)；④FOB Trimmed (FOB 平舱费在内)。

在许多标准合同中，为表明由卖方承担包括理舱费和平舱费在内的各项装船费用，常采用 FOBST (FOB Stowed and Trimmed)方式。

FOB 的上述变形，只是为了表明装船费用由谁负担而产生的，并不改变 FOB 的交货地点以及风险划分的界限。《2000 年国际贸易术语解释通则》指出，《通则》对这些术语后的添加词句不提供任何指导规定，建议买卖双方在合同中加以明确。

7) **the Institute Cargo Clause (Institute of London Underwriters):** 伦敦保险人协会《协会货物保险条款》。

5.10 Follow-up Practice

5.10.1 Review and Discussion Questions

1) What are trade terms? Why are they used in international trade?
2) What is the meaning of Incoterms? What is the significance of using Incoterms?
3) What are the benefits of organizing the terms in Incoterms 2000 into four basically different groups?
4) What are the differences between FOB and CFR?
5) Why does an export price need to contain a measuring unit, unit price, employed currency and trade term?
6) Why is it advisable to use CIF in export and use FOB in import?

5.10.2 Match the trade terms under Incoterms 2000 with their Chinese equivalents.

a. EXW (EX Works)	1. 船边交货
b. FAS (Free alongside Ship)	2. 运费付至
c. FCA (Free Carrier)	3. 目的港船上交货
d. FOB (Free on Board)	4. 未完税交货
e. CFR (Cost and Freight)	5. 工厂交货
f. CIF (Cost, Insurance and Freight)	6. 货交承运人
g. CPT (Carriage Paid to)	7. 运费、保险费付至
h. CIP (Carriage and Insurance Paid to)	8. 装运港船上交货
i. DAF (Delivered at Frontier)	9. 成本加运费
j. DES (Delivered Ex Ship)	10. 目的港码头交货
k. DEQ (Delivered Ex Quay)	11. 完税后交货

l. DDU (Delivered Duty Unpaid) 12. 边境交货
m. DDP (Delivered Duty Paid) 13. 成本、保险费加运费

5.10.3 Describe the differences and similarities of the following three trade terms and complete the table below.

Trade terms	Risks	Obligations		Costs	
	Who is responsible for all risks after the goods pass the ship's rail at the loading port?	Who charters the ship and books shipping space?	Who arranges marine insurance?	Who pays all costs and freight to the port of destination?	Who pays the insurance premium?
FOB					
CFR					
CIF					

5.10.4 Choose the right answer from each of the following.

1) Incoterms are a standard set of terms and abbreviations developed by ________.
   A. the International Law Association
   B. the International Chamber of Commerce
   C. the United Nations Conference on Trade and Development
   D. the United Nations Commission on International Trade Law
2) In the international trade practices regarding trade terms, which of the following is the most influential and widely used?
   A. Hague Rules (《海牙规则》).
   B. Warsaw-Oxford Rules 1932.
   C. Revised American Foreign Trade Definitions 1941.
   D. Incoterms.
3) Incoterms 2000 includes ________ trade terms.
   A. 6 B. 12
   C. 13 D. 14
4) As far as risks taken by the seller are concerned, ________.
   A. CIF is bigger than CFR B. CIF is as the same as CFR
   C. CFR is bigger than CIF D. FOB is bigger than CFR
5) The term FOB should be followed by ________.

A. point of origin B. port of importation

C. port of discharge D. port of exportation

6) The term CIF should be followed by ________.

A. point of origin B. port of shipment

C. port of destination D. port of exportation

7) The term CFR should be followed by ________.

A. point of origin B. port of shipment

C. port of destination D. port of exportation

8) The term EXW should be followed by ________.

A. point of origin B. port of shipment

C. port of importation D. port of exportation

9) The term DAF should be followed by ________.

A. point of origin B. port of importation

C. port of destination D. port of shipment

10) The term FAS should be followed by ________.

A. point of origin B. port of destination

C. port of shipment D. port of exportation

11) The term DES should be followed by ________.

A. point of origin B. port of shipment

C. port of exportation D. port of destination

12) The term DEQ should be followed by ________.

A. point of origin B. port of loading

C. port of destination D. port of shipment

13) The term FCA should be followed by ________.

A. point of origin B. seller's place of shipment

C. buyer's place of shipment D. buyer's railway station

14) The term DDP should be followed by ________.

A. point of origin B. port of shipment

C. port of buyer's premise D. place of destination

15) Which of the following prices quoted is correct?

A. US$1,000 per M/T CIF USA. B. US$200 per ton CIFC3 New York.

C. US$150 per case CIF. D. US$100 per doz. CIFC3 London.

5.10.5 Decide whether the following statements are true or false.

1) If the seller agrees to deliver the goods to a ship, but not to pay for loading them,

the term is FOB. ( )

2) Under FOB, the seller must bear all risks of loss of or damage to the goods until such time as they have passed the ship's rail at the named port of shipment. ( )

3) The only difference between CFR and CIF is that under a CFR contract the buyer must purchase a marine insurance contract to cover the goods while they are on the voyage. ( )

4) Under CFR, the seller must pay the usual freight rate and any additional costs that arise en route. ( )

5) The terms FOB, CFR and CIF are applicable to all modes of transport. ( )

6) DAF is only adopted when two countries have the land-connected borderline. ( )

7) Each term has a "liability point", which means that costs and risks are all moved over to another party from that very point. ( )

8) EXW contract is called "physical delivery" while CFR is "symbolic delivery". ( )

9) CFR states that the exporter is obligated to make all necessary arrangements to ship the goods all the way from the exporter's premises to the named port of debarkation. ( )

10) Under CIF the seller also has to procure marine insurance against the buyer's risk of loss of or damage to the goods during the carriage. ( )

5.10.6 Case Study

A Chinese exporter signed a CFR contract with an importer in America on canned meat for an amount of US$50,000, with payment by D/P at sight. On the morning of May 5, 2006, the goods were all loaded onto the named vessel. The Chinese salesperson in charge of this contract was so busy that he forgot to send the buyer the shipping advice until the next morning. Unexpectedly, when the American importer went to the local insurance company to insure the goods, the insurance company had already learned that the ship suffered a wreck on May 6 and refused to insure the shipment. The American importer immediately sent a fax to the Chinese exporter saying "Owing to your delayed shipping advice, we are unable to insure the goods. Since the vessel has been destroyed in a wreck, the loss of goods should be for your account. At the same time, you should compensate our profit and expense losses which amount to US$50,000." Soon all the shipping documents sent through the collecting bank were returned to the Chinese exporter, for the reason that the importer refused to take up the shipping documents.

Who should be responsible for the loss and why?

A Chinese international trade company exported a batch of walnut to England on the basis of CIF London. As it was a seasonal commodity, it was stipulated in the contract that the covering L/C should reach the seller before the end of September. The seller guaranteed that the vessel would reach the port of destination not later than December 2. If the vessel reached the port of destination later than that day, the buyer was entitled to cancel the contract. In case the payment had been made, the seller should return the payment to the buyer. Then, where do you think the crux lies in this case?

Web Links

1. http://www.exporteam.com 合众出口网
2. http://www.intl-trade.com 国际贸易
3. http://www.iccwbo.org 国际商会
4. http://www.mofcom.gov.cn 中国商务部
5. http://www.chinaintertrade.com 中国国际贸易网
6. http://www.tradehr.com 外贸英才网
7. http://www.iccwbo.org 国际商会

6 Chapter Six

International Cargo Transport

Learning Objectives

At the end of this chapter, you should be able to understand:

- the different modes of transport, esp. ocean transport
- the nature of liner transport
- general considerations on cargo transport
- the various kinds of B/L
- the contents of the transport clause

Transport is indispensable to international trade. It aids the realization of a transaction by moving goods between the import and export countries.

In international trade, both the seller and the buyer should negotiate and stipulate the terms and conditions of the shipment clause, such as shipment date, port of shipment and destination, partial shipment, transshipment, etc. Without specific stipulations of the shipment clause in the sales contract, disputes would arise from the performance of the sales contract and cause serious troubles. This chapter focuses on the different modes of transport and relevant aspects of the shipment clause.

6.1 Modes of Transport

There are different modes of transport. Where the import and export countries share common borders on land, land transport can do its part, using highways or railways. When the destination is far beyond the continent, other modes of transport are required. While air transport can be utilized to carry cargo abroad by planes to far places, its high cost lessens the chances of a successful sale. Then sea transport is undoubtedly the most economical means of transportation particularly when bulky commodities are involved.

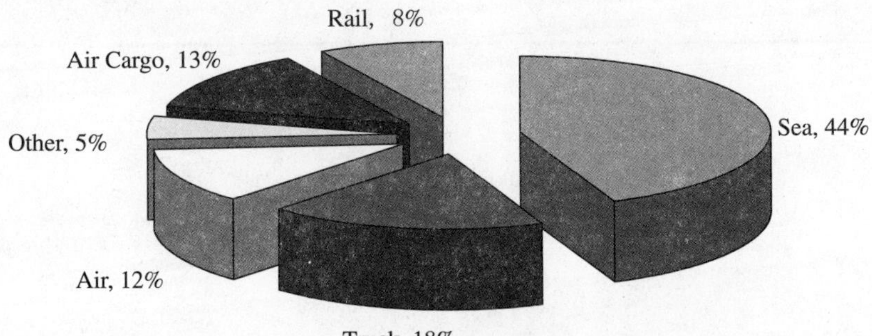

Transportation Segment

6.1.1 Ocean Transport

Ocean transport is the most widely used form of transportation in international trade. Two-thirds of the world total volume and over 80% of China's imports and exports now are transported by sea. It is generally considered as a cheap mode of transport for delivering large quantities of goods over long distances.

6.1.1.1 Features of Ocean Transport

Ocean transport has many advantages. The first advantage is the easy passage since about 70% of the earth is covered by water. Secondly, ocean transport has a large capacity. Thirdly, because of such large capacity, the unit distribution cost is reduced. And finally, ocean transport has good adaptability to cargoes of different sizes, weights, shapes, etc.

Of course, there are also disadvantages, one of which is the low passage of ocean transport. In addition, ocean transport is also vulnerable to bad weather and less punctual compared with road or air transport.

6.1.1.2 Types of Shipping Services

According to ways of operation, ocean transport can be divided into liner transport and charter transport.

(1) **Liner Transport**

A liner is a passenger or cargo vessel that operates over a regular route according to an advertised timetable. It has the following characteristics:

➢fixed route, ports, schedule and relatively fixed freight;

➢loading and unloading charges included in the freight;

➢simple procedures and ideal for cargoes of small quantity.

(2) **Charter Transport**

Charter here refers to the practice of paying money to a shipping company to use their boats. Charter rate is much cheaper than that of the liner. Shippers may choose direct route. Therefore it is widely used in transport of bulk cargoes.

Charter transport can be divided into voyage charter, time charter and demise charter. **Voyage charter** is the hire of a ship for a particular voyage. It can be further divided into single voyage charter, consecutive voyage charter and so on. The ship owner is responsible for fulfilling transportation according to the stipulated voyage, and for the operation and management of the ship, and should bear all costs in transit. The freight rate is usually charged by quantities of the goods carried, or at a fixed rate, regardless of the quantity. **Time charter** is the charter of a ship for a definite period of time. The ship owner is responsible for providing seaworthy ships and the related charges. The character has the right to dispatch the ship, but should bear all expenditures in transit, such as charges for fuels, port, loading and unloading. **Demise charter** is also called bareboat charter. Under demise charter, all what a shipper charters is the vessel itself. The charterer is responsible for crewing, provisioning, fuelling, maintaining and even paying various taxes or duties. The charterer has to pay an agreed sum of freight to the owner within the agreed time of charter. This kind of charter is less popular than time charter and voyage charter. It is mainly used when there is an unexpected or sudden increase of export goods to be shipped.

6.1.1.3 Freight Rates

Freight rate is a special unit used in calculating charges that must be paid for shipping the cargo. Shippers should be familiar with the rates in order to estimate and reduce, if possible, the cost of transport. Ocean freight may be broadly divided into liner freight and charter freight.

(1) **Liner Freight Rate**

Liner freight covers loading and unloading charges. The carrier is responsible for the loading and unloading. Freight rate is fixed and stipulated in the tariff. It contains basic freight rate and various kinds of surcharges. The following are the standards of liner freight calculations:

1) **Weight**: for items marked with "W" in the tariff, the freight thereon are to be calculated per metric ton on weight (weight ton).

2) **Measurement**: for items marked with "M", the freight is to be calculated per cubic meter on measurement of the cargo (measurement ton).

3) **Weight or Measurement**: for items marked with "W/M", the freight is to be calculated on the basis of either weight or measurement ton, subject to the higher one.

4) **Ad Val.**: for items marked with "AD Val.", the freight is to be calculated on the basis of the price or value of the cargo concerned. For some valuable goods like gold, silver, or expensive fur, the freight is usually 1%—5% of the price.

5) **W/M or Ad val.**: for items marked "W/M or Ad val." the highest rate is adopted.

In addition to the basic freight rates, there are many kinds of surcharges that cannot be ignored:

➢bunker adjustment factor;

➢port surcharges;

➢transshipment surcharges;

➢heavy lift and long length additional.

(2) **Charter Rate**

The freight rate for charter is usually charged by quantities of the goods carried and fluctuates with market conditions of supply and demand. In a boom period, the rates rise; in a period of recession, they decline.

As the charter freight does not cover loading and unloading charges, it should be made clear as to who will bear the loading and unloading charges. The stipulation of loading and unloading charges for charters should be in correspondence with the following derived trade terms.

1) **Liner terms/gross terms**: the freight includes loading and unloading charges. The ship owner shall be responsible for loading and unloading.

2) **Free in**: the ship owner bears the unloading charges, not loading charges.

3) **Free out**: the ship owner bears the loading charges, not the unloading charges.

4) **Free in and out**: the ship owner bears no unloading and loading charges.

5) **Free in and out and Stowed and Trimmed**: the ship owner is neither responsible for loading and unloading nor for stowed and trimmed charges.

6.1.2 Air Transport

Air transport is one of the modern forms of transport. It transports 1% of the total world trade volume, 20%—30% of the value and it is increasing at a rate of 7%—8% per year. Undoubtedly, it will continue to make contributions to the distribution of commodities throughout the world.

6.1.2.1 The Features of Air Transport

The main advantages of air transport are stated as follows:

(1) High speed and quick transit.

(2) Low risk of damage and pilferage.

(3) Reducing costs of logistics.

(4) Less capital tied up in transit.

(5) Ideal for consumer goods, seasonal goods and merchandise of high value.

(6) Simplified documentation system: One document—an air waybill—is used throughout air freight transit and is interchangeable between IATA accredited airlines.

(7) Major airports worldwide, compared with major seaports, tend to be located in the centers of commercial/industrial areas.

(8) The extensive air freight network worldwide, offering more frequent flights than the maritime services.

Although air transport has a number of advantages, there are some disadvantages which are stated below:

(1) Limited capacity and overall dimensions of acceptable cargoes with weight restrictions.

(2) High operating expenses and transport costs.

(3) Vulnerable to weather disruptions.

6.1.2.2 Types of Air Transport Services

Air transport services are divided into three categories: scheduled airlines, chartered carriers, and consolidated consignments by freight forwarders.

(1) **Scheduled airlines**: Scheduled airlines operate on the basis of a scheduled service, over a fixed airline and between fixed airports. They are suitable for conveying fresh, emergent and seasonal goods.

(2) **Chartered carriers**: Chartered carriers are the hire of an aircraft by a shipper or several shippers to deliver cargoes. They are ideal for carrying cargoes of large quantities or for carrying cargoes of different shippers to the same destination.

(3) **Consolidated consignments**: Consolidated consignments mean that the air freight forwarder assembles a number of individual shipments into one consignment and forwards them under one air waybill. A consolidated shipment made up of several shipments can be dispatched to one common destination. Many shippers prefer this kind of shipment as the freight rate is 7%—10% lower than that of a scheduled airline.

6.1.2.3 Airline Rates

Air freight is normally collected according to actual weight for heavy cargoes or measurement weight for large volume cargoes. The rates are normally quoted per kilogram. The air freight excludes other charges such as customs fees and storage fees.

In order to stimulate the business of transport, different types of air freight rates are designed. *General Cargo Rates* are the basic rates, while *Specific Commodity Rates* are reduced rates applicable to a wide range of commodities specified in the tariff of the carrier. Where no commodity rate is available for cargoes like live animals, human remains or valuable cargoes, Classification Rates apply.

6.1.3 Rail Transport

Rail transport is a major mode of transport in terms of capacity, only second to ocean transport. The modern railway system is a high capacity form of transport operating in a disciplined, controlled and reliable way. It is capable of attaining relatively high speeds and is most economical especially when it provides the complete trainload for a shipper on a regular basis. Besides, compared with other modes of transport, it is less prone to interruption by poor weather. However it is confined to railways and therefore less flexible.

Rail transport can be divided into international combined rail transport and domestic rail transport.

Different types of freight cars have been designed to suit the needs of different types of cargoes. A *shed car* is closed and provides complete protection for the cargo. An *open car* is an open-top wagon usually used for cargoes with water-proof packing or cargoes that will not be damaged in wet weather. A *flat car* does not have top and sides and is used for carrying cargoes with heavy weight and/or large measurement such as automobiles, timber, containers, etc. There are also special-purpose cars for carrying a specific type of cargo such as refrigerated cars, tank cars, ventilation cars, and live stock cars.

6.1.4 Road Transport

The road vehicle is very versatile unit of transport which is most flexible in operation. Road transport has become increasingly dominant between countries connected by roads and plays a very important role in shipping international cargoes to and from seaports and airports. Road transport is ideal for general merchandise and selective bulk cargoes in small quantities.

However the disadvantages are limited capacity, as well as relatively high operating cost. There is also a high risk of pilferage and damage although the driver accompanies the vehicle throughout the transit.

6.1.5 Containerization

Containerization is a method of distributing merchandise in a unitized form, suitable for ocean, rail and multi-modal transport. It is the most modern form of physical international distribution and overall is highly efficient in terms of reliability, cost, quality of service, advanced technology and so on.

6.1.5.1 Features of Containerization

Containerization offers a door to door service under FCL/FCL (Full Container Load/ Full Container Load), door to container freight station (CFS) service under FCL/LCL (Full Container Load/ Less than Container Load), CFS to CFS service under LCL/LCL, or CFS to door service under LCL/FCL conditions.

It can be handled quickly and easily by standardized equipment and can thus save labor and loading and unloading charges.

The low risk of cargo damage and pilferage enables more favorable cargo premium, compared with break-bulk cargo shipments.

Less packing is required for containerized consignments. In some cases, particularly with specialized ISO containers such as refrigerated ones or tanks, no packing is required. This cuts down costs substantially in the international transit and raises service quality.

Faster transit, coupled with more reliable maritime schedules, and ultimately increased service frequency, generates savings on warehouse accommodation, lessens risks of obsolescent stock and speeds up cash flow.

6.1.5.2 Types and Sizes of Containers

(1) **Types**

Different types of containers are available to suit different needs. They mainly comprise:

➢**Dry Cargo Container**—this type is designed for various kinds of dry cargoes, dry edibles, machines, precision instruments, medical apparatuses, valuable cargoes, etc.

➢**Refrigerated Container**—this type is fitted with a refrigerating machine, which is specially designed for frozen meat, eggs and fruits to be preserved at low temperature.

➤**Open Top Container**—this type is, as the term implies, open at the top and is normally covered by water-proof canvas after it is filled up. The open top container is fit for bulky and weighty cargoes including unbaled mineral ores, etc.

➤**Tanker Container**—this type is designed for vegetable oils, alcohol and other liquid cargo in bulk.

➤**Flat Rack Container**—this type is devoid of side and top pallets and, instead, grates are fitted at both sides. It is usually used for the carriage of livestock, fresh vegetables or certain types of machines.

(2) **Sizes**

The majority of containers used are built to the ISO specifications. The basic container is most commonly built of steel or aluminum. The 20-foot and 40-foot containers are most popular. Containers of other sizes and capacities are also available but not widely used.

Cross section: 2.60 m × 2.45 m
2.45 m × 2.45 m

Length: 3.05 m (10 ft)
6.10 m (20 ft)
9.15 m (30 ft)
10.70 m (35 ft)
12.20 m (40 ft)

Capacity (m)	Volume (cubic metre)	Weight (kg)
2.45×2.60×6.10	31.0	18,720
2.45×2.60×12.20	68.1	27,580
2.45×2.45×6.10	30.0	18,000
2.45×2.45×12.20	66.5	27,070

6.1.6 International Multi-modal Transport

Goods moving in international trade often have to pass through the hands of more than one carrier and over more than one mode of transport. International multi-modal transport refers to the carriage of goods by at least two different modes of transport on the basis of a multi-modal transport contract from a place in one country where the goods are taken in charge by the multi-modal transport operator to a place designed for delivery situated in a different country.

Although different modes of transport are used, a multi-modal transport operator is solely responsible to deliver the goods from the consignor to the consignee. This adds simplicity to the transport. Because of the simplicity and the use of containers in multi-modal transport, higher efficiency and better quality of transport service are also realized.

The multi-modal transport operator refers to any person, who on his own behalf, or through another person acting on his behalf, concludes a multi-modal transport contract, acts as a principal, not as an agent or on behalf of the consignor or of the carriers participating in the multi-modal transport operations, and assumes responsibility for the performance of the contract.

"Multi-modal transport contract" is a contract whereby a multi-modal transport operator undertakes, against payment of freight, to perform or to procure the performance of international multi-modal transport.

6.2 General Considerations on Cargo Transport

(1) **Reliability**

Reliability is the most essential requirement. Shippers must ascertain that goods will arrive before the import license expires and that goods will arrive in good condition.

(2) **Speed and Frequency**

Speed and frequency are important to shippers, manufacturers and importers alike. It is important for shippers to market the goods by an accurate arrival date, and to reduce costs and banking charges. Manufacturers need to avoid the risk and expense of obsolescence, especially for consumer goods. Importers want to reduce stocks, warehouse expenses and the amount of capital to reduce cost. Finally, consumers want to get the right commodities such as fresh fruits, and fashionable clothing, etc.

(3) **Cost**

Shipping costs vary according to time, directions, and carriers. It is worthwhile to study the market carefully to minimize transport cost to be more competitive in the world market.

Other considerations include the customer's choice and needs, the nature of the commodity to be shipped, the total time available, and the suitability of available transport services.

6.3 Major Transport Documents

6.3.1 Bill of Lading

A bill of lading is a shipping document that serves as a receipt from the shipping company for shipper's goods, a title document to the goods shipped, and an evidence of the contract of carriage between the shipping company and the shipper. The B/L is the most important document when shipping goods by ocean freight.

There are a number of different types of bills of lading, as listed below:

(1) **Shipped/On Board B/L & Received for Shipment B/L**

Shipped B/L is issued by the shipping company after the goods are actually shipped on board the designated vessel. Both the name of the vessel and the date of issue of the B/L are indicated on the shipped B/L. It proves that the goods have been loaded or shipped.

Received for shipment B/L merely confirms that the goods have been handed over to, and are in the custody of the ship owner. It proves only the receipt but not the loading or shipment of the cargo. It therefore has no date of shipment and generally no name of a vessel.

(2) **Clean B/L & Unclean B/L or Foul B/L**

A *clean B/L* is the one issued by a carrier for goods which were received in good condition without any unfavorable remarks. A clean B/L provides proof that up until the time goods were transferred to the carrier, no damage has occurred.

When goods are received in damaged condition for shipment on a vessel, the master of the ship will note the damage on the B/L. A bill of lading with such a notation is referred to as an unclean B/L. Unclean B/L is usually not acceptable to the buyer and banks.

(3) **Straight B/L, Blank B/L & Order B/L**

Straight B/L has a specified name in the column of consignee in B/L. Under this bill, only the consignee at the destination is entitled to take delivery of the cargo. As it is not transferable, it is not commonly used in international trade and normally applies to high-value shipments or goods for special purposes.

Blank B/L, also called Open B/L or Bearer B/L, means that there is no definite consignee of the goods. There usually appear in the box of consignee words like "To bearer". Anyone who holds the bill is entitled to the goods the bill represents. No endorsement is needed for the transfer of the blank bill. Due to the exceedingly high risk involved, this bill is rarely used.

Order B/L is widely used in international trade. It means that the goods are consigned or destined to the order of a named person. In the column of consignee, "To order", "To order of the shipper", or "To order of the consignee" is marked. This type of bill of lading is a negotiable instrument. That is, it may be used to transfer title to the goods being shipped to another party. The transfer may occur at any time during the transit process simply by endorsing the order bill to another party.

(4) **Direct B/L, Transshipment B/L & Through B/L**

Direct B/L means that the goods are shipped from the port of loading direct to the port of destination without transshipment.

Transshipment B/L means the goods need to be transshipped at an intermediate port as there is no direct service between the shipment port and the destination port.

Through B/L is issued when the entire voyage involves more than two modes of transportation. More than one carrier is involved during the transportation. Each carrier is responsible only for its own distance although he contracts for further carriage as an agent of the shipper with the next carrier. The consignee will obtain the first B/L through the bank, exchange it for the B/L issued by the last carrier at destination, and take delivery of the cargo.

(5) **Long Form B/L & Short Form B/L**

Long Form B/L refers to the B/L on the back of which all the detailed terms and conditions about the rights and obligations of the carrier and the consignor are listed as an integral part of the B/L.

Short Form B/L, as the name implies, is an abbreviated type of document, not containing the long list of detailed clauses that generally appear on the back of the B/L.

(6) **On Deck B/L & Stale B/L**

When the cargo is placed on the deck of a ship for delivery, an *On Deck B/L* is issued to the consignor when the ship leaves the port. The bill provides a list of goods loaded on the deck of the ship. It applies to goods like livestock, plants, dangerous cargoes that cannot fit into the ship's hold. On deck transit is more dangerous than carriage in the hold of a ship. Insurance and financing for such transit may be more difficult to obtain or may be more costly.

The B/L presented to the consignee or his bank after the stipulated expiry date of presentation or after the goods are due at the port of destination is described as "*Stale B/L*". It is important that the B/L is available at the port of destination before the goods arrive or at the same time. Otherwise, the buyer cannot collect the goods. The late arrival of this all-important document may have undesirable consequences such as warehouse rent, and therefore should be avoided. Sometimes in the case of short sea voyages, it is necessary to add a clause of "Stale B/L is acceptable".

(7) **Ante-dated B/L & Advanced B/L**

Ante-dated B/L means when the actual shipment date is later than that stipulated in the L/C, the carrier sometimes, at the shipper's request, issues and signs a B/L with a date of shipment that suits the requirement so as to avoid non-acceptance by the bank. Due to the risk of the goods being rejected by the consignee arising from the issuance of such a bill, it is advisable to avoid this malpractice even when it seems necessary in certain circumstances

Advanced B/L is issued when the expiry date of the L/C is due but the goods are not got ready for shipment. The purpose of issuing such a bill is to negotiate payment with the bank in time within the validity of the L/C. It is also regarded as unlawful and risky and therefore should be avoided.

6.3.2 Air Waybill

The air waybill is the consignment note used for the carriage of goods by air. It is basically a receipt of the goods for dispatch and evidence of the contract of carriage between the carrier and the consignor. This document is approximately the equivalent to the sea freight bill of lading, but the air waybill is not a negotiable title to goods in the same way as is an ocean bill of lading.

There are two types of air waybills: Master Air Waybill (MAWB) and House Air Waybill (HAWB). The former is issued by the air company to the consignor or freight forwarder after loading the goods on board, and the latter is issued by the freight forwarder.

Air waybills are made out in three originals. Normally the consignor would retain the No. 1 original, the No. 3 would be retained by the airline and the No. 2 would automatically go forward with the consignment to the consignee at the destination.

6.3.3 Multi-modal Transport Document (MTD)

The multi-modal transport document is a document which evidences a multi-modal transport contract, and the taking charge of the goods by the multi-modal transport operator who is responsible for delivering the goods in accordance with the terms of that contract.

When the multi-modal transport operator takes charge of the goods, he shall issue a multi-modal transport document which, at the option of the consignor, shall be either negotiable or non-negotiable. A negotiable multi-modal transport document is made out to order or to bearer. A non-negotiable multi-modal transport shall indicate a named consignee.

It is quite similar to a "through B/L". A through B/L is always connected with sea, used for any transport combined with sea, while MTD can be applied to any kind of combined transport. Several carriers are involved in a through B/L, while MTD is issued by only one carrier, that is, the multi-modal transport operator.

6.4 Clause of Shipment

The clause of shipment specifies all the details regarding the shipment of the goods. The details include the time of shipment, port of shipment, port of destination, advice of shipment, partial shipment and transshipment, etc.

(1) **Time of Shipment**

Time of shipment is the period or deadline by which the consignor must effect the shipment of the contracted goods. Time of shipment is a very important clause in a contract. Any delay or advance of delivery constitutes violation of the contract.

There are basically two ways to set the time of shipment. One is to clearly specify a period of time. For instance, *shipment not later than 31st December, 2007*. The other is to create a link between the time of shipment and the deadline by which the relevant L/C must reach the seller. For example, *Shipment within* ×× *days after receipt of L/C.* The first method is straightforward and easy to understand. The second provides more security for the transaction as shipment will not be made until payment is guaranteed.

(2) **Port of Shipment and Port of Destination**

Port of shipment and port of destination can be specified when a contract is signed. In case a decision cannot be made by that time, several alternatives can be listed and a time limit be set by which the seller or the buyer must notify the counterpart which port is to be the port of shipment or destination.

In choosing the port of shipment and port of destination, the following must be taken into consideration:

Firstly, try to make the port of shipment and port of destination clear and specific. Ambiguous terms, such as "European Main Ports", "Japanese Ports" shall be avoided.

Secondly, allow some flexibility by allowing optional ports because sometimes when the sales contract is concluded, it might not be possible to decide precisely on the exact points of departure and destination. It is thus usually stipulated that the buyer has the right or duty to name later the more specific point.

Thirdly, port regulations, facilities and charges should be considered. Ports with unfamiliar regulations, poor facilities and high charges should be avoided.

Lastly, there is a possibility that different ports may have the same name and that inland cities might be used as loading or unloading ports. Therefore, it might be wise to specify the area where the intended port is located and to find out if an inland city has been used as the port of shipment or the port of discharge.

(3) **Advice of Shipment**

Advice of shipment is required to coordinate the responsibilities of the exporter and the importer.

When the goods are shipped on board the vessel, the seller needs to give the buyer prompt notice of the port of shipment, the date of sailing, the name of the carrying vessel, the estimated time of arrival of the vessel and send the buyer the copies of the necessary documents to enable the buyer to get ready to take delivery of the goods.

In the event of the seller failing to send the advice of shipment to the buyer within the prescribed time frame, the seller would bear the consequential cost incurred.

(4) **Partial Shipment and Transshipment**

Partial shipment means a large amount of export goods are involved in one transaction and are shipped in several lots by several carriers onto different means of conveyance. There are several reasons for partial shipments, such as the limitation of means of conveyance or shipping space, loading and unloading facilities at the port, etc. The clause of shipment must specify whether partial shipment is allowed by using a phrase such as "*Partial shipment (not) to be allowed*".

Transshipment means that the cargo being shipped will change ships before reaching the port of destination. The clause must also specify whether transshipment is allowed by using a phrase such as "*To be transshipped at* ×××" or "*Transshipment not to be allowed*".

6.5 Vocabulary Check

classification rates 分类货运费
consignment note 托运单
consecutive voyage charter 连续程租合同
container freight station (CFS) 集装箱货物集散站
container yard (CY) 集装箱货物堆场
deviation surcharge 绕航附加费
demise charter 光船租船
dry container 杂货集装箱
FCL (full container load) 整箱货
flat rack container 框架集装箱
free out (F.O.) 船方管装不管卸
free in (F.I.) 船方管卸不管装
free in and out (F.I.O.) 船方不管装卸
free in and out, stowed and trimmed (F.I.O.S.T.) 船方不管装卸、理舱和平舱
general cargo rates 普货运价
LCL (less than container load) 拼箱货
liner terms/gross terms 班轮条件
multi-modal transport 多式联运
open top container 敞顶集装箱
refrigerated container 冷藏集装箱
round voyage charter 往返程租合同
specific commodity rates 特定商品运价
tanker container 罐式集装箱
time charter 定期租船
voyage charter 定程租船

6.6 Notes and Key Terms

1) **liner:** 班轮，即轮船公司按照固定的船期、航线和港口往来行驶的船舶。这样的运输叫班轮运输。
2) **freight rates:** 运输费率。在运输业中，freight 一词有两个意思：一是指船舶、车辆运输的货物（goods carried by a vessel)，相当于 cargo 一词；二是指运费 (the charge for transporting goods)。
3) **scheduled airline:** 班机运输，是指定期开航的，定航线、定始发站、定目的港、定途经站的飞机。一般航空公司都使用客货混合型飞机(Combination Carrier)，一方面搭载旅客，一方面又运送少量货物。但一些较大的航空公司在一些航线上开辟定期的货运航班，使用全货机(All Cargo Carrier)运输。
4) **chartered carriers:** 包机运输，可分为整包机和部分包机两类。整包机，即包租整架飞机，指航空公司按照与租机人事先约定的条件及费用，将整架飞机租给包机人，从一个或几个航空港装运货物至目的地。由几家航空货运公

司或发货人联合包租一架飞机或者由航空公司把一架飞机的舱位分别卖给几家航空货运公司装载货物，就是部分包机，适用于托运不足一架整飞机舱，但货量又较重的货物运输。

5) **consolidated consignment:** 集中托运，即将若干票单独发往同一方向的货物集中起来作为一票货，填写一份总运单发运到同一目的站的做法。

6) **bill of lading:** 提单，是由船长或承运人或其代理人签发的，证明收到特定的货物，或已装船，并将约定的货物运至特定的目的地，并交付于收货人或提单持有人的物权凭证，也是承运人和托运人之间运输合同的证明。提单可以作为收取运费的证明和向船公司或保险公司索赔的重要依据。

7) **shipped B/L & received for shipment B/L:** 已装船提单，指承运人向托运人签发的货物已经装船的提单。收货待运提单或备运提单，指承运人虽已收到货物但尚未装船时签发的提单。

8) **clean B/L & unclean B/L:** 清洁提单指提单上未附加表明货物表面状况有缺陷的批注的提单。承运人如签发了清洁提单，就表明所接受的货物表面或包装完好，承运人不得事后以货物包装不良等为由推卸其运送责任。在签发清洁提单的情况下，如交货时货物受损，就说明货物是在承运人接管后受损的，承运人必须承担赔偿责任。货物交运时，若其包装及表面状态出现不坚固、不完整等情况，船方可以批注，即为不清洁提单。

9) **straight B/L, blank B/L & order B/L:** 记名提单，指规定将货物运给记名人而不载明待指定或待分配的提单。不记名提单，即提单内没有任何收货人或ORDER字样，提单的任何持有人都有权提货。指示提单，是指在提单正面“收货人”一栏内载明“凭指示”(To Order)或“凭某人指示”(To order of)字样的提单。前者称为托运人指示提单，这种提单在托运人未指定收货人或受让人之前，货物所有权仍属于卖方。在跟单信用证支付方式下，托运人以议付银行或收货人为受让人，通过转让提单而取得议付货款。后者称为记名指示提单，即由载明的“某人”通过背书方式指定收货人。收货人可以通过背书将提单再次转让，也可以凭提单请求承运人交付货物。

10) **direct B/L, transshipment B/L & through B/L:** 直达提单，指货物自装货港装船后，中途不经换船直接驶到卸货港卸货而签发的提单。直达提单上仅列有装运港和目的港的港口名称。转船提单，是指货物须经中途转船才能到达目的港而由承运人在装运港签发的全程提单。转船提单上注有“在某港转船”字样，承运人只对第一程运输负责。在联运方式中由第一承运人签发的包括全程在内并收取全程费用的提单称为联运提单。联运提单分为海上联运提单与多式联运提单。前者是指为海海联运签发的一票到底的提单，即转船提单；后者指海河、海陆、海空两种或两种以上运输方式进行联运而签发的一票到底的提单。

11) **long form B/L & short form B/L:** 全式提单，指在提单上列有承运人和托运人权利、义务、责任和豁免等详细条款的提单。由于提单正反面均列有烦琐的条款，所以又有繁式提单之称。这是一种在实际业务中应用较广的提单格式。简式提单，是指仅保留提单正面的必要记载事项，而无背面详细条款的提单。这种提单一般都列有“本提单货物的收受、保管、运输和运费等项，均按本公司全式提单内所印的条款为准”的字样。此外，租船合同项下所签发的提单通常是简式提单，在这种简式提单上应注明“所有条件根据×年×月×日签订的租船合同办理”。

12) **on deck B/L & stale B/L:** 舱面货提单，又称甲板货提单。这是指货物装于露天甲板上承运时，并于提单注明“装于舱面”(On Deck)字样的提单。在贸易实践中，有些体积庞大的货物以及某些有毒货物和危险物品不宜装于舱内，只能装在船舶甲板上。货物积载于甲板承运，遭受灭失或损坏的可能性很大，除商业习惯允许装于舱面的货物如木材，法律或有关法规规定必须装于舱面的货物，承运人和托运人之间协商同意装于舱面的货物外，承运人或船长不得随意将其他任何货物积载于舱面承运。如果承运人擅自将货物装于舱面，一旦灭失或损坏，承运人不但要承担赔偿责任，而且还将失去享受的赔偿责任限制的权利。但是，如果签发的是表明承、托双方协商同意的，注有“装于舱面”字样的舱面提单，而且实际上也是将货物积载于舱面，那么，只要货物的灭失或损坏不是承运人的故意行为造成的，承运人仍可免责。如果货物装在甲板上而没有批注，承运人对此要像装舱内货一样负责。为了减轻风险，买方一般不愿意把普通货物装在舱面上，有时甚至在合同和信用证中明确规定，不接受舱面货提单。银行为了维护开证人的利益，对这种提单一般也予以拒绝。过期提单，即出口商向银行交单结汇的日期与装船开航的日期相去甚远，以致无法于船到目的地以前送达目的港收货人的提单，银行一般不接受这种提单。

13) **ante-dated B/L & advanced B/L：** 倒签提单和预借提单，前者指承运人应托运人的要求，签发提单的日期早于实际装船日期的提单，以符合信用证对装船日期的规定，便于在信用证下结汇；后者指由于信用证规定的结汇日期已到，而货主因故未能及时备妥货物装船，或因为船期延误，影响了货物装船，托运人要求承运人先行签发已装船提单，以便结汇。倒签提单和预借提单被认为是典型的海运欺诈行为。不论出于什么原因，承运人通过倒签和预借提单，总是向收货人或提单持有人传达了一个关于装船时间的虚假情况。如果是应托运人的要求所为，那么从买卖关系上说，承运人则是帮助卖方掩盖了未能按时交运的违约事实。倒签和预借提单的主要原因是卖方不能按照买卖合同的约定时间交运货物，有时也因为承运人船期延误。

14) **Master Air Waybill (MAWB):** 航空主运单，凡由航空运输公司签发的航空运单称为主运单。它是航空运输公司据以办理货物运输和交付的依据，是航空公司和托运人订立的运输合同，每一批航空运输的货物都有自己相对应的航空主运单。

15) **House Air Waybill (HAWB):** 航空分运单，集中托运人(货运代理人)在办理集中托运业务时签发的航空运单被称作航空分运单。在集中托运的情况下，除了航空运输公司签发主运单外，集中托运人还要签发航空分运单。

6.7 Follow-up Practice

6.7.1 Review and Discussion Questions

1) What are the major types of transportation in international cargo transport?
2) What are the characteristics of liner transport?
3) What are the differences between voyage charter and time charter?
4) What are the main functions of a B/L?
5) What should be considered when choosing a port of shipment and a port of destination?
6) Why can the advice of shipment coordinate the responsibilities of the exporter and the importer?
7) What are the main responsibilities of a multi-modal transport operator?
8) What should the clause of shipment specify?

6.7.2 Choose the right answer from each of the following.

1) ________ can be freely bought and sold just like commodities.

A. Railway bill　　B. Airway bill

C. Shipping advice　　D. Ocean bill of lading

2) Freight under liner transportation ________.

A. needs to stipulate demurrage and dispatch money between the shipper and the carrier

B. does not include loading and unloading cost

C. consists of basic charges and additional charges

D. is collected based on gross weight of the goods

3) Airway bill is NOT ________.

A. a transport contract between the consignor and the carrier

B. a document for customs clearance

C. a document for bank negotiation

D. a document of title

4) ________ is the most commonly used transportation mode, which occupies 2/3 of international transportation.

A. Railway transportation B. Maritime transportation

C. Air transportation D. Parcel transportation

5) In international trade, the importer often does not require ________.

A. shipped B/L B. clean B/L C. blank B/L D. order B/L

6) ________ can be transferred after endorsement.

A. Straight B/L B. Blank B/L C. Order B/L D. Through B/L

7) A multi-modal transport operator is responsible for ________.

A. the first voyage B. the whole voyage

C. the ocean transport C. the last voyage

8) Under ________ character, the ship-owner only rents the charterer the boat.

A. demise B. time C. voyage D. booking

9) ________ is suitable for conveying fresh, emergent and seasonal goods.

A. Scheduled airlines B. Chartered carriers

C. Consolidated consignment D. Liners

10) If items are marked with "AD Val.", the freight is to be calculated on the basis of ________ of the cargo concerned.

A. weight B. price or value

C. measurement D. volume

6.7.3 Judge whether the following statements are true or false.

1) The loading and unloading charges are included in the freight of the liners. (   )

2) Demurrage is the extra charges a shipper pays for detaining a freight ship beyond the time permitted for loading or unloading. (   )

3) Dispatch money is a fine imposed on the charterer for the delay in the loading and unloading of the goods. (   )

4) A straight B/L can be transferred through endorsement. (   )

5) A bill of lading is both a receipt for merchandise and an evidence of contract to deliver it as freight. (   )

6) Advantages of containerization include less handling of cargo, more protection against pilferage, less exposure to the elements, and reduced time of shipping. (   )

7) An order B/L can be transferred with or without endorsement. (   )

8) In international multi-modal transportation, a multi-modal transport operator will issue a combined transport document and be responsible for the safe carriage of the whole voyage. ( )

9) In order to clarify who will bear the loading and unloading charges in voyage charter transportation, the clause "Free in and out" is set forth in the Voyage Charter Party. This means the charterer shall be responsible for both loading and unloading charges. ( )

10) Free in and free out means that ship-owner is responsible for both loading and unloading charges. ( )

6.7.4 Fill in the blanks in the following passage with the words or phrases given below.

bills of lading	cargo	consignments	commercial invoice
cleared	Clearing and forwarding		Customs and Excise
documents	destination	dock services	identifying
insurance policy	loading and unloading	inspected	manifest
shipping marks	stenciled	transportation	unloaded

The ________ carried by a ship is listed in the ________, which is a list in the ________ covering all the ________ on that vessel for that voyage. It is just one of the ________ that are involved in the shipping of goods; the ________ and ________ are among the others. The ________ authorities will examine all these.

________ agents are often used to handle the ________ of goods. They will arrange for the ________ of the goods and arrange all the ________ that are needed.

The ________, which are ________ on the cases, provide an easy way of ________ the items in a consignment when they are ________. The marks are described in the manifest, which is again ________ when the goods are ________ through Customs on reaching their ________.

6.7.5 Case Study

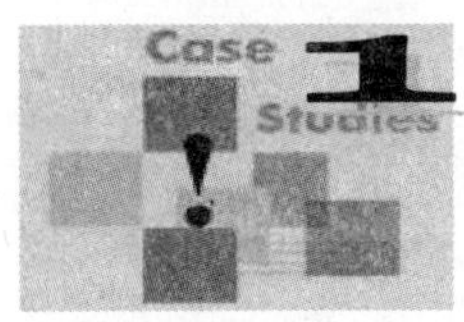

A Chinese company (Company A) signed a sales contract with a Brazilian company (Company C). Company A entrusted a shipping company (Company B) to ship 10,000 sacks of coffee beans from the Shanghai Port to a port in Brazil. Company B issued a clean B/L evidencing that each sack weighed 60 kgs in apparent good condition. When the goods arrived at the destination, Company C found that 600 sacks of the goods were 25% less in weight than contracted and the packages were loosened.

Therefore, Company C sued Company B for the quantity discrepancy between the delivered goods and the descriptions on the B/L, and asked Company B to compensate for the loss. Company B later provided evidence to prove that the loosened packages and the shortweight had existed when the goods were loaded on board, and the company issued the clean B/L because of failure in checking every package. Since the discrepancy in delivered quantity was not caused by Company B, the company need not compensate for the loss. Investigation also confirmed that the shortweight of 600 sacks was not caused by the carrier but by the shipper, Company A.

Which party should compensate Company C? Give reasons to support your answer.

A bill of lading issued by Cosco was required by the credit. Shantou Cosco Container Transportation Co., the agent of the carrier, issued a B/L to the beneficiary, Shanghai Golden Dragon Company. The B/L indicated that Cosco was the carrier. However, Shanghai Golden Dragon Company was dishonored by the issuing bank.

Please analyze the case and find out the reason for dishonor.

Web Links

1. http://training.mofcom.gov.cn/video2.asp?ClassID=136 商务培训网
2. http://www.china-56.com 中国物流网
3. http://www.xa-rail.com.cn 深圳货运物流网
4. http://www.crct.com/ztmh/index.jsp 中铁集装箱运输网

Cargo Transport Insurance

Learning Objectives

At the end of this chapter, you should be able to understand:

- the concept of cargo transport insurance
- risks and losses in marine cargo transport
- the basic risks coverage and additional risks coverage
- the notion of overland, air and postal transport insurance
- the insurance practice in international trade

Human beings are subject to various unpredictable risks—risk of death or disability due to natural disasters or accidents, risk of loss of or damage to one's property, etc. Risk has the element of unpredictability, but losses can be mitigated through insurance.

Insurance is a contract made by a company, society, or the state, to provide a guarantee of compensation for loss, damage, sickness, death, etc. in return for regular payment. The regular payment here refers to insurance premium, which is the money the insured pays to the insurer for taking out an insurance policy. An insurance policy is the document issued by the insurer to the insured after premium is paid. It sets out the exact terms in an insurance transaction such as the insurance coverage, the insured amount, the premium rate, and the insurance duration. The insurance policy is the key document for the insured to lodge a claim in the event of misfortune or loss. If all the required documents are found in order and the cause of the loss is an insured risk, the insurer pays indemnity, which is expressed as the insured value.

There are many types of insurance products available for life and non-life: property insurance, life insurance, liability insurance, bond insurance, to name just a few. Cargo insurance comes under property insurance.

Cargo insurance covers physical damage to or loss of goods whilst in transit by land, sea or air and offers considerable opportunities and cost advantages if managed properly. It brings the potential loss of or damage to the goods into cost and the insurer, on the basis of the premium received, undertakes to indemnify the insured against the loss from certain risks or perils to which the cargo insured may be exposed. Cargo insurance has become a must in international trade. Without it, international trade cannot be guaranteed.

7.1 Fundamental Principles of Cargo Insurance

There are three main principles of insurance, two subsidiary principles and a doctrine: A basic understanding of the underlying principles of cargo insurance will facilitate the process of claims.

7.1.1 Insurable Interest

A contract of insurance effected without insurable interest is null. It means that the insured must have an actual pecuniary interest and not a mere anxiety or sentimental interest in the subject matter of the insurance. The insured must be so situated with regard to the thing insured that he would have benefit by its existence and loss from its destruction. The owner of a ship runs a risk of losing his ship, the charterer of the ship runs a risk of losing his freight and the owner of the cargo incurs the risk of losing his goods and profit. So, all these parties have something at stake and all of them have insurable interest. It is the existence of insurable interest in a contract of insurance.

7.1.2 Utmost Good Faith

Since risks are shifted from one party to another through insurance, it is crucial that there must be utmost good faith and mutual confidence between the insured and the insurer. In a contract of insurance the insured knows more about the subject matter of the contract than the insurer. Consequently, he is bound to disclose accurately all material facts and nothing should be withheld or concealed. Any fact is material, which goes to the root of the contract of insurance and has a bearing on the risk involved. It is only when the insurer knows the whole truth that he is in a position to judge (a) whether he should accept the risk and (b) what premium he should charge.

7.1.3 Indemnity

A contract of insurance contained in a fire, marine, burglary or any other policy is a contract of indemnity. This means that the insured, in the event of loss against which the policy has been issued, shall be paid the actual amount of loss not exceeding the amount of the policy, i.e. he shall be fully indemnified. The object of every contract of insurance is to place the insured in the same financial position, as nearly as possible, after the loss, as if his loss had not taken place at all. It would be against public policy to allow the insured to make a profit out of his loss or damage.

7.1.4 Two Subsidiary Principles

Under the indemnity principle, there are two sub-principles:

(1) **Contribution**

According to this sub-principle, a person has no right to insure twice for the same risk, or to compensation from both insurers. But when two policies cover the same event, the insurance companies contribute pro rata to the loss, and the insured is only restored to the indemnity position. This is unlikely to happen very frequently in cargo insurance, though.

(2) **Subrogation**

This sub-principle is quite important in cargo insurance. It places the insurer in the shoes of the insured and entitles the insurer to all rights and remedies which the insured may have against any third parties.

For example, Company A has insured its cargo with Insurance Company B. But the cargo is damaged through a third party's negligence, say, the carrier. Company A will claim against Insurance Company B, who will pay up for the loss suffered. However, because the damage was due to the negligence of a third party, a legal action by Company A against the third party would almost certainly lead to an award of damages against the third party. In this way, Company A would get two compensations, and this would be a breach of the principle of indemnity. In order to prevent this from happening, Insurance Company B is substituted for Company A, the insured, in any legal action against the third party. The insurance company is entitled to the advantage of every right of the insured, which diminishes the loss they have been forced to bear, be it a contractual right, an action in tort for negligence, a right over property or a statutory right.

7.1.5 The Doctrine of Proximate Cause

The proximate cause is the direct cause of the loss. When an insurance policy covers a certain risk, a claim becomes payable only if that risk which occurred as the proximate cause of the loss suffered.

Sometimes it is hard to decide the true cause when there is more than one. Careful considerations are therefore needed. Where there are several causes which are covered under the insurance, the insurer must compensate for the loss suffered. Where there are several causes which are not all covered by the insurance, it would be rather complicated. If the first cause is covered, and the second cause is not, but the second cause is the inevitable outcome caused by the first cause, the first cause is regarded as the proximate cause. Thus, the insurer must make compensation for the loss suffered.

7.2 Risks and Losses in Cargo Transport

7.2.1 Cargo Transport

Goods may be subject to all kinds of risks or losses in transit, so they must be insured against all these. The widespread ways of cargo transport are marine, land, air and postal. Among them, marine cargo transport has the greatest ascendancy, importance and influence.

The insurance company is responsible for indemnifying the insured goods in accordance with the loss or damage caused by risks included in different coverages and the expenses involved. Apparently, risk, loss and coverage are interconnected; and their causal relations must be found in order to have a clear understanding of cargo transport insurance.

7.2.2 Risks in Marine Cargo Transport

The cargo may encounter all kinds of perils in its traveling to another country, which could bring about loss of one kind or another. Marine risks in connection with cargoes in transit can be classified into two types: perils of the sea and extraneous risks. The former is caused by natural calamities and fortuitous accidents, and the latter, by general and special extraneous reasons.

7.2.2.1 Perils of the Sea

Perils of the sea are those caused by natural calamities and fortuitous accidents.

(1) **Natural calamities** refer to the disasters such as vile weather, thunder and lighting, tsunami, earthquake, floods, etc.

(2) **Fortuitous accidents** refer to the accidents such as stranding, striking upon the rocks, sinking, collision, colliding with icebergs or other objects, fire, explosion, ship missing, etc.

7.2.2.2 Extraneous Risks

Extraneous risks are risks caused by extraneous reasons, including general extraneous risks and special extraneous risks.

(1) **General extraneous risks include:** theft or pilferage, rain, shortage, contamination, leakage, breakage, taint of odor, dampness, heating, rusting, hooking, etc.

(2) **Special extraneous risks include**: war risks, strikes, non-delivery of cargo, refusal to receive the cargo, etc.

7.2.3 Losses in Marine Cargo Transport

Marine losses are the damages to or losses of the insured goods incurred by perils of the sea. Losses sustained by the insured include two parts, one is the loss of the goods or the damage done to the goods, the other is the expenses the insured sustained in rescuing the goods in danger. According to the extent of damage, losses in marine insurance fall into two types: total loss and partial loss. The former may be subdivided into actual total loss and constructive total loss, and the latter, general average and particular average.

7.2.3.1 Total Loss

Total loss refers to the loss of the entire shipment caused by the occurrence of the perils of the sea, fire, or some other reasons. It consists of two different losses: Actual Total Loss and Constructive Total Loss.

(1) **Actual Total Loss**

The actual total loss occurs when the insured goods have been totally lost or damaged, or found to be totally valueless on arrival.

(2) **Constructive Total Loss**

Constructive total loss is found in the case where an actual total loss appears to be unavoidable or the cost to be incurred in recovering or reconditioning the goods together with the forwarding cost to the destination named in the policy would exceed their value on arrival.

7.2.3.2 Partial Loss

Partial loss refers to the loss of part of a consignment. According to different causes, partial loss can be classified as either general average or particular average.

(1) **General Average (GA)**

In the insurance business the term "average" simply means "loss" in most cases. It all goes back to the situation where a ship is in danger, somebody's cargo has to be abandoned and one of the shippers will suffer. To cover this situation the concept of general average was introduced. It means that whichever shipper loses all or part of his cargo, all the others will club together to recompense him for his loss. All policies the insured takes out automatically cover them against it.

(2) **Particular Average**

A particular average means a partial loss which is suffered by the one whose goods are partly lost or damaged. When there is a particular average loss, other interests in the voyage (such as the carrier and other cargo owners whose goods were not damaged) do not contribute to the partial recovery of the one suffering the loss. An example of a particular average occurs when a storm or fire damages part of the shipper's cargo and no one else's cargo has to be sacrificed to save the voyage. The cargo owner whose goods were damaged turns to his insurance company for payment, provided, of course, his policy covers the specific type of loss suffered.

Since most of losses encountered by shippers are partial, that is, of the particular average nature, it is important to know exactly what provisions for such partial losses are in the insurance policy.

7.2.4 Expenses

Losses of the insured cargoes not only come from the risk of the loss of the goods or the damage done to the goods, but also from the expenses the insured spends in rescuing the goods in danger. Therefore, losses, damages, and expenses are all covered by the transportation insurance. The main expenses are as follows.

7.2.4.1 Sue and Labor Expense

These expenses are the expenses arising from measures properly taken by the insured, the employee and the assignee, etc., to minimize or avoid losses caused by the risks covered in the insurance policy. The insurer is held responsible to compensate for such expenses.

7.2.4.2 Salvage Charges

Salvage charges are expenses resulting from measures properly taken by a third party other than the insured, the employee and the assignee, etc.

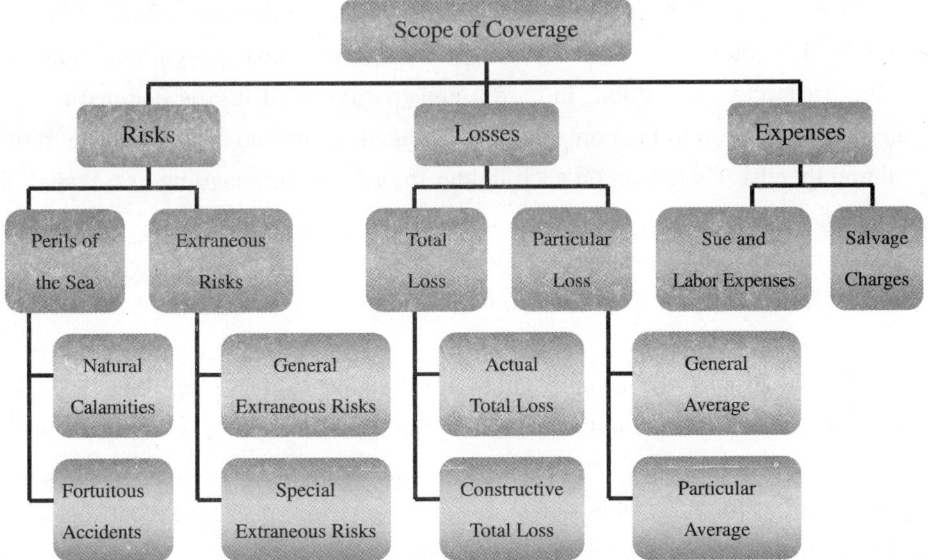

7.3 Ocean Marine Insurance under C.I.C.

The China Insurance Clauses (C.I.C.) issued by People's Insurance Company of China (PICC) provides both basic risks coverage and additional risks coverage for marine cargo transport. The former can be further divided into three conditions: Free From Particular Average (F.P.A.), With Particular Average (W.P.A.) and All Risks (A.R.) and the latter includes general additional risks and special additional risks.

7.3.1 Basic Risks Coverage

(1) **Free from Particular Average (F.P.A.)**

Free from particular average, basically, is a limited form of cargo insurance cover in as much as that no partial loss or damage is recoverable from the insurers unless that actual vessel or craft is stranded, sunk or burnt. Under the latter circumstances, the F.P.A. cargo policy holder can recover any losses of the insured merchandise which was on the vessel at the time as would obtain under the more extensive W.P.A. policy. The F.P.A. policy provides coverage for total losses and general average emerging from actual "marine perils".

According to *PICC's Ocean Marine Cargo Clauses* revised in January 1, 1981, F.P.A. insurance covers:

1) Total or constructive total loss of the whole consignment hereby insured caused in the course of transit by natural calamities—heavy weather, lightning, tsunami, earthquake and flood. In case a constructive total loss is claimed for, the insured shall abandon to the company the damaged goods and all his rights and title pertaining thereto. The goods on each lighter to or from the seagoing vessel shall be deemed a separate risk.

2) Total or partial loss caused by accidents—the carrying conveyance being grounded, stranded, sunk or in collision with floating ice or other objects as fire or explosion.

3) Partial loss of the insured goods attributable to heavy weather, lightning and/or tsunami, where the conveyance has been grounded, stranded, sunk or burnt, irrespective of whether the event or events took place before or after such accident.

4) Partial or total loss consequent on falling of entire package or packages into sea during loading, transshipment or discharge.

5) Reasonable cost incurred by the insured in salvaging the goods or averting or minimizing a loss recoverable under the policy, provided that cost shall not exceed the sum insured of the consignment so save.

6) Losses attributable to discharge of the insured goods at a port of distress following a sea peril as well as special charges arising from loading, warehousing and forwarding of the goods at an intermediate port of call or refuge.

7) Sacrifice and contribution to General Average and Salvage Charges.

8) Such proportion of losses sustained by the ship owners as is to be reimbursed by the cargo owner under the Contract of Affreightment "Both to Blame Collision" clause.

(2) **With Average/With Particular Average (W.A./W.P.A.)**

This insurance covers wider than F.P.A. Apart from the risks covered under F.P.A. conditions as mentioned above, this insurance also covers partial losses of the insured goods caused by heavy weather, lightning, tsunami, earthquake and/or flood.

(3) **All Risks (A.R.)**

All Risks is the most comprehensive of the three in coverage. Aside from the risks covered under F.P.A. and W.P.A., this insurance also covers all risks of loss of or damage to insured goods whether partial or total. Arising from external causes in transit, it should be noted that "All Risks" does not, as its name suggests, really cover all risks. The "All Risks" clause excludes coverage against damage caused by war, strikes, riots, etc. These perils can be covered by a separate clause. And it covers only physical loss or damage from external causes.

7.3.2 Additional Risks Coverage

The above-mentioned three covers can be chosen in accordance with the nature of goods insured. If more protections are needed, the applicant may further insure his goods against one or several additional risks. Additional risks are complements to the basic risks and all additional risks cannot be covered independently because they should be underwritten depending on one of the basic risks. Additional risks consist of general additional risks and special additional risks.

(1) **General Additional Risks**

General additional risks cover the losses caused by extraneous risks. If the goods are covered against All Risks, it is not necessary to ask for general additional risks. General additional risks under C.I.C. fall into the following 11 types:

1) Theft, Pilferage and Non-delivery (TPND);

2) Fresh water and/or rain damage;

3) Shortage;

4) Intermixture and contamination;

5) Leakage;

6) Clash and breakage;

7) Taint of odor;

8) Sweat and heating;

9) Hooks damage;

10) Breakage of packing;

11) Rust.

(2) **Special Additional Risk**

Special additional risks cover losses caused by special extraneous risks. Normally, they fall into 8 types:

1) War Risk;

2) Strike Risk;

3) On Deck Risk;

4) Import Duty Risk;

5) Rejection Risk;

6) Aflatoxin Risk;

7) Failure to Deliver Risk;

8) Fire Risk Extension Clause for Storage of Cargo at Destination HongKong, including Kowloon or Macao.

7.3.3 Exclusions

Besides the above three types of basic risks, there are conditions of exclusions. Exclusions refer to losses and expenses for which the insurance company declares clearly not to be responsible. They usually include:

1) Loss or damage caused by the intentional act or fault of the insured;

2) Loss or damage falling within the liability of the consignor;

3) Loss or damage arising from the inferior quality or shortage of the insured goods prior to the attachment of this insurance;

4) Loss or damage arising from normal loss, inherent vice or nature of the insured goods, loss of market and/or delay in transit and any expenses arising

therefrom;

5) Risks and liabilities covered and excluded by the war risks clause and strikes, riot and civil commotion clauses under C.I.C.

7.3.4 Commencement and Termination of Basic Insurance

The commencement and termination of basic insurance are usually stipulated by adopting the customary Warehouse to Warehouse Clause, W/W.

By the clause warehouse to warehouse, the liability of the insurer is extended to cover pre-shipment and post-shipment risk. The insured goods are covered from the time when they leave the warehouse at the place named in the policy for the commencement of the transit and continue to be covered until they are delivered to the final warehouse at the destination named in the policy, but the policy provides an overriding time limit of 60 days after the completion of discharge of the insured goods from the seagoing vessel at the final port of discharge. On the expiration of that time limit of 60 days the cover ceases to protect the goods even though they have not reached the final warehouse.

7.4 Insurance of Land, Air and Parcel Post Transport

The cargo shipped by sea must be insured, and the cargo transported by land, air and parcel post should also be insured, for risks also lie in these means of transport. However, the insurance company may have different clauses and terms to meet the needs of different modes of transport.

7.4.1 Overland Transport Cargo Insurance

Rail and road is now responsible for a high volume of business. It is crucial that adequate cover be obtained for the land carriage. Insurance coverage for land transport can be divided into two categories: land transport risks, almost equivalent to WPA, and all risks for land transport, almost equivalent to All Risks of marine transport.

7.4.2 Air Transport Insurance

Air transport has the nature of air movements, shorter transit time, lighter packing, quicker clearance at destination points and, in most places, stricter theft-pilferage control. Therefore, a significant number of export dispatches are sent by air these days. Though an air disaster is spectacular and attracts the public attention exceptionally, it is true that air traffic is one of the safest methods of moving goods. Obviously, the speed and ease of handling air freight makes an insurance risk attractive to the insurer and premium rates attractive to the insured. There are also two types of coverages: air transport risk and air transport all risks. Air transport risk is similar to W.P.A., while air transport all risks is similar to All Risks of marine transport.

7.4.3 Parcel Post Insurance

Parcel post insurance covers the losses of or damage to the parcels caused by natural calamities, fortuitous accidents or external risks. It includes parcel post risk and parcel post all risks. On the basis of these two basic covers, some additional risks may also be added when required.

7.5 Insurance Practice of International Trade

7.5.1 Choice of Insurance Coverage

As to who is to arrange the insurance, it depends on the terms of trade of the particular cases. Under CIF terms, for instance, insurance is arranged by the exporter, whereas under FOB or CFR terms, it is borne by the importer. The bearer approaches an insurance company; inquires and chooses the right coverage and then negotiates insurance premium rates. Sometimes, brokers may play the role of the applicant, for they are highly skilled specialists and can obtain sound and reliable coverage, together with competitive premium rates. The most frequently used trade terms which affect insurance arrangements are FOB, CFR, and CIF. Where the contract between the exporter and the importer is a FOB contract, it is the importer's responsibility to insure the goods. If the goods are contracted to be sold on a CIF basis, then it is the exporter's turn to take out the policy and pay the costs of insurance.

As to what kind of insurance coverage should be adopted, the following factors should be taken into account:

1) The characteristics of the cargo;

2) The packing of the cargo;

3) The mode of transport;

4) The line and port of transport;

5) The season of transport;

6) Possible losses and damages in transit.

Understanding the distinctions between F.P.A., W.P.A. and A.R. is of great practical significance and may help exporters choose the right coverage.

For exporters who want to have the widest coverage they can get A.R. coverage. However because of the nature of the goods, underwriters may agree to provide only a more limited form of cover. Moreover, even though an exporter can get A.R. coverage, he may well decide that it is uneconomical. An experienced exporter will come to predict the losses he can expect, and may find it cheaper to write them off as trade losses than to pay the relatively higher A.R. premium.

Products should be insured in the appropriate category. A good rule of thumb is that an exporter should insure for the coverage accepted in his particular trade. Now let's examine which type of insurance cover a smart exporter would choose for the following items.

1) A consignment of shoes.

2) Wood logs.

3) Wooden toys.

4) Heavy machinery.

5) Plywood.

6) Bicycles.

Probably, you will give the following answers: 1), 3), 4) and 6) would probably be insured against A.R. because they are likely to be damaged in transit. Most manufactured goods fall into this category; 2) would be insured against F.P.A., for while it could be lost it is not likely to be damaged; 5) on the other hand would be insured against W.P.A. because it could be damaged in transit, but is less prone to damage than the finished products mentioned. Normally the insurance company will advise the exporter in this respect.

7.5.2 Insured Amount and Insurance Premium

(1) **Insured Amount**

The insured amount is the highest compensation amount undertaken by the insurer, and it is also the foundation for calculating the insurance premium.

According to the international insurance practice, the insured amount is usually calculated on the basis of the CIF invoice value plus 10% or 15 % representing an anticipated profit for the buyer. Such amount is usually agreed upon first, and the insurer will not, generally, accept additional percentage of more than 30%. The formula for calculating the insured amount under CIF trade terms is as follows:

Insured amount = CIF price × (1 + markup percentage)

(2) **Insurance Premium**

The insurance premium is the amount of money paid by the insured in order to make the insurance contract come into force and the basic proceeds cared by the insurer.

The insurance premium is usually calculated according to two kinds of rates: the general premium rate and the named cargo premium rate. Under CIF trade terms, the formula for calculating the premium is:

Insurance premium = insured amount × premium rate
= CIF price × (1+markup percentage) × premium rate

7.5.3 Insurance Documents

The insurance documents are the evidence documents on the strength of which the insurance contract is signed by and between the insurer and the insured. The following are insurance documents used in international trade:

(1) **Insurance policy:** It is the most commonly used insurance document that contains all the details concerning the goods, coverage, premium, and the insured value. It is also called formal insurance document.

(2) **Insurance certificate:** It is a simplified insurance document. The certificate carries the same contents as the insurance policy except for the obligations and rights of the insurer and the insured. Besides, the insurance certificate has the same legal force as the insurance policy. It must be pointed out that the insurance certificate is less often used in recent years.

(3) **Combined certificate:** This certificate is the combination of the invoice and insurance policy. It is much simpler than the insurance certificate. It is not often used now.

(4) **Open policy:** Open policy is also known as open cover. It is the general contract between the insured (normally the importer) and the insurer. It is often used in import transactions in China.

(5) **Endorsement:** After the insurance policy is issued, if the insured wants to add or change some items of the policy, the insured can, with the insurance company's consent, apply for the addition and change. The document issued to state the additional items or changes is known as endorsement, which is considered an indispensable part to the policy.

7.5.4 Insurance Clauses of the Sales Contract

Being an indispensable part of a sales contract, the insurance clause should be stipulated explicitly and reasonably. The insurance clause in a sales contract under different trade terms may vary. Normally, it should specifically stipulate the insured amount, basic risk and additional risks to be covered, the insurance document required and standard of insurance coverage, etc. The examples are shown as follows:

Insurance to be covered by the seller for 110% of the CIF invoice value against all risks and war risk as per the relevant Ocean Marine Cargo Clauses of the People's Insurance Company of China dated 1st Jan. 1981.

Insurance shall be effected for the amount of the seller's CIF invoice value plus 10% against W.P.A. Any additional insurance required by the buyer shall be at his own expense. The seller may insure against War Risk at the buyer's request and at his expense. In case the rate of relevant insurable premium shall be raised between the time of concluding contract and that of shipment, this excess premium shall be on the buyer's account.

Marine insurance to be effected by the seller against W.P.A. for CIF invoice amount plus ten percent only, any additional insurance required by the buyer shall be effected by the buyer himself and at his own expense.

The insurance should be effected by the buyer if the contract is concluded on a FOB or CFR basis. However, the seller should, immediately after the goods are completely loaded at port of shipment, fax to notify the buyer or the consignee of the contract number, name of the commodity, quantity, gross weight, measurement, invoice value and number of B/L, name of the vessel, the date of shipment, etc. In case the goods are not insured in time, owing to the seller's failure to give a shipping advice in time, any and all consequent losses should be borne by the seller.

In case the contract is concluded on a CIF basis, the insurance should be effected by the seller for 110% of the invoice amount against all risks, war risk, strikes, riot and civil commotion risk as per Ocean Marine Cargo Transportation Clause of the People's Insurance Company of China.

7.6 Vocabulary Check

absolute total loss 绝对全损
actual total loss 实际全损
ascendancy 优势；权势
average 海损
constructive total loss 推定全损
cover *n. v.* 承保；投保
diminish *v.* 减少；缩小
doctrine 学说；原则
mitigate *v.* 缓解；减轻
indemnify *v.* 赔偿；偿付
indemnity *n.* 赔偿
insurance coverage 保险范围
insurance premium 保险费
insured amount 保险金额
the insured 投保人
the insurer 承保人
partial loss 部分损失
pecuniary 金钱的
premium 保险费
proceeds 收入；收益
pro rata 按比例地
statutory 法律的；法规的
tsunami 海啸
utmost good faith 最大诚信

7.7 Notes and Key Terms

1) **insurable interest:** 可保利益，也称保险利益。指投保人或被保险人对其所保标的具有法律所承认的权益或利害关系。

2) **contribution:** 分摊。避免投保人因购买多于一份财物或财务保险而从该项损失中获益。当投保人购买多份保单而出现下列情况时，便会采用分摊原则：一、在同类受保危险的同一损失或破坏；二、同一事故；三、同一投保人的相同利益。

3) **subrogation:** 代位追偿。在保险业务中，为了防止被保险人双重获益，保险人在履行全损赔偿或部分赔偿后，在其赔付金额内，要求被保险人转让其对造成损失的第三者责任方要求全损赔偿或相应部分赔偿的权利。这种权利称为代位追偿权(right of subrogation)或称代位权。

4) **the doctrine of proximate cause:** 近因原则，是保险理赔过程中必须遵循的重要原则。按照这一原则，只有当被保险人的损失是直接由于保险责任范围内的事故造成的，保险人才能予以赔偿，即保险事故的发生与损失事实的形成，两者之间必须有直接因果关系的存在，才能构成保险赔偿的条件。

5) **basic insurance coverage and additional insurance coverage:** 基本险和附加险。基本险指可以单独投保的保险险种。我国海洋运输货物保险的基本险有平安险(Free From Particular Average, F.P.A.)、水渍险(With Particular Average, W.P.A.)和一切险(All Risks, A.R.)。附加险指不能单独投保，只能附加于基本险投保的保险险种。基本险因失效、解约或满期等原因效力终止或中止时，附加险效力也随之终止或中止。

6) **perils of the sea：**海上风险，又称海难，是指船舶或货物在海上运输过程中所遇到的自然灾害和意外事故。它包括自然灾害(natural calamities)和意外事故(fortuitous accidents)两类。自然灾害是指不以人的意志为转移的自然界力量所引起的灾害，但在海运保险业务中，它并不是泛指一切由于自然力量造成的灾害，而是仅指恶劣气候、雷电、地震、海啸或火山爆发等人力不可抗拒的自然力量造成的灾害。意外事故是指由于偶然、非意料的原因所造成的事故，并不是泛指海上所有的意外事故，而仅指运输工具搁浅、触礁、沉没、船舶与流冰或其他物体碰撞以及失踪、失火、爆炸等。

7) **extraneous risk：**外来风险，是指由于自然灾害和意外事故以外其他外来原因造成的风险，但不包括货物的自然损耗和本质缺陷。它包括一般外来风险和特殊外来风险。一般外来风险指由于一般外来原因所造成的风险，主要包括：偷窃、渗漏、短量、碰损、钩损、生锈、雨淋、受热受潮等。特殊外来风险是指由于社会、政治原因所造成的风险，主要包括：战争、罢工、拒收以及交货不到等。

8) **general average:** 共同海损，简称G.A.，是指载货的船舶在海上遇到自然灾害或意外事故，危及船、货等各方的共同安全时，为了解除这种共同危险，维护船货安全，或者使航程得以继续完成，由船长有意识地、合理地采取措施，造成某些特殊的损失或者支出的额外费用。

9) **particular average:** 单独海损，是指在海上运输途中因海上风险而造成的不能列入共同损失的部分损失。单独海损是意外发生的，损失仅指保险标的物本身的毁损，并不包括由此而引起的费用。单独海损一定是部分损失。单独海损不涉及其他各方利益，由受损者单独承担。

10) **Warehouse to Warehouse Clause:** 仓至仓条款，是保险责任起讫的条款。保险责任自被保险货物运离保险单所载明的起运地仓库或储存处所开始，包括正常运输中的海上、陆上、内河和驳船运输在内，直至该项货物运抵保险单所载明的目的地收货人的最后仓库或储存处所或被保险人用作分配、分派或非正常运输的其他储存处所为止。但被保险的货物在最后到达卸载港卸离海轮后，保险责任以60天为限。

11) **sue and labor expense:** 施救费用，指在保险范围内，由被保险人、雇用人员和受让人等为抢救保险货物，以防止损失扩大而采取措施所支出的合理费用。

12) **salvage charges:** 救助费用，是指在货物保险范围内，由被保险人、雇佣人员和受让人以外的第三者采取救助行为而向其支付的报酬费用。

13) **basic insurance coverage:** 基本险。可以单独投保，被保险人投保时，必须选择一种基本险投保。海洋货运保险的基本险包括平安险(F.P.A)、水渍险(W.P.A 或 W.A)和一切险(All Risks)。平安险的承保范围，包括除了由自然灾害造成的单独海损以外的海上风险所造成的一切损失和费用。水渍险的承保范围，包括海上风险所造成的一切损失和费用，即在平安险的基础上，加上自然灾害造成的单独海损。一切险的承保范围，包括水渍险的所有责任，还包括由一般外来风险所造成的损失。

14) **additional risks:** 附加险，承保由外来风险所造成的损失，可分成一般附加险和特殊附加险，分别对应于一般外来风险和特殊外来风险。一般附加险包括：偷窃、提货不着险(Theft Pilferage and Non-Delivery, TPND)、淡水雨淋险(Rain Fresh Water Damage, FWRD)、渗漏险(Risk of Leakage)、短量险(Risk of Shortage)、钩损险(Hook Damage)、破碎碰损险(Risk of Clash and Breakage)、锈损险(Risk of Rust)、混杂玷污险(Risk of Intermixture and Contamination)、串味险(Risk of Odour)、受潮受热险(Damage Caused by sweating and Heating)、包装破裂险(Loss and Damage Caused by Breakage of

Packing)等 11 种。特殊附加险主要有战争险(War Risks)、罢工险(Strike Risks)、舱面险(On Deck)、拒收险(Rejection)、交货不到险(Failure to Deliver)、黄曲霉素险(Aflatoxin Risk)、进口关税险(Import Duty)以及货物出口到港澳地区的存仓火险责任扩展条款(Fire Risk Extension Clause, F.R.E.C.—for storage of cargo at destination Hong Kong, including Kowloon, or Macao)等 8 种。附加险不能单独投保，可在投保一种基本险的基础上，根据货运需要加保其中的一种或若干种。投保了一切险后，因一切险中已包括了所有一般附加险的责任范围，所以只需在特殊附加险中选择加保。

15) **exclusions**: 除外责任，是指保险公司明确规定不予赔偿的损失和费用范围。其内容有：被保险人的故意行为或过失所造成的损失；发货人的责任引起的损失；保险责任开始，保险货物已存在的品质不良或数量短差；保险货物的自然损耗、本质缺陷、市价跌落以及运输延迟所引起的损失和费用；战争险和罢工险条款承保的责任范围和除外责任。

16) **insurance documents**: 保险单证。保险单证是保险人与被保险人之间订立保险合同的证明文件，它确认并规定了保险人与被保险人之间的权利与义务关系，是保险人出具的承保证明。当被保险货物遭受损失时，它是向保险公司索赔的主要依据，也是保险公司理赔的主要依据，此外还是进出口企业通过银行结汇的重要单据。常用保险单证可分为保险单(Insurance Policy)、保险凭证(Insurance Certificate)、联合凭证(Combined Certificate)、预约保单(Open Policy)、批单(Endorsement)。保险单证可以转让。

7.8 Follow-up Practice

7.8.1 Review and Discussion Questions

1) Why is insurance indispensable to international trade?
2) What are the fundamental principles of insurance?
3) What are the major types of risks in marine cargo transport?
4) What is constructive total loss and what is the difference between actual total loss and constructive total loss?
5) What's the difference of General Average and Particular Average?
6) What are the major types of basic risks coverage and additional risks coverage?
7) Explain the scope of coverage of F.P.A. and W.P.A.
8) What is W/W Clause?
9) What is the difference between the insurance policy and insurance certificate?
10) What should be considered in choosing the right insurance coverage?

7.8.2 Choose the right answer from each of the following.

1) ________ is defined as loss arising in the consequence of extraordinary and intentional sacrifice made, or expenses incurred, for the common safety of the ship and cargo.

A. Particular average　　B. General average

C. Without average　　D. With average

2) Which of the following risks is NOT covered by the All Risks coverage of marine cargo transport insurance?

A. Delay.　　B. Flood.

C. Lightning.　　D. Heavy weather.

3) W.P.A. is one of the ________.

A. basic risks　　B. additional risks

C. special additional risks　　D. general additional risks

4) Which of the following risks is NOT covered by the A.R. coverage of marine cargo transport insurance?

A. Marine perils.　　B. Stranding.

C. Pilferage.　　D. Inherent vice.

5) Which of the following risks are covered by the All Risks coverage of PICC Ocean Marine Cargo Clauses?

A. War and fire.　　B. Strike and delay.

C. Aflatoxin and on deck.　　D. Heavy weather and fire.

6) As far as risks taken by the seller is concerned, ________.

A. CIF is bigger than CFR　　B. CIF is as the same as CFR

C. CFR is bigger than CIF　　D. FOB is bigger than CFR

7) In insurance, the party who insures for other parties against possible loss or damage and promises to effect payment in case of loss or damage is called the ________.

A. insured　　B. consignee

C. insurer　　D. consignor

8) A.R. covers risks of ________.

A. war and strike　　B. rejection

C. inherent vice of goods　　D. ship stranding

9) Under the trade term CFR, the ________ must contract for the cargo transport insurance.

A. buyer　　B. seller

C. consignee　　D. carrier

10) General perils refer to natural ________ and fortuitous accidents.

A. calamities B. damages

C. losses D. franchises

7.8.3 Decide whether the following statements are true or false.

1) An insurance contract is essentially a contract between the insurer and the insured. ( )

2) The amount of money the insurer agrees to cover by insurance against the subject matter is the insured amount, which is normally 110% of the CIF value of the consignment. ( )

3) Under CIF term, the seller has to procure insurance against the buyer's risk of loss of or damage to the goods during the carriage. ( )

4) F.P.A. coverage includes total losses resulting from marine perils and other specific accidents, like an earthquake. ( )

5) All additional risks can also be covered independently. ( )

6) General average and salvage charges are covered both in F.P.A. and W.A. coverage. ( )

7) A.R. does not cover risks of war and special additional risks but covers the general additional risks. ( )

8) Three types of risks are covered by ocean marine insurance, namely the perils of the sea, the extraneous risks and the force majeure. ( )

9) If you have insured your goods against A.R., you will get compensated whatever risks occur to your goods. ( )

10) A.R. covers all losses and damages to the goods caused by perils of the sea, fortuitous accidents and general extraneous risks.

7.8.4 Translate the following terms into Chinese.

No.	English	Chinese	No.	English	Chinese
1	G.A.		6	W/W Clause	
2	particular average		7	insurance premium	
3	insurance policy		8	proximate cause	
4	F.P.A.		9	C.I.C.	
5	T.P.N.D.		10	W.P.A.	

7.8.5 Case Study

A cargo ship was sailing from the Shanghai port to Singapore, when suddenly a fire broke out in the ship's hold and soon spread to the engine room. The captain, for the safety of the ship and the consignments on board, ordered his men to pour water into the hold and the fire was put out. But the engine was damaged, unable to sail. So the captain decided to hire a towboat to drag the ship to a nearby port for repair. The losses caused by this accident were: (1) 1,000 cartons of goods were burnt; (2) 600 cartons of goods were wet; (3) the main engine and some decks were damaged; (4) towing charges; (5) the extra cost of fuel and the wages of the crew. What are the types of the above-mentioned losses in terms of their characteristics?

A Chinese company exported 600 cases of tableware on a CIF basis. The export company covered the insurance on the goods against F.P.A. for 110% of the CIF value. Before the goods were loaded on the ship, 20 cases fell off the hook and fell into the sea. Do you think the insurance company should undertake to compensate for the loss? If this transaction was concluded on a FOB or CFR basis, should the insurance company compensate for the loss? Why or why not?

Web Links

1. http://www. picc.com.cn 中国人民保险公司网站
2. http://www.mofcom.gov.cn 中国商务部网站

International Payments

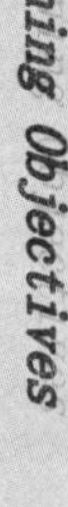

At the end of this chapter, you should be able to understand:

- the importance of payment in international trade
- the functions and uses of common instruments
- three main payment methods—remittance, collection and L/C
- the advantages and disadvantages of each payment method
- other payment methods, e.g. factoring, forfaiting and L/G

All the effort put by the seller into marketing, market research, pricing, physical distribution, documentation and so on and so forth will be for nothing if he does not receive payment for the goods or services sold. So it is universally acknowledged that international payment is the most important aspect of international trade in that the seller is most interested in getting paid for the goods he sells. Only after the seller has received the full sum of payment without claims can we say the transaction is concluded and will the seller feel at ease. In other words, getting paid as the seller desires is the most important. On the other hand, the buyer's first obligation is to pay or to promise to pay for the goods he buys from the seller.

In international trade practice, the buyer is obliged to pay the seller the agreed amount, in the agreed currency, within the agreed period of time and by the agreed method of payment. Therefore, it is of essential importance to stipulate in the contract the various terms of payment.

This chapter therefore aims to explain the different types of payment methods used in international transactions, including the mechanisms to facilitate the actual transfer of funds between the buyer and the seller, and will highlight the relative safety of each payment method.

8.1 Payment Amount

Generally speaking, the actual amount of payment is the same as what is given in the written contract. However sometimes they differ, for the actual payment of the goods may be adjusted in accordance with the more or less clause, the price adjustment clause, or the exchange clause. Also, some contracts may stipulate that additional charges or expenses, such as the optional port charges and port congestion surcharges under CFR or CIF terms, additional expenses for special packing upon the request of the buyer, should not generally be included in the price of the goods and should be paid by the buyer separately. It is the general practice that the actual payment will be effected against the full invoice of the goods and the receipts of the seller who has paid the additional charges of expenses.

8.2 Payment Currency

Payment currency is an important part of payment terms of a sales contract.

Usually there is quite a long time between the conclusion of a sales contract and the settlement of the payment. During this time, the payment currency may depreciate or appreciate in the international financial market, sometimes to quite a great degree. So the exporter should consider the exchange risks while determining what currency is to be used for the payment of the consignment.

In international payment practice, either the currency of the seller's, the buyer's, or a third can be used. But it must be considered what currency is to be used for the sake of lessening risks of foreign exchange rate fluctuation. The following are the ways to determine the evaluation currency and the payment currency.

(1) An exporter would generally choose a hard currency for evaluation and payment, while an importer would try to use a soft currency. Hard currency refers to the currency that is fully convertible and strong or relatively stable in value in comparison with other currencies while soft currency indicates a type of currency whose value may depreciate rapidly or that is difficult to convert in other currencies.

(2) If soft currency is used in export and hard currency is used in import, the price for exported goods should be raised and the price for import reduced so as to offset the possible depreciation or appreciation of the currency used.

(3) Both soft currency and hard currency are to be used. That is, the payment is to be made partially in soft currency and partially in hard currency.

(4) An exchange clause is to be constructed in a sales contract. There are several ways to do this:

1) Both the evaluation currency and the payment currency are soft currency. This is converted into hard currency according to the exchange rate at the time when the sales contract is concluded. Upon payment, the hard currency is converted into soft currency.

2) The price is evaluated in soft currency and paid in hard currency. In this way, the soft currency will be converted into hard currency at the rate when the deal is concluded.

3) The same currency is used for the evaluation and payment. When the sales contract is concluded, an exchange rate is determined between this currency and a few other currencies. When the payment is effected, if the exchange rate between this currency and the other currencies has fluctuated beyond a certain percentage, then the actual amount of the payment will be adjusted accordingly.

8.3 Payment Instruments

In international trade, payment can be made by various means including draft, promissory note, check, money order or credit card. They are used for the payment or transfer of money. Among them, draft is used as the most common payment instrument, although check and promissory note are also sometimes used.

8.3.1 Draft / Bill of Exchange

A draft or bill of exchange is defined as an unconditional order in writing, addressed by one person to another and signed by the first person, requiring the second person to whom it is addressed to pay on demand, or at a fixed or determinable future time, a certain sum of money to the order of a specified person, or to the order of him.

It is understood from the above definition that a draft is an unconditional written order drawn by the drawer (the exporter or the seller) and accepted by the drawee (the importer or buyer), who then is responsible for paying on presentation of the bill at the appropriate time.

8.3.1.1 Basic Contents of a Draft

A draft involves three parties: the drawer (i.e. the party that issues a draft, usually the seller in an international trade transaction), the drawee (the recipient of the draft for payment or acceptance, usually the buyer in an international trade transaction), and the payee (the party to whom the draft is payable, usually the seller or their bankers). Usually the drawer and the payee are the same person.

The following is an example of a draft:

BILL OF EXCHANGE

Drawn under Bank of China, London (1)
Irrevocable L/C No. 200710020 (2) **Dated** 12th Oct.2007 (3)
Payable with interest @ **** (4) per annum
No. CB0710102 (5) **Exchange for** US$ 9980.00 (6) Hangzhou China 12th Nov. 2007 (7)
At 30 days (8) sight of this FIRST of EXCHANGE (Second of Exchange being unpaid) pay to the order of Bank of China, Hangzhou (9) the sum of U.S.DOLLAR NINE THOUSAND NINE HUNDRED AND EIGHTY ONLY (10)

To: Kimpton Brothers Limited
10-14 Hewett Street
London EC2A 3HA UK (11)

Zhejiang Chinabase Impex Co., Ltd (12)

(1) The issuing bank of the L/C according to which the bill of exchange is drawn.

(2) The number of the L/C.

(3) The issuing date of the L/C.

(4) The interest rate of the bill of exchange.

(5) The number of the bill of exchange.

(6) The amount of the bill of exchange in figures.

(7) The drawing date of the bill of exchange.

(8) The payment date of the bill of exchange.

(9) The payee of the bill of exchange.

(10) The amount of the bill of exchange in words.

(11) The drawee of the bill of exchange.

(12) The drawer of the bill of exchange.

The forms of a bill of exchange might be different, but according to *Article 1 of Bills of Exchange Act (1882)—United Kingdom*, a bill of exchange must contain:

1) The term "Bill of Exchange" inserted in the body of the instrument and expressed in the language employed in drawing up the instrument;

2) An unconditional order to pay a determinate sum of money;

3) The name of the person who is to pay;

4) A statement of the time of payment;

5) A statement of the place where payment is to be made;

6) The name of the person to whom or to whose order payment is to be made;

7) A statement of the date and of the place where the bill is issued;

8) The signature of the person who issues the bill.

8.3.1.2 Types of Drafts

Drafts or bills of exchange can be sorted according to different criteria. They may be classified into the following types:

Classification Criteria	Description	Types
According to the drawer	It is a draft drawn by a bank on another bank.	Banker's bill / bank's bill
	It is a bill issued by a trader on another trader or on a bank.	Trade bill / commercial bill
According to the acceptor	It is a time bill drawn on a trader and accepted by him.	Trader's acceptance bill / commercial acceptance bill
	It is a time bill drawn on a bank and accepted by this bank. This kind of bill is more preferable and negotiable than the trader's acceptance bill and is more acceptable in the discount market.	Banker's acceptance bill
According to the tenor	It is a bill payable on demand or at sight or on presentation,	Sight bill or demand bill
	It is a bill payable at a fixed or determinable future time.	Time bill or usance bill
According to whether or not the shipping documents are attached	It is a bill without shipping documents attached thereto.	Clean bill
	It is a bill with shipping documents attached thereto.	Documentary bill
According to the currency denominated:	It is a bill on which the amount is denominated in local currency.	Local currency bill
	It is a bill on which the amount is denominated in foreign currency.	Foreign currency bill
According to the place of acceptance and place of payment	It is a bill on which the place of acceptance is the same one as the place of payment.	Direct bill
	It is a bill on which the place of acceptance is not the same one as the place of payment. So far as the indirect bill is concerned, when the drawee accepts the draft he usually writes the place of payment thereon such as "Payable in…with…Bank."	Indirect bill
According to the place of issuance and place of payment	It is a bill drawn and payable in the same country.	Inland bill or domestic bill
	It is a bill drawn in one country and payable in another country.	Foreign bill

8.3.1.3 Functions of the Bill of Exchange in International Trade

The bill of exchange performs many functions in international trade including:

(1) Facilitating the granting of trade credit in a legal format by permitting payments on agreed future dates.

(2) Providing formal evidence of the demand for payment from a seller to a buyer.

(3) Providing the seller with an access to finance by permitting them to transfer their debts to a bank or other financier by merely endorsing the bill of exchange to that bank or financier.

(4) Permitting the banker or financier to retain a valid legal claim on both the buyer and the seller. In certain circumstances a bank or financier may have a stronger legal claim under a bill than the party that sold them the debt.

(5) Permitting a seller to obtain greater security over the payment by enabling a bank to guarantee a drawee's acceptance (guarantee to pay on the due date) by signing or endorsing the bill.

(6) Allowing a seller to protect their access to the legal system in the event of problems, while providing easier access to that legal system.

8.3.2 Promissory Note

A promissory note is defined as an unconditional promise in writing made by one person (the maker) to another (the payee or the holder) signed by the maker engaging to pay on demand or at a fixed or determinable future time a certain sum of money to or to the order of a specified person or to bearer.

A promissory note can be issued by a person, a firm, or a bank. But promissory notes issued by individuals and firms are not widely used in trade today.

The following is an example of a promissory note issued by a bank:

ASIA INTERNATIONAL BANK, LTD.
18 Queen's Road, Hong Kong
CASHIER'S ORDER
Hong Kong, Oct. 20, 2007

Pay to the order of ANGAD CO., LTD. The sum of U.S. Dollars Fifty Thousand Only.

For Asia International Bank, Ltd.
US$50,000.00

Manager

8.3.3 Check / Cheque

A check is defined as an unconditional order in writing addressed by the customer (the drawer) to a bank (the drawee) signed by the customer authorizing the bank to pay on demand a specified sum of money to or to the order of a named person or to bearer (payee).

A check is a special kind of draft in that the drawee is always a bank with which the drawer has an account. Besides, a check is always paid upon presentation. If the drawer wants to write a check now but does not want the payee to collect the money immediately, the drawer can postdate the check.

A check can be made to order, to bearer, crossed with two parallel lines for account deposit only, or certified by a bank that is going to pay. If a check is issued by a bank, it is called a banker's demand draft.

The following table shows the differences between the above three payment instruments:

	Draft	Check	Promissory Note
Drawer or Maker	For the banker's draft, the drawer is a bank; for the trade draft, the drawer is a person or a business organization	The banker's check is made by a bank; a general check is made by a depositor	A commercial promissory note is made by a person or business organization; a cashier's order is made by a bank
Payer	A banker's draft is paid by a bank; a trade draft is paid by a person, business organization or a bank	A bank	A commercial promissory note is paid by a person or business organization; a cashier's order is paid by a bank
Parties Involved	Three: drawer, payer and payee	Three: drawer, payee and payer	Two: maker and payee
Number of Copies	Generally two originals	One single original	One single original
Tenor	Sight or time	Sight	Sight or time
Acceptance	A time draft must be accepted	No acceptance	No acceptance
Applicable Areas	Widely used in international trade	Local cities or domestic areas	Domestic and international

8.4 Payment Methods

To succeed in today's global marketplace, exporters must offer their customers attractive sales terms supported by the appropriate payment method to win sales against competitors. As getting paid in full and on time is the primary goal for each export sale, an appropriate payment method must be chosen carefully to minimize the payment risk while also accommodating the needs of the buyer. There are three main methods of international payment–remittance, collection and letter of credit, each providing a different level of protection and cost. The choice will depend upon the relationship with the trading partner, the level of risk in the transaction, and, in some cases, the regulatory requirements of different countries. During or before contract negotiations, it is advisable to consider which method is mutually desirable for the exporter and the importer. The following table provides a comparison of the payment methods, outlining the risks involved in each payment method for both the exporter and the importer.

Method	Usual Time of Payment	Goods Available to the Buyer	Exporter's Risks	Importer's Risk
Cash in Advance	Before shipment	After payment	None	Completely relies on exporter to ship goods as ordered
L/C/Confirmed /Sight	When shipment is made	After payment	Credit Risk with Confirming Bank and Documentary Risk	Completely relies on exporter to ship goods as ordered
L/C/Confirmed /Time	On maturity of draft	Before payment	Credit Risk with Confirming Bank and Documentary Risk	Completely relies on exporter to ship goods as ordered
Sight draft, D/P	On presentation of draft to buyer	After payment	Disposition of goods if shipment not accepted. Involves many side risks such as exchange availability	Is assured shipment made but relies on exporter to ship goods described in documents unless he can inspect goods before payment
Time draft, D/A	On maturity of draft	Before payment	Disposition of goods if shipment not accepted. Relies on buyer to pay draft at maturity	Is assured shipment made but relies on exporter to ship goods described in documents unless he can inspect goods before payment
Open account	As agreed	Before payment	Relies completely on buyer to pay his account as agreed upon	None

Key points to be considered

1) International trade presents a spectrum of risks, causing uncertainty over the payments between the exporter (seller) and importer (buyer).

2) To exporters, any sale is a gift until payment is received. Therefore, the exporter wants payment as soon as possible, preferably as soon as an order is placed or before the goods are sent to the importer.

3) To importers, any payment is a donation until the goods are received. Therefore, the importer wants to receive the goods as soon as possible, but to pay as late as possible, preferably until after the goods are resold to have generated enough income to make payments to the exporter.

8.4.1 Remittance

Remittance refers to the transfer of funds from the importer to the exporter via the bank. It is one of the most simple, convenient and common terms of payment in international trade. In remittance, there are four parties involved: the remitter (the person who requests his bank to remit funds to a beneficiary), the beneficiary (the person who is addressed to receive the remittance), the remitting bank (the bank transferring funds at the request of a remitter to its correspondent or its branch in another country and instructing the latter to pay a certain amount of money to a beneficiary), and the paying bank (the bank entrusted by the remitting bank to pay a certain amount of money to a beneficiary named in the remittance advice).

Generally, there are three types of remittance: Telegraphic Transfer (T/T), Demand Draft (D/D) and Mail Transfer (M/T), of which T/T is the mainstay means. It is a method of transferring funds by telecommunication system such as telex or cable. The advantage is the fast speed. A payment can be made within two or three banking days. The disadvantage is the relatively high cost. However, SWIFT (Society for Worldwide Interbank Financial Telecommunication) members are able to transfer funds within their own telecommunication network at a much lower cost. This has made T/T very popular as most international banks are SWIFT members. The transfer can also be made by a check that is sold to its customer by a bank instructing another branch/bank to pay upon demand a certain amount to the payee as specified on the check. This check is called a banker's demand draft (D/D). It is a cheaper but slower method of transferring funds since the purchaser of the check must mail it to the beneficiary, who is to get the funds from a local bank. M/T is a remittance method in which the remitting bank, based on the application by the remitter, sends the mail transfer trust deed to the receiving bank through the post office or express companies, and authorizes the receiving bank to pay the remittance to the receiver. It is slow and has more paper work than D/D. So it has almost been replaced by demand draft or telegraphic transfer.

In international trade, remittance is mainly used for payment in advance, cash on delivery, cash with order, open account trade, down payment, installment and commission payment. To avoid loss from bill forgery or cheating, the exporter should make sure that the payment has been received from the buyer before delivering the goods. In essence, remittance is a kind of commercial credit, which is less secure than a banker's credit and hence in using this method, the parties involved must have trust in each other.

8.4.2 Collection

Under the method of collection, the seller ships the goods and submits a draft and/or shipping documents to the seller's local bank, entrusting the local bank to collect the proceeds through its branch or corresponding bank in the buyer's country. Title to the goods does not pass to the buyer until the draft is paid or accepted by the buyer. In collection, there are generally four parties involved: the principal, the payer, the remitting bank and the collecting bank. The principal is the exporter, also called the drawer, for the exporter usually draws a draft to collect payment for the goods. The payer is the importer, also called the drawee, for the importer is generally the drawee of the draft. The remitting bank is the seller's local bank which sends instructions to its branch bank or a correspondent bank in the importing country to collect payment for the goods. The collecting bank is the bank in the buyer's country entrusted by the remitting bank with collecting the money from the buyer.

8.4.2.1 Types of Collection

Collection may be divided into two categories: Clean Collection and Documentary Collection. In clean collection, the amount owed is evidenced by a bill of exchange, promissory note, undertaking, or a simple receipt denoting the amount required by the exporter/seller. There are no commercial documents, such as invoices or transport documents. Most trade collections are documentary, comprising commercial documents, which include transport documents giving title and/or control to the underlying goods and may or may not be accompanied by a financial document, a bill of exchange.

(1) **Clean Collection**

Clean collection refers to the collection which is made with financial documents only. In other words, by clean collection, it is meant that financial documents such as a bill of exchange are presented to the bank which is entrusted by the principal for the collection without commercial documents such as a B/L, which is a document of title to the goods. Clean collection is seldom used in international trade except for the case where a small amount is to be collected. It is chiefly used for "open account" transactions or services.

(2) **Documentary Collections**

Documentary collection is a method of effecting payment for goods whereby the seller/exporter ships goods to the buyer, but instructs his bank to collect a certain sum from the buyer/importer in exchange for the transfer of shipment title and other documents enabling the buyer/importer to take possession of the goods.

By virtue of the way the documents are released, documentary collection can be further divided into documents against payment (D/P) and documents against acceptance (D/A).

In the case of documents against payment, the documents are released to the importer only after the payment. If the importer pays at the sight of the documents, it is documents against payment at sight (D/P at sight); when a time draft is drawn and the importer accepts the draft and pays at a determinable future time, it is documents against payment after sight (D/P after sight).

In the case of documents against acceptance, the collecting bank releases the documents to the importer after the latter has accepted the time draft. The importer makes payment when the draft matures.

➢**Advantages and Disadvantages of Documentary Collection**

The major advantage of a "cash against documents" payment method for the buyer is the low cost, versus opening a letter of credit. The advantage for the seller is that he can receive full payment prior to releasing control of the documents, although this is offset by the risk that the buyer can, for some reason, reject the documents. Since the cargo would have already been loaded (to generate the documents), the seller has little recourse against the buyer in case of non-payment. An arrangement of payment against documents involves a high level of trust between the seller and the buyer and should be adopted only by parties well known to each other.

➢**Risks in Documentary Collection**

For the exporter: If it is a sight draft, the exporter will reduce the risk of non-payment but will not eliminate it totally since the importer may not be in a position to pay for the goods or may not be able to procure sufficient foreign exchange to make the payment. In this case the exporter may be forced to either call back the goods or negotiate sales to some other interested party, which may be at a reduced rate.

In the case of term draft, the risk to the exporter is higher since the buyer might take possession of the goods and may not pay at due date, forcing therefore the exporter to try and collect payment from the buyer in a foreign country.

For the importer: The importer faces the risk of paying for goods of sub-standard quality or even with shortages. In such a circumstance, it would take some time to get refunds from the exporter. It could also happen that the exporter refuses to make refunds, leading the importer to lengthy legal proceedings.

➢**When to Use Documentary Collection**

Since documentary collection transactions entail some measure of trust, it is advisable to use this mechanism only when the following conditions apply:

1) When the exporter and importer have a well established relationship;

2) When there is little or no threat of a total loss resulting from the buyer's inability or refusal to pay;

3) When the political and economic situation of the importing country is stable;

4) When a letter of credit is too expensive or not available.

8.4.3 Letter of Credit

A letter of credit (L/C) is one of the most common and safest payment methods for international sales transactions. It is basically a mechanism which allows importers/buyers to offer secure terms of payment to exporters/sellers in which a bank (or more than one bank) gets involved. The technical term for "letter of credit" is "documentary credit". At the very outset one must understand that letters of credit deal with documents, not goods. This idea is to shift the risk from the actual buyer to a bank. Thus an L/C is a payment undertaking given by a bank to the seller and is issued on behalf of the applicant i.e. the buyer. The buyer is the applicant and the seller is the beneficiary. The bank that issues the L/C is referred to as the issuing bank which is generally in the country of the buyer. The bank that advises the L/C to the seller is called the advising bank which is generally in the country of the seller.

The specified bank makes the payment upon the successful presentation of the required documents by the seller within the specified time frame. Note that the bank scrutinizes the "documents" and not the "goods" for making payment. Thus the process works in favor of both the buyer and the seller. The seller gets assured that if documents are presented on time and in the way that they have been requested on the L/C, the payment will be made. The buyer, on the other hand, is assured that the bank will thoroughly examine these presented documents and ensure that they meet the terms and conditions stipulated in the L/C.

8.4.3.1 Types and Uses of Letters of Credit

Letters of credit can be categorized into different types depending on the payment conditions. Traders choose the one they find proper for import and export financing. The main letters of credit and their uses are briefly described as follows:

(1) **Clean L/C & Documentary L/C**

The L/C can be clean or documentary. A clean L/C refers to the L/C according to which the issuing bank makes payment against only the draft drawn by the beneficiary or some ordinary documents which do not include the important shipping documents. A clean L/C is not so commonly used in international trade because the importer may run greater risks. Letters of credit used by traders are always documentary. This means that the exporter is required to produce documents (A draft to which the documents are attached, accompanied by a collection letter. Usually, these documents include a commercial invoice and shipping documents) stated in the letter of credit evidencing the current shipment of the goods ordered before the money is released. A documentary L/C is most commonly used in international trade settlement. With a documentary L/C, the importer would feel it safer to pay money.

(2) **Revocable L/C & Irrevocable L/C**

A revocable L/C may be revoked without the consent of the exporter, meaning that it may be canceled or changed up to the time the documents are presented. As it affords the exporter little protection, it is rarely used. On the other hand, an irrevocable L/C cannot be canceled or changed without the consent of all parties, including the exporter. An L/C therefore should clearly indicate whether it is revocable or irrevocable. In the absence of such indication, the L/C shall be deemed to be irrevocable.

(3) **Unconfirmed L/C & Confirmed L/C**

An unconfirmed L/C contains the commitment of the issuing bank only. There is no undertaking on the part of the advising bank or other bank, while a confirmed credit has the commitment of the confirming bank besides that of the issuing bank. The confirming bank guarantees payment if the issuing bank cannot pay provided the terms and conditions of the credit are met. Remember, only the issuing bank may request another bank to add its confirmation.

(4) **Sight L/C & Time L/C**

A sight L/C means that payment is made immediately to the beneficiary/seller/exporter upon presentation of the correct documents in the required time frame. A time L/C, also called a usance L/C, or a date L/C, will specify when payment will be made at a future date upon presentation of the required documents.

(5) **Transferable L/C & Non-transferable L/C**

A transferable L/C is a credit that can be transferred (only once) by the original (first) beneficiary to another (second) beneficiary. If partial shipments are permitted, different portions of such a credit not exceeding the total amount of the credit can be transferred to different beneficiaries. A transferable L/C is often used when the beneficiary is not the ultimate supplier of merchandise but the middleperson between the supplier and a buyer. For a credit to be transferable, the beneficiary must arrange for the buyer to have a credit opened expressly stipulating that it is transferable. Additionally, before any transfer can be made, the beneficiary must send a written request to the transferring bank to effect such a transfer. The transferring bank, however, is under no obligation to execute the transfer until it is paid for its services.

A non-transferable L/C is a credit in which the beneficiary cannot transfer part or all of his right and obligations thereunder to another party. If the word transferable is not indicated in the credit, it is deemed to be a non-transferable credit.

(6) **Back-to-Back L/C**

The beneficiary (the seller or middle person in a purchase transaction) of an irrevocable L/C occasionally wants to use the L/C as a form of credit support for having its bank open a companion irrevocable L/C in favor of the manufacturer or supplier of the goods being purchased under the first credit. Back-to-back credits are usually requested by middle persons who do not have sufficient credit available at their banks to open their own L/Cs to the ultimate suppliers. The middle person will ask the bank to issue a second L/C in favor of the ultimate supplier, while using the L/C issued by the buyer as collateral. When an L/C is used as security to obtain the issuance of a second L/C covering the same transaction, and when all terms and conditions of both credits are identical, except for amounts and dates in the second L/C which must be smaller and earlier, the arrangement is defined as a back-to-back L/C.

There are inherent risks associated with every back-to-back credit arrangement since performance under the original L/C is contingent upon timely and perfect execution of the second L/C. For this reason, banks generally are averse to issuing back-to-back L/Cs.

The parties involved in the example of a transferable L/C may arrange the transaction on a back-to-back basis instead.

(7) **Red Clause L/C (Anticipatory L/C)**

A red clause L/C, also called anticipatory L/C, is an irrevocable L/C containing a clause authorizing the advising or confirming bank to pay an amount in advance to the beneficiary, before presenting any document that may be required under the terms of the L/C. The reason for it being called "red" is that such a clause used to be written in red ink.

A red clause L/C allows an exporter to receive payments in advance against the exporter's clean draft or receipt prior to the shipment. The advances can be used as deposits to the exporter's suppliers to obtain the products for exports or as working capital to complete the exportation of the goods ordered.

(8) **Standby L/C**

This type of credit is not specifically related to the movement of goods, but it acts more like a guarantee. Like a performance guarantee, a standby letter of credit allows the beneficiary to draw in the event of default on a contract, provided that the complying documents (usually a sight draft) are presented.

(9) **Revolving L/C**

When a buyer and a seller operate under an arrangement for goods to be shipped on a continuing basis over a stipulated period, it may be desirable to establish a single or revolving L/C to handle the shipments as they occur, rather than an individual L/C for each shipment. The credit will contain instructions allowing the beneficiary to draw designated amounts over a specified period of time and may also restrict the amount available for each shipment or control the frequency of shipments during a specified period. Revolving L/Cs are either cumulative or noncumulative. The difference lies in the amounts available for drawing against the L/C during a specified time period.

(10) **Deferred Payment L/C**

A deferred payment L/C is normally used by the buyer to obtain extended payment terms from the seller for a period usually beyond six months after delivery, while providing the seller the flexibility of obtaining funds sooner. Under this type of L/C the exporter, after shipment, presents complying documents to the buyer's bank, which acknowledges that delivery of the goods has taken place. The actual draw-down, however, cannot occur for six months or some other designated period. When requiring interim financing, the seller can use the paying bank's promise of future payment to obtain credit from other banks. However the seller will not be able to discount the draft to obtain financing without a banker's acceptance.

8.4.3.2 Basic Elements of an L/C

The form of an L/C may vary to some extent. Several standard L/C forms have been recommended by the *International Chamber of Commerce*, which are however not quite often used by the issuing banks. Most banks use their own forms with reference to the standard forms. The legal document concerning the use of L/C is the *Uniform Customs and Practice for Commercial Documentary Credits*. In general, an L/C includes the following elements, which can be seen from the example of a credit below:

1) The type of the L/C;

2) The L/C number, the date of issue, the date of expiry, the place of expiry, and the period of presentation of the documents;

3) The parties involved with the L/C, such as the issuing bank, the applicant, the advising bank, the beneficiary and so on;

4) The types of draft, the drawer, drawee, the duration to effect payment and so on;

5) The description of goods, quantity, unit price, specification, price terms, packing, shipping mark and so on;

6) The payment currency;

7) Terms and conditions of shipment and insurance;

8) Full details of the documents required;

9) Special terms and conditions;

10) The undertaking clause of the issuing bank.

INTERNATIONAL BANKING GROUP

ORIGINAL

Megabank Corporation

P.O. BOX 1000, ATLANTA, GEORGIA 30302-1000
CABLE ADDRESS: MegaB
TELEX NO. 1234567
SWIFT NO. MBBABC 72

OUR ADVICE NUMBER: EA00000091
ADVICE DATE: 08MAR97
ISSUE BANK REF: 3312/HBI/22341
EXPIRY DATE: 23JUN97

****AMOUNT****
USD****25,000.00

BENEFICIARY:
THE WALTON SUPPLY CO.
2356 SOUTH N.W. STREET
ATLANTA, GEORGIA 30345

APPLICANT:
HHB HONG KONG
34 INDUSTRIAL DRIVE
CENTRAL, HONG KONG

WE HAVE BEEN REQUESTED TO ADVISE TO YOU THE FOLLOWING LETTER OF CREDIT AS ISSUED BY:
THIRD HONG KONG BANK
1 CENTRAL TOWER
HONG KONG

PLEASE BE GUIDED BY ITS TERMS AND CONDITIONS AND BY THE FOLLOWING:
CREDIT IS AVAILABLE BY NEGOTIATION OF YOUR DRAFT(S) IN DUPLICATE AT SIGHT FOR 100 PERCENT OF INVOICE VALUE DRAWN ON US ACCOMPANIED BY THE FOLLOWING DOCUMENTS:

1. SIGNED COMMERCIAL INVOICE IN 1 ORIGINAL AND 3 COPIES.

2. FULL SET 3/3 OCEAN BILLS OF LADING CONSIGNED TO THE ORDER OF THIRD HONG KONG BANK, HONG KONG NOTIFY APPLICANT AND MARKED FREIGHT COLLECT.

3. PACKING LIST IN 2 COPIES.

EVIDENCING SHIPMENT OF: 5000 PINE LOGS – WHOLE – 8 TO 12 FEET
FOB SAVANNAH, GEORGIA

SHIPMENT FROM: SAVANNAH, GEORGIA TO: HONG KONG
LATEST SHIPPING DATE: 02JUN97

PARTIAL SHIPMENTS NOT ALLOWED TRANSHIPMENT NOT ALLOWED

ALL BANKING CHARGES OUTSIDE HONG KONG ARE FOR BENEFICIARYS ACCOUNT.
DOCUMENTS MUST BE PRESENTED WITHIN 21 DAYS FROM B/L DATE.

AT THE REQUEST OF OUR CORRESPONDENT, WE CONFIRM THIS CREDIT AND ALSO ENGAGE WITH YOU THAT ALL DRAFTS DRAWN UNDER AND IN COMPLIANCE WITH THE TERMS OF THIS CREDIT WILL BE DULY HONORED BY US.

PLEASE EXAMINE THIS INSTRUMENT CAREFULLY. IF YOU ARE UNABLE TO COMPLY WITH THE TERMS OR CONDITIONS, PLEASE COMMUNICATE WITH YOUR BUYER TO ARRANGE FOR AN AMENDMENT.

The above example of a confirmed irrevocable letter of credit illustrates the various parts of a typical letter of credit. In this sample, the letter of credit is forwarded to the exporter, the Walton Supply Company, by the confirming bank, Megabank Corporation, as a result of the letter of credit being issued by the Third Hong Kong Bank, Hong Kong, for the account of the importer, HHB Hong Kong. The date of issue is March 8, 1997, and the exporter must submit the proper documents (e.g., a commercial invoice in one original and three copies) by June 23, 1997 in order for a sight draft to be honored.

8.4.3.3 How an L/C Operates

The basic chain of operations of letters of credit is almost the same with some slight differences owing to different types of L/Cs. The following flow chart shows the operation processes of a documentary L/C.

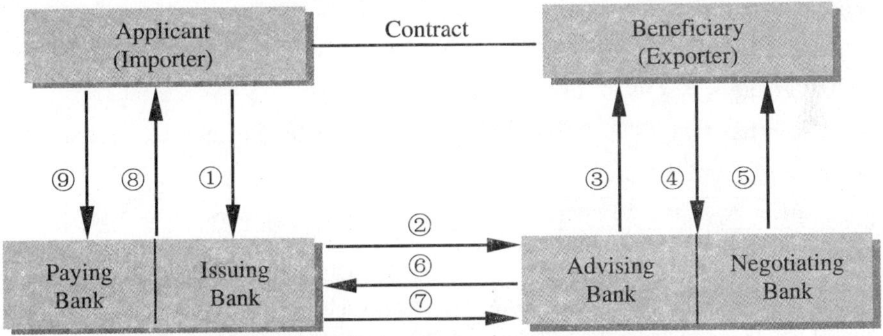

The flow chart of a documentary credit

①After the sales contract has been established between the exporter and importer, agreeing to settle the payment by L/C, the applicant (the importer) applies to their bank for a letter of credit in favor of the exporter (beneficiary).

②The issuing bank (opening bank) issues an L/C and forwards it to the advising bank in the exporter's country.

③The advising bank passes the documentary credit to the beneficiary after verifying the genuineness of the credit.

④On receiving the L/C, the exporter checks the terms and conditions of the credit based on the sales contract. If there is a discrepancy, the beneficiary may have the option to accept it as it stands or to ask the applicant to have it amended so as to be in line with the contract. The exporter prepares the documentation as per the terms and conditions of the L/C, and have the goods shipped. The exporter then presents the documents to the negotiating bank for the negotiation of the draft.

⑤ After receiving the documents, the negotiating bank will check the documents against the terms and conditions of the L/C. If all are in order, the above bank will effect payment to the beneficiary.

⑥The negotiating bank forwards the documents to the paying bank or the bank authorized by the issuing bank to ask for reimbursement.

⑦The paying bank, after receiving the documents from the negotiating bank, will examine them carefully to see whether the documents are in compliance with the terms of the L/C. If the documents conform to the L/C, the paying bank will reimburse the negotiating bank.

⑧The issuing bank will notify the importer of the arrival of the documents and ask him to pay the bank for the documents.

⑨The importer will pay money to the bank and get the documents for claiming the merchandise.

8.4.3.4 Advantages & Disadvantages of L/C Payment

As a coin has two sides, payment by L/C has advantages and disadvantages for both the exporter and the importer as shown below:

Advantages for the Exporter	Disadvantages for the Exporter
➢Shift credit risk from the importer to the importer's bank (the issuing bank). ➢An undertaking from the issuing bank that payment will be made under the letter of credit, provided that all terms and conditions of the credit are met. ➢If the L/C is not issued as agreed, the exporter is not obligated to ship against it.	➢Documents must be prepared in strict compliance with the requirements stipulated in the letter of credit. Non-compliance exposes the exporter to the risk of non-payment and removes the protection afforded by the issuing bank since the final decision on the documents then rests with the importer. ➢A revocable L/C does not provide an adequate payment guarantee.
Advantages for the Importer	**Disadvantages for the Importer**
➢Reduce commercial risks by ensuring that the supplier will not be paid until evidence has been provided that the goods have been dispatched. ➢The bank will refuse payment to the seller if the documents presented do not comply with the terms and conditions of the credit. ➢Conserve the company's cash flow by eliminating the need to make advance payments or deposits. ➢Demonstrate the importer's creditworthiness to the supplier. ➢The L/C with deferred payment provides a credit facility.	➢In L/C transactions, banks deal only in documents, not in goods and services. The goods may not be as represented in the documents. ➢The importer must bear the cost of arranging the L/C and may be asked to deposit money in a special account as a margin to cover the L/C, which will tie up the importer's capital.

8.4.4 Other Payment Methods

Apart from the above three common payment methods, there are also some other methods such as factoring, forfaiting and letter of guarantee.

8.4.4.1 Factoring and Forfaiting

Factoring is the discounting of a foreign account receivable that does not involve a draft. The exporter transfers title to its foreign accounts receivable to a factoring house (an organization that specializes in the financing of accounts receivable) for cash at a discount from the face value. Forfaiting is the selling, at a discount, of longer term accounts receivable or promissory notes of the foreign buyer.

(1) **Comparisons between Factoring and Forfaiting**

Both factoring and forfaiting involve the purchasing of receivables. They both aim at creating a source of finance by the purchase from a seller/exporter of receivables due from a buyer at a future date.

The UNIDROIT Convention on International Factoring (Ottawa, 28 May 1988) defines factoring as the assignment by a supplier of receivables arising from contracts of sale of goods made between the supplier and its customers (debtors) to a factor, in which the factor is to perform at least two of the following functions:

1) finance for the supplier, including loans and advance payments;

2) maintenance of accounts (ledgering) relating to the receivables;

3) collection of receivables;

4) protection against default in payment by debtors.

Factoring can therefore be an operation in which financing and credit collection functions are combined, or it can be the "outsourcing" of credit management and collection functions, without any finance provided to the supplier. In practice, however, the majority of factoring operations are done for financing purposes, and many factors stress this element in their publicity, to the extent that many define factoring as a primarily "cash for invoices" operation.

(2) **Similarities**

For the seller both factoring and forfaiting maximize cash flow, reduce transaction risks, and may enhance competitiveness by offering flexible payments terms to the buyer.

In both cases, the risk of the delivery of satisfactory goods or services and the fulfillment of the underlying contract remains with the seller, while the purchaser of receivables (whether a forfaiter or a factor) assumes the commercial, political and economic risks of the buyer's country.

(3) **Differences**

The differences, however, are that factoring deals mainly with non-negotiable instruments like book receivables, whereas forfaiting deals mainly with negotiable instruments, like bills of exchange, promissory notes, and letter of credit.

Forfaiting deals with one single existing and known transaction whereas factoring deals with a group of present and future receivables on the books of the seller. In factoring, the seller assigns all or part of the receivables to the factor, including those in the future. In factoring, the service of collecting receivables always represents part of the contract, whereas forfaiting offers this service indirectly for individual transactions handled in any agreement. In factoring, it is quite common not to finance 100% of the value of the receivables but to retain a certain amount. In forfaiting 100% of the present value (future value minus the interest discount) is always disbursed.

Factoring often covers domestic short- to medium-term business whereas forfaiting is mostly used for medium- and long-term deals involving cross-border transactions. However, nowadays forfaiters are discounting short-term deals mainly in commodity transactions.

Forfaiting usually uses a main document called the promissory note that has the following characteristics:

1) An unconditional (an irrevocable) promise in writing;

2) Made by one person to another;

3) Engaging to pay:

➢at a fixed future dated

➢a certain sum of money

➢to or to the order of a specified person or to the bearer/order.

8.4.4.2 Letter of Guarantee (L/G)

In international trade, on the one hand, the buyer wants to be certain that the seller is in a position to honour his commitment as offered or contracted. The former therefore makes it a condition that appropriate security be provided. On the other hand, the seller must find a way to be assured of receiving payment if no special security is provided for the payment such as in open account business and documentary collections. Such security may be obtained through banks in the form of a guarantee. A bank guarantee is used as an instrument for securing performance or payment especially in international business.

A letter of guarantee is a written promise issued by a bank at the request of its customer, undertaking to make payment to the beneficiary within the limits of a stated sum of money in the event of default by the principal. It may also be defined as the irrevocable obligation of a bank to pay a sum of money in the event of non-performance of a contract by the principal. Distinguished from a letter of credit, a bank guarantee is an undertaking which will be brought into effect by the guarantor, namely the bank, only if the principal fails to pay or perform and so the bank is secondarily liable to the beneficiary. However, under a payment guarantee, it is stipulated that the bank undertakes to pay, provided the documents presented are in compliance with the terms and conditions of the guarantee. In that case, the issuing bank is primarily liable to the beneficiary.

8 .5 Vocabulary Check

appreciate *v.* 升值
appreciation *n.* 升值
applicant / opener 开证申请人/开证人
advising bank / notifying bank 通知行
account receivable 应收账款
at a discount 打折扣
beneficiary 受益人
bank's draft / bill 银行汇票
banker's acceptance bill 银行承兑汇票
commercial draft / bill 商业汇票
clean draft / bill 光票
convertible 可转换的
commercial acceptance bill 商业承兑汇票
collecting bank 代收行
cash flow 现金流量

cross-border transactions 跨境交易
confirming bank 保兑行
debtor 债务人；借方
discount 贴现；折扣
default 诈骗
distribution 经销；分销
depreciate *v.* 贬值
depreciation *n.* 贬值
drawer 出票人
drawee 受票人
documentary draft / bill 跟单汇票
evaluation currency 估价货币
finance *v. n.* 融资
margin 押金；保证金
mechanism 机制

negotiating bank 议付行
non-negotiable 非议付的
opening bank/issuing bank 开证行
optional port charges 选港费
port congestion surcharges 港口拥挤附加费
payment instrument 支付工具
paying bank 付款行
principal 委托人
presenting bank 提示行
receivables 应收款项
remittance 托收
remitting bank 托收行
sight draft / bill 即期汇票
spectrum 范围；领域
time draft / bill 远期汇票

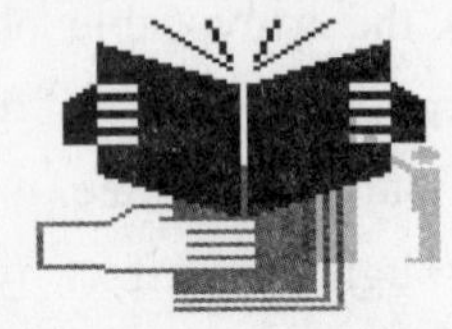

8.6 Notes and Key Terms

1) **hard currency and soft currency**：硬通货和软通货。前者是指国际信用较好、币值稳定、汇价呈坚挺状态的货币；后者是指币值不稳、汇价呈疲软状态的货币。实际上，硬通货与软通货只是相对而言，它会随着该国经济状况和金融状况的变化而变化。此外，硬通货和软通货还有另一层含义。第二次世界大战后，国际金融市场上某些不实施外汇管制、可以自由和无限地兑换黄金和其他国家货币的货币，被称作硬通货。软通货则是指实施外汇管制、不能自由兑换黄金和其他国家货币的货币。

2) **draft/bill of exchange:** 汇票。《英国票据法》对汇票的定义是： 汇票是由一人向另一人签发的，要求即期或定期或在可以确定的将来的时间，对某人或其指定人或持票人支付一定金额的无条件书面支付命令。

3) **promissory note:** 本票，是出票人签发的，承诺自己在见票时无条件支付确定的金额给收款人或持票人的票据。

4) **money order**：统指汇票，是由开票机构(一般为实力雄厚、信誉卓著的金融机构或公司)开出的在见票时按照实际结算金额无条件支付给收款人的保付票据，可从银行、邮局或 MoneyMart 购买。money order 和银行汇票(bank draft)不同的是，银行汇票是由出票银行签发的，由其在见票时按照实际结算金额无条件支付给收款人或者持票人的保付票据。银行汇票的出票银行为银行汇票的付款人。单位和个人各种款项的结算，均可使用银行汇票。通常 money order 是指金额 1000 元或以下的汇票，bank draft 是指金额 1000 元(视乎不同银行的规定)以上的汇票。所以 bank draft 也可以理解为大额的 money order。两者的不同之处在于 money order 只要由银行的柜台工作人员签名即可生效，而

bank draft 则需要由银行的柜台工作人员和值班经理两人同时签名方可生效。

5) **SWIFT (Society for World-wide Inter-bank Financial Telecommunication):** 环球银行金融电讯协会，该组织成立于 1973 年，总部在比利时的布鲁塞尔。从事传递各国之间非公开性的金融电讯业务，包括外汇买卖、证券交易、开立信用证、办理信用证项下的汇票业务和托收、国际间财务清算和银行间资金调拨。SWIFT 提供的服务除快速、标准、安全、可靠外，其运转和管理效率也很高，当前银行间的业务往来已经广泛使用 SWIFT。

6) **payment methods:** 随着国际贸易的发展，形成了多样化的支付方式。不同的支付方式所涉及的信用不同，付款时间、地点也各不相同。国际贸易支付方式主要有汇付、托收和信用证三种。

汇付(Remittance)，又称汇款，是债务人(即进口商)通过银行，将款项交债权人(即出口商)的结算方式，也是最简单的国际货款结算方式。汇付有三种：电汇(Telegraphic Transfer, T/T)，信汇(Mail Transfer, M/T)和票汇(Remittance by Banker's Demand Draft, D/D)。

汇付方式常用于预付现金(cash in advance)、随订单付款(cash with order)、交货付款(cash on delivery)和赊账(open account)等业务。此外，汇付方式还用于支付定金(down payment)、分期付款(installment)以及佣金(commission)等费用。汇付方式的使用，取决于交易双方中一方对另一方的信任，因此属于商业信用。另外，当出口商扩大其市场时，汇付可用于出口商提供给进口商的一种优惠待遇。

托收(Collection)，是指由卖方根据发票金额开立汇票，委托银行向进口商收取货款。托收可分为光票托收(Clean Collection)和跟单托收(Documentary Collection)。光票托收主要用于小额交易货款、部分预付货款、分期付款及贸易从属费用的收取。在大多数情况下，采用跟单托收。跟单托收可分为两类：付款交单(Documents against Payment, D/P)和承兑交单(Documents against Acceptance, D/A)。付款交单指进口商付了货款后才会得到货运单据。根据付款时间的不同，付款交单可分为即期付款交单(Documents against Payment at Sight, D/P Sight)和远期付款交单(Documents against Payment after Sight, D/P after Sight)。即期付款条件下，托收行(Remitting Bank)得到汇票和单据后，向进口商出示汇票，进口商应立即对出口商开出的跟单汇票付款，付款后交单。如果规定了远期付款交单，进口商应立即承兑出口商开出的提示××天内付款的跟单汇票，到期时付款，汇款后交单。承兑交单指出口商交单以进口商承兑为条件。进口商承兑汇票后，即可向银行取得货运单据，待汇票到期时才付款。承兑交单只适用于远期的汇票托收。此外，在远期付款交单条件下，还有付款交单凭信托收据借单(D/P after sight against Trust Receipt, D/P-T/R)的做法，即代收行对于资信较好的进口人，允许进口人凭信托收据借取货运单据，先行提货。这种做法在西方发达国家比较流行。

信用证(Letter of Credit, L/C)是指银行应买方(进口商)的要求开给卖方(出口商)的一种有条件的承担付款责任的书面保证文件。出口商采用信用证方式可以保证安全收汇；而进口商的付款是以付款银行取得全部合格、有效的单据为前提条件，因此也免除了预付货款所要承担的风险。信用证可以根据其性质、形式、付款期限和用途分为许多种类。但从银行信用角度来分，主要有两种：可撤销信用证(Revocable L/C)和不可撤销信用证(Irrevocable L/C)。在不可撤销信用证的基础上，一般又可分为以下主要几种：即期信用证(Sight L/C)、远期信用证(Usance L/C)、保兑信用证(Confirmed L/C)、可转让信用证(Transferable L/C)、可分割信用证(Divisible L/C)、循环信用证(Revolving L/C)、对开信用证(Reciprocal L/C)、对背信用证(Back to Back L/C)和预支信用证(Anticipatory L/C)。

7) **UNIDROIT Convention on International Factoring：** 国际统一私法协会《国际保理公约》，该《公约》对保理的定义是：卖方或供应商或出口商与保理商之间存在的一种契约关系。根据该契约，卖方(供应商、出口商)将其现在或将来的基于其与买方(债务人)订立的货物销售、服务合同所产生的应收账款转让给保理商，由保理商为其提供下列服务中的至少两项：(1)贸易融资；(2)销售分账户管理；(3)应收账款的催收；(4)信用风险控制与坏账担保。
8) **forfaiting:** 福费廷，通常是指买进因商品和劳务的转让(主要是出口交易)而产生的在将来某一个日子到期的债务，这种购买对原先的票据持有人无追索权。
9) **Letter of Guarantee:** 保函，又称银行保函(Bank Guarantee)，是银行向受益人开立的保证文件。由银行作为担保人，以第三者的身份保证被保证人如未向受益人履行某项义务时，由担保银行承担保证书中所规定的付款责任。

银行保函与信用证的区别：

信用证	银行保函
开证行负第一付款责任	一般来说保证行负第二责任
合同正常履行时，支付必然发生	合同正常履行时，保函不必使用
使用时与实际合同履行无关，只要求单单一致，单证一致	使用时必须对合同违约行为调查取证

8.7 Follow-up Practice

8.7.1 Review and Discussion Questions

1) Why are payment arrangements for international trade more complicated than those of home trade?
2) What currency will the importer choose to make payments, hard currency or soft currency? Why?
3) What payment instruments are used in international trade? Please list at least 3 of them and explain them briefly.
4) What is the difference between a bill of exchange and a promissory note?
5) Describe the types of remittance and their advantages and disadvantages.
6) What is the difference between clean collection and documentary collection?
7) Describe the types of documentary collection and their advantages and disadvantages.
8) What is L/C? Which types of L/C are commonly used? Why?
9) What is the relationship between the L/C and the sales contract?
10) What is the difference between a letter of credit and a letter of guarantee?
11) What is the difference between factoring and forfaiting?

8.7.2 Give the Chinese equivalents to the following English terms and match their definitions given below.

a. clean L/C	________	b. deferred L/C	________
c. irrevocable L/C	________	d. red clause L/C	________
e. confirmed L/C	________	f. a sight draft	________
g. D/P	________	h. a letter of guarantee	________
i. open account	________	j. cash in advance	________

1) ________ is a credit available by deferred payment, under which payment must be effected on a specified future date.
2) ________ is one with a clause inserted into the credit authorizing the negotiating bank to make an advance of the amount under the credit, whole or part, to the beneficiary.
3) ________ is a credit under which payment will be effected only against a draft without any shipping documents attached thereto or sometimes, against a draft with an invoice alone attached thereto.

4) ________ is a credit that constitutes a definite undertaking of the issuing bank and can be amended or cancelled by the issuing bank only on condition that all parties concerned have agreed.

5) ________ is a credit that is advised to the beneficiary with another bank's confirmation added thereto.

6) ________ is the bill of exchange that is payable the moment the bill is presented to the drawee of it.

7) ________ means that the principal gives the draft and the shipping documents to the bank and entrusts the bank to collect the payment from the importer on condition that the importer effects payment.

8) ________ is a term of payment in which no banks are involved. It is just an agreement between the seller and the buyer that payment will be made within a specified period of time.

9) Under ________, the exporter is paid when the importer places his order or when the goods are ready for shipment to the importer.

10) ________ is a written promise issued by the bank to compensate (pay a sum of money) to the beneficiary (third party, local or foreign) in the event that the obligor (the bank's customer) fails to honor its obligations in accordance with the terms and conditions of the guarantee/agreement/contract.

8.7.3 Choose the right answer from each of the following.

1) Documentary collection seeks ________ from the bank.

A. guarantee　　B. no guarantee
C. no protection　　D. insurance

2) Documentary credit seeks ________ from the bank.

A. guarantee　　B. no guarantee
C. no protection　　D. insurance

3) The most important documents in documentary collection is ________.

A. commercial invoice　　B. certificate origin
C. bill of exchange　　D. certificate of inspection

4) The bill of exchange is only drawn by the ________.

A. seller　　B. agent
C. buyer　　D. bank

5) A bank informs the beneficiary that another bank has opened a letter of credit in his favor. The bank informing the beneficiary does not add its engagement. This

bank is acting as ________.

A. an advising bank
B. a confirming bank
C. an issuing bank
D. a negotiating bank

6) How will a bank honor a sight draft?

A. Pay the beneficiary at once.
B. Accept the draft for payment at a future date.
C. Discount the draft.
D. Return the draft to the seller.

7) How will a bank honor a time draft?

A. Pay the beneficiary immediately.
B. Accept the draft for payment at a future date.
C. Discount the sight draft.
D. return the draft to the seller.

8) In a documentary credit transaction, payment is made in exchange for ________.

A. goods
B. shipping documents
C. commercial invoice
D. bill of exchange

9) The most common and safest payment method for international sales transactions is ________.

A. cash in advance
B. remittance
C. collection
D. L/C

10) Which of the following is NOT an advantage of an L/C?

A. Shift credit risk from the importer to the importer's bank.
B. L/C is as good as an advanced payment.
C. An undertaking from the issuing bank that payment will be made under the L/C, provided that all terms and conditions of the credit are met.
D. If the L/C is not issued as agreed, you are not obligated to ship against it.

11) In terms of the risk for the exporter to get payment, the risk spectrum of the payment methods from the highest to the least is: ________.

A. L/C, D/P, D/A, and O/A
B. O/A, D/A, D/P and L/C
C. L/C, D/A, D/P and O/A
D. L/C, O/A, D/A and D/P

12) Under ________, the importer borrows the shipping documents from the collecting bank and takes the goods. When the draft matures, he effects payment.

A. D/P at sight
B. D/P after sight
C. D/A
D. D/D

13) According to UCP500, which of the following documents must be issued /drawn

by the beneficiary unless otherwise stipulated by the Credit?

A. Draft. B. Packing list.

C. Inspection certificate. D. Insurance policy.

14) L/C embodies the contractual relationship between ________.

A. the applicant and the issuing bank

B. the issuing bank and the beneficiary

C. the applicant and the beneficiary

D. the paying bank and the negotiating bank

15) If a buyer has goods delivered to him in installments at specified intervals, ________ is often used so as to simplify formalities and reduce expenses.

A. a back-to-back L/C B. a revolving L/C

C. a standby L/C D. a deferred payment L/C

8.7.4 Decide whether the following statements are true or false.

1) In international trade, the exporter generally chooses soft currency and the importer tries to use hard currency. ( )

2) Most of the promissory notes in use today are issued by individuals rather than by firms. ( )

3) A draft involves three parties: the drawer, the drawee and the payee. ( )

4) A time bill is sometimes called a usance bill. ( )

5) Of the three types of remittance, T/T is most commonly used because of the fast speed. ( )

6) Remittance belongs to commercial credit while collection and letter of credit belong to banker's credit. ( )

7) A revocable L/C is more secure than an irrevocable L/C and thus it is more often used. ( )

8) A clean L/C is favoured by the importers in international trade, because if it is used, the importers run no risks. ( )

9) An L/C should indicate whether it is revocable or irrevocable. In the absence of such indication, the L/C shall be deemed to be revocable. ( )

10) By using a sight L/C, the buyer is financing the transaction while the goods are in transit since the buyer pays before he gets the goods. ( )

11) The letter of credit is usually forwarded to the exporter by the importer. ( )

12) The exporter will run more risks to adopt D/A at 30 days sight than D/P at 30 days after sight. ( )

13) Exporters always insist on payment by cash in advance when they are trading with old customers. ( )
14) Factoring is usually used for short-term export financing while forfaiting is used for medium-term and long-term financing. ( )
15) A letter of guarantee is different from an L/C because under the L/C, the issuing bank holds itself responsible for the payment of the goods, but under a letter of guarantee, the issuing bank holds itself responsible only after the principal has not fulfilled its obligations. ( )

8.7.5 Case Study

On May 8, 2005, a remitting bank accepted an outward collection business of D/P at sight with the amount of US$80,000. Instructed by the exporter, the remitting bank mailed the full set of documents together with a collection instruction to the collecting bank in a Middle East country. A week later, the exporter required the remitting bank to change "D/P at sight" into "D/A at 30 days sight" according to the importer's request, despite the remitting bank's warning about the high risk of D/A. So the remitting bank sent a modification instruction. However, the collecting bank didn't send them the notice of acceptance. On August 15, the exporter asked the remitting bank to instruct the collecting bank to return the documents. On August 25, the remitting bank received the returned documents but found that one of the three original bills of lading was missing. The exporter soon learned that the goods had been picked up by the importer. The remitting bank required that the collecting bank either send back the documents in full or make payment by acceptance, but the collecting bank paid no attention to it. Furthermore, the exporter was unwilling to settle the problem by legal means. The exporter has still not received the payment after several years. What are the lessons we can learn from this case?

A Chinese company concluded a contract with a European country for exporting dehydrated carrot flakes of the second grade. The L/C established by the bank of the importing country described the goods as "Dehydrated Carrot Flakes Grade 2". Before the goods were ready for shipment, the goods of this quality were out of stock. The exporter decided to ship "Grade 1" instead of "Grade 2" to meet the demand of the market. The invoice marked "Dehydrated Carrot Flakes Grade 1, price as per

Grade 2."

The exporter took it for granted that the importer would not show any objection to this, so would the negotiating bank. However, on the contrary, the importer refused to make the payment because of "nonconformity between documents and terms of the credit". What was more, the importer even demanded compensation for the loss caused by the exporter's failure to ship the goods according to the agreed specification. What does this case show us?

Web Links

1. http://www. china.org.cn/law 中国网
2. http://info.jctrans.com 进出口资讯网
3.http://www.chinaim-ex.com 中国进出口网
4. http://www. boc.cn 中国银行网
6. http://www.swift.com 环球银行金融电讯协会网
7. http://www.iccwbo.org/policy/banking/iccjjdi/index.html 国际商会网

Chapter Nine

Inspection, Claims, Force Majeure and Arbitration

Learning Objectives

At the end of this chapter, you should be able to understand:

- the inspection practice in international trade
- the three ways of stipulating the place and time of inspection
- disputes, claims and the settlement of disputes
- the ways of stipulating the claim clause in the contract
- the consequences of force majeure
- the concept of arbitration

With the development of international trade, commodity inspection has become an indispensable link in the chain of smooth handling of international trade transactions and how to stipulate the place and time of inspection and to exercise the right of inspection is the core of constructing the inspection clause of the contract. In case of a claim, the party involved should try to settle it on the basis of integrity. It is best to settle international trade disputes through friendly negotiations. If no agreement can be reached, the parties to the disputes may choose arbitration, which is another widely used alternative of settling disputes. In case of a force majeure event after the conclusion of the contract, the party who suffers the event is allowed to be relieved liabilities of the non-performance or termination of the contract.

9.1 Commodity Inspection

The inspection of goods is of great significance in international trade. In international trade, the quality and quantity of the goods delivered by the seller should be in conformity with the terms of the contract and should be packed in the manner required by the contract. In this sense, the commodity inspection and the issuance of certificate of inspection are necessary steps in the transfer of the goods.

9.1.1 Place and Time of Inspection

The place and time of inspection is the first item in an inspection clause. It stipulates where and when the inspection should be conducted and is associated with the terms of delivery used, the nature of the commodity and packaging, and the laws or regulations of different countries.

In general, there are three ways to stipulate the place and time of inspection.

(1) **Shipping Quality and Weight**

With this method, inspection at the seller's factory or at the port of shipment is final. Theoretically, buyers can re-inspect the goods at the port of destination. However, the buyer will bear all the risks once the goods leave the factory or the port of shipment and cannot claim for compensation unless there is a big discrepancy in quality. Therefore, this method is not favorable to the buyer.

(2) **Landed Quality and Weight**

This means inspection carried out at the port of destination is to be final. This

(3) **Inspection at the Port of Shipment and Re-inspection at the Port of Destination**

It means after inspection at the port of shipment, the buyer retains the right to re-inspect and claim for compensation if the goods delivered don't comply with the contract. This method is favorable to both sides and therefore is widely used in international trade.

9.1.2 Inspection Body

The sale or use of import commodities is not allowed until they have undergone inspection, and the export of commodities is not allowed until they have been found to be up to standard through inspection. The commodity inspection authorities are supposed to go through the procedures for inspection and issue an inspection certificate within the period of validity of claims prescribed in a sales contract.

There are mainly two types of inspection bodies: governmental and non-governmental. The governmental inspection bodies such as the Food and Drugs Administration (FDA) in the USA, specialize in the inspection of particular merchandise (grain, drug, etc.). The international inspection of commodity is mainly undertaken by non-governmental bodies which have the same legal status as notary organizations. The notable bodies are Societe General De Surveillance S. A. (SGS) in Geneva, Swiss, Underwriters Laboratory (UL) in the USA, Lloyd Surveyor, B.V. in Britain and Japan Marine Surveyor & Sworn Measurer's Association (NKKK), etc.

In China, it is the State Administration for Commodity Inspection who is in charge of the inspection of import and export commodities throughout the country. The State Administration for Commodity Inspection, in the light of the needs in the development of foreign trade, makes, adjusts and publishes a List of Import and Export Commodities Subject to Inspection by the Commodity Inspection Authorities. The commodity inspection authorities and other inspection organizations designated by the State Administration for Commodity Inspection perform the inspection of import and export commodities in accordance with the law.

9.1.3 Inspection Certificate

The commodity inspection authorities issue inspection statements called the inspection certificate after the commodities have undergone inspection. The inspection certificates are used to verify whether the goods are in conformity with the terms of the contract. If the verification is positive, the certificates are the supporting documents for payment. If not, they are the documents for refusal of the goods and claim for compensation.

The inspection certificates issued by Chinese Inspection and Quarantine Organizations are mainly as follows:

- ➢Inspection Certificate of Quality
- ➢Inspection Certificate of Quantity
- ➢Inspection Certificate of Packing
- ➢Inspection Certificate of Disinfection
- ➢Veterinary Inspection Certificate
- ➢Sanitary Inspection Certificate
- ➢Inspection Certificate on Damaged Cargo
- ➢Inspection Certificate on Tank/Hold
- ➢Inspection Certificate on Cargo Weight

9.1.4 The Inspection Clause of the Contract

The inspection clause in the sales contract usually contains stipulations on the inspection right, the time and place of inspection or re-inspection, the inspection organization, the inspection items and the inspection certificate. The following are two examples:

➢It is mutually agreed that the Certificate of Quality and Weight (Quantity) issued by the China Exit and Entry Inspection and Quarantine Bureau at the port/place of shipment shall be part of the documents to be presented for negotiation under the relevant L/C. The buyers shall have the right to re-inspect the quality and weight (quantity) of the cargo. The re-inspection fee shall be borne by the buyers. Should the quality and or weight (quantity) be found not in conformity with that of the contract, the buyers are entitled to lodge with the sellers a claim which should be supported by survey reports issued by a recognized surveyor approved by the sellers. The claim, if any, shall be lodged within…days after arrival of the cargo at the port/place of destination.

➢It is mutually agreed that the Certificate of Quality and Weight (Quantity) issued by the manufacturer shall be part of the documents for payment under relevant L/C. In case the quality, quantity or weight of the goods is found not in conformity with those stipulated in this contract after re-inspection by the China Exit and Entry Inspection and Quarantine Bureau within…days after discharge of the goods at the port of destination, the buyers shall return the goods to or lodge claim against the sellers for compensation of losses upon the strength of Inspection Certificate issued by the said Bureau, with the exception of those claims for which the insurers or the carriers are liable. All expenses (including inspection fees) and losses arising from the return of the goods or claims should be borne by the sellers. In such case, the buyers may, if so requested, send a sample of the goods in question to the sellers, provided that the sampling is feasible.

9.2 Claims

When one party to a contract fails to fulfill his obligations and causes the other party financial losses, the latter would demand the former to compensate him for the losses. This demand is called a claim.

9.2.1 Breach of Contract

Before the settlement of the claim, however, the nature of the breach should be determined according to the trade terms of the contract or the consequence of the breach, for different remedies are to be used for different breaches. Normally, there are two ways to determine the nature of breach. One is based on the terms and conditions of the contract; the other is based on the consequence of breach.

(1) **On the Basis of Terms and Conditions of the Contract**

There are two types of undertakings entered into every sales contract. The more important one of the two types is called a condition which is a clause associated with the essence of the contract. This clause actually goes to the root of the contract. If one party breaks a condition, he will break the foundation of the contract and leads to an action for fundamental breach of the contract.

The less important type of undertaking is called a warranty. Since a warranty does not go to the root of the contract, the injured party cannot cancel the contract, but he is entitled to the compensation for breach of warranty.

(2) **On the Basis of Consequence of Breach of the Contract**

If one party breaks the contract and makes the other party unable to obtain the main profit, then this is called “material breach”. In this case, the injured party has the right to cancel the contract. Meanwhile, he may also have the right to ask for compensation for losses.

If one party breaks the contract, but the case is not so serious and the other party will not lose any main profit, this is called "minor breach". In this case, the injured party cannot cancel the contract. However, he may ask for compensation for losses.

9.2.2 Important Tips in Handling Claims

To file or to settle a claim, the following points should be first considered:

➢whether the claim is justified by the contract

➢whether the claim is made in time

➢whether the claim is well supported by good documentation

Failing to have positive answers to all the above would mean difficulties in settling the claim. If it is justified, timely and well-supported, a claim can be settled in one of the following ways:

➢making refund with compensation for direct losses and expenses such as banking charges, storage and inspection charges, etc;

➢devaluating the goods according to the degree of inferiority, extent of damage and amount of losses;

➢replacing the defective goods with new ones that conform to the specifications, quality and performance as stipulated in the contract.

9.2.3 Claim Clause of the Contract

In the import or export contract, the most commonly used claim clauses are the discrepancy and claim clause and the penalty clause or the liquidated damage clause. The former is stipulated in case the quality, quantity or packing of the goods delivered by the seller is not in conformity with the relevant contract provisions while the latter is directed against delayed delivery by the seller or the buyer's delay in opening an L/C. The following are examples of claim clauses and penalty clauses respectively:

➢Any claim by the buyers regarding the goods shipped shall be filed within 30 days after arrival of the goods at the port of destination specified in the relative B/L and supported by a survey report issued by a surveyor approved by the sellers.

➢Should the buyers for its own sake fail to open the letter of credit on time stipulated in the contract, the buyers shall pay a penalty to the sellers. The penalty shall be charged at the rate of 0.5% of the amount of the L/C for every ten days of delay in opening the L/C, however, the penalty shall not exceed 5% of the total valued of the L/C which the buyers should have opened. Any fractional days less than ten days shall be deemed to be ten days for the calculation of penalty. The penalty shall be the sole compensation for the damage caused by such delay.

9.3 Force Majeure

9.3.1 Definition of Force Majeure

Force majeure is an event or effect that cannot be reasonably anticipated or controlled. Certain natural disasters and social disturbances are considered as force majeure events.

A force majeure event should have the following features:

➢it happens after the contract is signed;

➢it is not due to the negligence of the buyer or the seller;

➢neither the buyer nor the seller can control the situation.

A force majeure clause is mainly a protection for the seller to enable him to avoid his contractual obligations without paying a compensation or penalty, although it protects the buyers as well.

9.3.2 Consequences of Force Majeure

There are usually two consequences of force majeure: termination of the contract and postponement of the contract.

(1) **Termination of the Contract**

In cases of natural disasters or other events that have made it impossible to fulfill the contract, the contract can be terminated.

(2) **Postponement of the Contract**

In cases of events (such as transportation stoppage caused by an earthquake) that will only delay the fulfillment of a contract, the contract can be postponed but not terminated since it is still possible for the seller to carry out his contract obligations.

9.3.3 Force Majeure Clause

The following points should be remembered when drafting the force majeure clause:

(1) **The Scope of Force Majeure Clause**

The kinds of events that are to be considered as force majeure should be specified as clearly as possible. For instance, some people include social disturbances or strikes as force majeure events, but some other people disagree. If the scope of the event is not clearly defined, there might be difficulties in using the clause.

There are basically three ways to set the scope as shown in the samples below:

1) The general type

If the shipment of the contracted goods is prevented or delayed in whole or in part *due to Force Majeure*, the seller shall not be liable for non-shipment or late shipment of the goods of this contract. However, the seller shall notify the buyer by cable or telex and furnish the latter within...days by registered airmail with a certificate issued by the China Council for the Promotion of International Trade attesting such event or events.

2) The listing type

If the shipment of the contracted goods is prevented or delayed in whole or in part *by reason of war, earthquake, flood, fire, storm, heavy snow*, the seller shall not be liable for non-shipment or late shipment of the goods of this contract. However, the seller shall notify the buyer by cable or telex and furnish the latter within...days by registered airmail with a certificate issued by the China Council for the Promotion of International Trade attesting such event or events.

3) The comprehensive type

If the shipment of the contracted goods is prevented or delayed in whole or in part *by reason of war, earthquake, flood, fire, storm, heavy snow or other causes of Force Majeure*, the seller shall not be liable for non-shipment or late shipment of the goods of this contract. However, the seller shall notify the buyer by cable or telex and furnish the latter within...days by registered airmail with a certificate issued by the China Council for the Promotion of International Trade attesting such event or events.

(2) **Time Limit of Notifying the Other Party**

In case of a force majeure event, the party seeking to use the clause of force majeure has a duty to promptly notify the other party of "the impediment and its effect on his ability of performance."

(3) **The Issuer of the Certificate**

A force majeure event should be verified by a certificate that attests such an event. The issuer of the certificate should be mentioned in the clause.

9.4 Arbitration

When disputes arise between the exporter and the importer, they can be settled through friendly negotiation, consultation, arbitration, or litigation. Friendly negotiation is an important tool in the process of dispute settlement, and undoubtedly the one most commonly relied on. The majority of the disputes are settled this way and friendly business relations are thus maintained between exporters and importers. Arbitration is the next best alternative. It is a means of settlement between two parties through the medium of a third party who is not partial to either of the parties to the dispute. Litigation means lawsuit, a process in law instituted by one party to compel another to do him justice. It is usually costly and time-consuming. This section will focus on arbitration.

9.4.1 Definition of Arbitration

Arbitration means a method of resolving disputes arising from the two parties who voluntarily render their disputes to a third party agreed by themselves to deal with in accordance with certain arbitration rules and make a final decision binding each of the parties based on the arbitration clause concluded previously by them or based on the arbitration agreement the parties have reached after the disputes arose.

Arbitration should have the following features:

➢Voluntariness: The litigants submit themselves voluntarily to an arbitrator who is a private, disinterested person, or nonofficial government organization chosen by the parties to a disputed question.

➢An arbitration agreement in written form between the parties concerned is the prerequisite for arbitration. An arbitration agreement is a contract between two or more parties whereby they agree to refer the subject in dispute to others and to be bound by their award.

➢More simple in procedures, less costly and time-consuming than litigation.

➢The award is final and binding on both parties.

9.4.2 Arbitration Procedures

The general arbitration procedures are as follows:

(1) **Application for Arbitration**

When applying for arbitration, the claimant must submit to the Secretariat of the Arbitration Commission an arbitration agreement, an application for arbitration in writing, and the facts and evidence on which his claim is based, and the claimant shall pay an arbitration fee in advance to the arbitration commission according to the Arbitration Fee Schedule of the Arbitration Commission.

(2) **Composition of Arbitration Tribunal**

According to the Arbitration Rules of the Arbitration Commission, there are two types of arbitral tribunals, i.e. sole-arbitrator tribunal composed of one arbitrator and collegiate tribunal with three arbitrators. The parties may agree on the ways to form the tribunal.

(3) **Hearing**

Generally, case hearings are conducted by face-to-face reply. However, in some countries, the arbitration tribunal may examine the case and make an award on the basis of documents only at the request of the parties or with their consent.

(4) **Award**

An award is the decision made by the arbitration tribunal. It must be in written form with explanations or reasons. The date on which the arbitral award is made is the date on which the arbitral award comes into effect. The arbitral award is final and binding upon both parties. Neither party may bring a suit before a law court or make a request to any other organization for revising the arbitral award.

9.4.3 Arbitration Clause

An arbitration clause expresses the willingness of the parties to submit the disputes to arbitration and excludes the jurisdiction of courts.

Under the condition of institutional arbitration, an eligible, effective, complete and accurate arbitration clause or arbitration agreement should have the following elements.

➤**The intention of requesting for arbitration**

The intention of requesting for arbitration is the explicit written action of desire for requesting for arbitration by all the parties. The willingness of asking for arbitration should be clear, exact, sure and in accordance with the essence of the finality of arbitration and possess the effect of excluding the jurisdiction of courts without any ambiguity, indistinctness or speciousness.

➢**Arbitration bodies**

There are two forms of arbitration: institutional arbitration and ad hoc arbitration. What the major difference between an ad hoc arbitration and an institutional arbitration falls on the fact that it is unnecessary for an ad hoc arbitration to have an institutional arbitration body to administrate a case. That is to say, an arbitration body is not the element that all forms of arbitration or arbitration clause must have.

➢**Arbitration place**

The arbitration place is not only a matter of convenience. It is also related to the application of the law system under which the dispute is settled. The location can be anywhere in the seller's country, the buyer's country or a third country. No matter where the arbitration takes place, the location must be politically and professionally acceptable.

➢**Rules of arbitration procedure**

An arbitration agreement must provide the rule of arbitration procedure, which is of vital importance in the arbitration agreement or arbitration clause, because the rule of arbitration procedure governs the whole process of the arbitration case from the beginning of accepting the case to the end of making an award.

➢**Effect of arbitral award**

An arbitration clause must provide that the arbitral award is final. This is the incarnation of excluding the jurisdiction of litigation of courts by the arbitration clause.

➢**Arbitration fee**

An arbitration clause shall provide that the arbitration fees shall be borne by the losing party.

The following is an example of an arbitration clause in the contract:

Any dispute, controversy or claim arising out of or relating to this contract, or the breach, termination of invalidity thereof, shall be settled amicably through negotiation. In case no settlement can be reached through negotiation, the case shall then be submitted to the China International Economic and Trade Arbitration Commission of the China Council for the Promotion of International Trade, Beijing for arbitration in accordance with its Rules of Arbitration. The arbitral award is final and binding upon both parties. The arbitration fees shall be borne by the losing party.

9.5 Vocabulary Check

ad hoc 特别的；专门的
arbitration 仲裁
arbitration tribunal 仲裁庭
arbitrator 仲裁员
attest *v.* 证明；表明
award 裁决结果
breach of condition 违反要件
breach of warranty 违反担保
claimant (根据权利)提出要求者；原告
comprehensive type/way 综合式
consultation *n.* 协商
devaluate/devalue *v.* 降价
disturbance *n.* 骚动；动乱
eligible 适任的；合格的
fundamental breach 重大违约
general type/way 概括式
hearings 审理；审讯
incarnation *n.* 具体化；化身
invalidity *n.* 无效
jurisdiction 权限；管辖范围
lawsuit *n.* 诉讼
litigant 诉讼人
liquidated damage clause 清算损失条款
litigation 诉讼
material breach 重大违约
minor breach 轻微违约
notary 公证人
postponement of the contract 合同延期
sole arbitrator 独任仲裁员
terminate *n.* 终止；解除

9.6 Notes and Key Terms

1) **commodity inspection:** 商品检验，是指在国际货物买卖中，对卖方交付给买方货物的质量、数量和包装进行检验，以确定合同的标的是否符合买卖合同规定；有时还对装运技术条件或货物在装卸运输过程中发生的残损、短缺进行检验或鉴定，以明确事故的起因和责任的归属；商检还包括根据一国的法律或行政法规对某些进出口货物或有关的事项进行质量、数量、包装、卫生、安全等方面的强制性检验或检疫。

在国际货物买卖中，由于买卖双方分处两个国家(地区)，一般不是当面交接货物，且进出口货物需要经过长途运输，多次装卸，如到货出现品质缺陷、数量短缺等，容易引起有关方面的争议。为了保障买卖双方利益，避免争议的发生，以及发生争议后便于分清责任和进行处理，就需要由一个有资格的、有权威的、独立于买卖双方以外的公正的第三者，即专业的检验检疫机构负责对卖方交付的货物的质量、数量、包装进行检验，或对装运技术、货物残损短缺等情况进行检验或鉴定。检验机构检验或鉴定后出具相应的检验证书，作为买卖双方交接货物、支付货款和进行索赔、理赔的重要依据。因此，进出口货物检验是买卖双方交接货物过程中必不可少的重要业务环节。

2) **inspection certificate:** 商检证书，是各种进出口商品检验证书、鉴定证书和其他证明书的统称，是对外贸易有关各方履行契约义务、处理索赔争议和仲裁、诉讼举证，具有法律依据的有效证件，也是海关验放、征收关税和优惠减免关税的必要证明。以下是常见的商检证书：

Inspection Certificate of Quality　质量检验证书
Inspection Certificate of Quantity　数量检验证书
Inspection Certificate of Weight　重量检验证书
Inspection Certificate of Packing　包装检验证书
Veterinary Inspection Certificate　兽医检验证书
Sanitary Inspection Certificate　卫生检验证书
Inspection Certificate of Disinfection　消毒检验证书
Inspection Certificate of Fumigation　熏蒸证书
Inspection Certificate of Temperature　温度检验证书
Inspection Certificate on Damaged Cargo　验残检验证书
Inspection Certificate on Tank/Hold　船舱检验证书
Inspection Certificate of Value　价值检验证书
Inspection Certificate of Origin　产地检验证书
Inspection Certificate of Health　健康检验证书

3) **arbitration:** 仲裁，从字面上看，"仲"就是居于中间，"裁"就是裁定解决，合起来"仲裁"的含义就是居中裁决。这很形象地说明了仲裁的特点。法律意义上的仲裁，就是指争议双方的当事人自愿将他们之间的纠纷提交仲裁机关，由仲裁机关以第三者的身份进行裁决。仲裁并不是一种法定的诉讼程序，仲裁机构也不是国家机关，但仲裁裁决具有法律效力，当事人必须执行。

4) **force majeure:** 不可抗力，从法律上来讲是指人力所不能预见、不能抗拒的情形。包括两类，一类是自然灾害，包括水灾、火灾、地震等等，另一类是政治事件，如战争、武装冲突、暴乱等等。

5) **Food and Drugs Administration (FDA):** 美国食品和药物管理局。它是由美国国会即联邦政府授权，专门从事食品与药品管理的最高执法机关，负责美国所有有关食品、药品、化妆品及辐射性仪器的管理。它也是美国最早的消费者保护机构。约有 1 万名正式员工，管理美国市场的制造、进口、运送和储藏，所管辖的动物、食物与药品业者超过 12 万家，其中以食品业者最多，约 5 万家，其次便是医疗器材业者有 3.2 万余家，影响美国每个纳税义务人约 3 美元，可以说与社会大众的生活和生命安全息息相关。FDA 之中约有 1100 名检查员，每年要赴海内外 15000 个工厂，去确认他们的各种活动均符合美国的法律规定；同时他们也必须搜集 80000 项美国境内制造或进口的产品样品并施以检验。

6) **Societe General De Surveillance S.A. (SGS)**：通用公证行。它创建于 1887 年，是目前世界上最大、资格最老的民间第三方从事产品质量控制和技术鉴定的跨国公司。总部设在日内瓦，在世界各地设有 251 家分支机构、256 个专业实验室和 27000 名专业技术人员，在 142 个国家开展产品质检、监控和保证活动。

7) **Underwriters Laboratory (UL)**：保险商实验室。UL 安全试验所是美国最有权威的，也是世界上从事安全试验和鉴定的较大的民间机构。它是一个独立的、非营利的、为公共安全做试验的专业机构。它采用科学的测试方法来研究确定各种材料、装置、产品、设备、建筑等对生命、财产有无危害和危害的程度；确定、编写、发行相应的标准和有助于减少及防止造成生命财产受到损失的资料，同时开展实情调研业务。总之，它主要从事产品的安全认证和经营安全证明业务，其最终目的是为市场得到具有相当安全水准的商品，为人身健康和财产安全得到保证做出贡献。就产品安全认证作为消除国际贸易技术壁垒的有效手段而言，UL 为促进国际贸易的发展也发挥着积极的作用。UL 始建于 1894 年，初始阶段 UL 主要靠防火保险部门提供资金维持运行，直到 1916 年，UL 才完全自立。经过近百年的发展，UL 已成为具有世界知名度的认证机构，其自身具有一整套严密的组织管理体制、标准开发和产品认证程序。UL 由一个安全专家、政府官员、消费者、教育界、公用事业、保险业及标准部门的代表组成的理事会管理，日常工作由总裁、副总裁处理。目前，UL 在美国本土有五个实验室，总部设在芝加哥北部的 Northbrook 镇，同时在中国的台湾和香港分别设立了相应的实验室。

8) **Lloyd Surveyor**：劳合社，英国最大的保险组织。劳合社本身是个社团，更确切地说是一个保险市场，与纽约证券交易所相似，但只向其成员提供交易场所和有关的服务，本身并不承保业务。伦敦劳合社是从劳埃德咖啡馆演变而来的，故又称“劳埃德保险社”。1871 年经议会通过法案，劳合社才正式成为一个社团组织。劳合社由其社员选举产生的一个理事会来管理，下设理赔、出版、签单、会计、法律等部，并在 100 多个国家设有办事处。该社为其所属承保人制订保险单、保险证书等标准格式，此外还出版有关海上运输、商船动态、保险海事等方面的期刊和杂志，向世界各地发行。在历史上，劳合社设计了第一张盗窃保险单，为第一辆汽车和第一架飞机出立保单，近年又是计算机、石油能源保险和卫星保险的先驱。劳合社设计的条款和保单格式在世界保险业中有广泛的影响，其制定的费率也是世界保险业的风向标。劳合社承保的业务包罗万象。劳合社对保险业的发展，特别是对海上保险和再保险做出的杰出贡献是世界公认的。

9) **Japan Marine Surveyor & Sworn Measurer's Association (NKKK)**：日本海事检定协会(Nippon Kaiji Kentei Kyokai，英文名 Japan Marine Surveyors & Sworn Measurer's Association)创立于 1913 年，是一个社团法人检验协会，主要是为社会公共利益服务。NKKK 总部设在东京，除在本国各主要港口设有检验所外，还在泰国、新加坡、马来西亚、菲律宾和印度尼西亚等国设有海外事务所。目前，NKKK 在国内外设立的分支机构有 70 多个，业务范围很广，主要检验项目有：舱口检视、积载鉴定、状态检验、残损鉴定、水尺计重、液体计量、衡重衡量及理化检验等，还接受从厂家到装船或从卸货到用户之间的连续检验。NKKK 与中国商品检验机构签订长期委托检验协议，多年来，双方有着密切的相互委托检验业务和频繁的技术交流。

9.7 Follow-up Practice

9.7.1 Review and Discussion Questions

1) Why must there be the inspection clause in sales contracts? What does the inspection clause generally include?
2) Please explain the three major ways of stipulating the place and time of inspection.
3) How disputes are settled in international trade?
4) What are some of the major characteristics of a force majeure event?
5) Please give examples of three ways to set the scope of force majeure.
6) Why is arbitration a commonly used settlement of disputes in international trade?

9.7.2 Decide whether the following statements are true or false.

1) Should cargo be damaged or lost during transit, the carrier bears no responsibility whether or not the damage or loss is due to the carrier's negligence. ( )
2) For one contract, only one method and one standard should be used to ensure consistency in inspection. ( )
3) In international trade, the party that has failed to implement the contract may choose not to carry out his contract obligations if he has paid the required penalty. ( )
4) Arbitration can be used to settle criminal cases as well as civil cases. ( )
5) Usually an arbitration tribunal can consist of one, two or three arbitrators. ( )

6) An arbitration award must be in written form with or without explanations or reasons. (   )

7) When the departure term (EXW) is used, the commodity should be inspected at the factory or warehouse where the delivery is made. (   )

8) If shipping quality is used in inspection, the inspection must be conducted at the seller's factory only. (   )

9) The party who suffers a force majeure event can decide to terminate the contract without notice to the other party. (   )

10) All inspection bodies are governmental. (   )

9.7.3 Complete the following diagram according to what you have learnt about arbitration.

Procedures of Arbitration

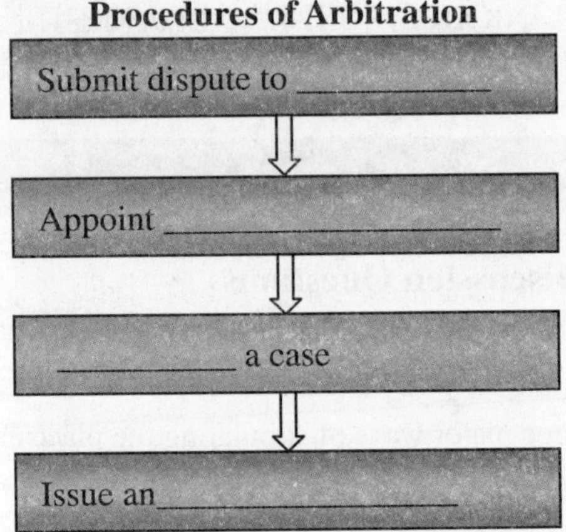

9.7.4 Choose the right answer from each of the following.

1) The necessary precondition of settling disputes by arbitration is that ________.

A. there must be a sales contract between the disputing parties

B. there must be an arbitration agreement between the disputing parties

C. there must be mediation taking place first

D. there must be litigation taking place first

2) To make inspection after shipment, if a quality problem was found when goods were inspected at the port of destination, ________ should be responsible for the loss?

A. the seller   B. the buyer

C. the carrier   D. the insurer

3) Which of the following statements is NOT true about a force majeure event?

A. A force majeure event may occur before the conclusion of the contract.

B. A force majeure event may lead to cancellation of the contract or delayed performance of the contract.

C. A force majeure event can be caused by natural forces.

D. A force majeure event can be caused by social forces.

4) The most widely used way of stipulating the place and time of inspection in the contract is ________.

A. shipping quality and weight

B. landed quality and weight

C. inspection at the port of shipment and re-inspection at the port of destination

D. gross weight

5) The award of arbitration is usually ________.

A. final B. not binding on all parties

C. amendable D. rejective

6) Which of the following events is usually stipulated in the contract as force majeure?

A. War.

B. Rise of price.

C. Manufacturer's refusal to supply to the seller.

D. Late delivery.

7) Generally, there is/are ________ way(s) to stipulate "force majeure" clauses.

A. 1 B. 2 C. 3 D. 4

8) Which of the following is a governmental inspection body?

A. Underwriters Laboratory. B. Lloyd Surveyor.

C. Food and Drugs Administration. D. Societe General De Surveillance.

9) Which of the following is NOT true about the features of arbitration?

A. The litigants should submit themselves voluntarily to an arbitrator.

B. An arbitration agreement in written form between the parties concerned is the prerequisite for arbitration.

C. The award is final and binding on both parties.

D. Once the arbitration body is chosen, there is no need to stipulate the rule of arbitration procedure in the arbitration agreement because the rule of the arbitration body is applicable.

10) Normally, there are ________ ways to determine the nature of breach.

A. 1 B. 2 C. 3 D. 4

9.7.5 Case Study

Company A in the U.S.A and Company B in Britain signed a contract in 2006, in which Company A sold 100 M/T of wheat at the price of ￡400 M/T CFR London to Company B. The total contract value was ￡40,000 and the delivery time was from May to September in 2006. After the conclusion of the contract, there was a flood in the region where Company A had planned to buy the wheat. Company A asked to be exempted from the goods delivery obligation because of force majeure. Company B denied Company A's demand.

Do you think Company A can be exempted from delivery obligation and cancel the contract because of force majeure? Provide your reasons.

A Chinese company (Company X) signed a contract with a Japanese company (Company Y) in 2004. Company Y exported a second-hand cigarette production line to Company X. As the production line was second-hand, it was stipulated in the contract that the production line should operate normally before disassembly; otherwise, it should be replaced or refunded. And claims should be made by the buyer within 14 days after the discharge of the goods at the port of destination. When it arrived, Company X found out that the production line could not be put into operation. Furthermore, they discovered that the production line had not been normally used before disassembly. Therefore, Company X lodged a claim against Company Y 20 days after the arrival of the production line. However, Company Y refused to compensate Company X because the claim was made beyond the agreed effective period. Is Company Y's refusal reasonable? Why?

1. http://www.ulonline.com.cn 中国 UL 在线信息网
2. http://www.ul.com 保险商试验所
3. http://www.ahtvu.ah.cn/jxc/39zcfx/index.html 仲裁法学网上教学系统
4. http://met.fzu.edu.cn/tradepractices/index.asp 国际贸易实务网
5. http://www.aqsiq.gov.cn 国家质量监督检验检疫总局
6. http://www.customs.gov.cn 中国海关网

Chapter Ten

Performance of the Contract

Learning Objectives

At the end of this chapter, you should be able to understand:

- basic export procedures
- basic import procedures
- preparation of major import and export documents

In international trade, as soon as a sales contract is signed it becomes a legally binding agreement with rights and obligations set out for each party. The successful performance of a sales contract, which involves the smooth coordination of different parties, is not only of serious concern for the buyer and seller, but also for the national image on both sides.

In practice, the rights and obligations vary according to customer requirements, trade terms, customary procedures, and so on. However, there are always the basic obligations for both parties in each sales contract, which are for the seller to deliver goods as specified in all related documents for the transfer of ownership of the goods and for the buyer to pay and take delivery of the goods.

10.1 Export Procedures

The performance of an export contract involves mainly the steps illustrated in the flow chart below:

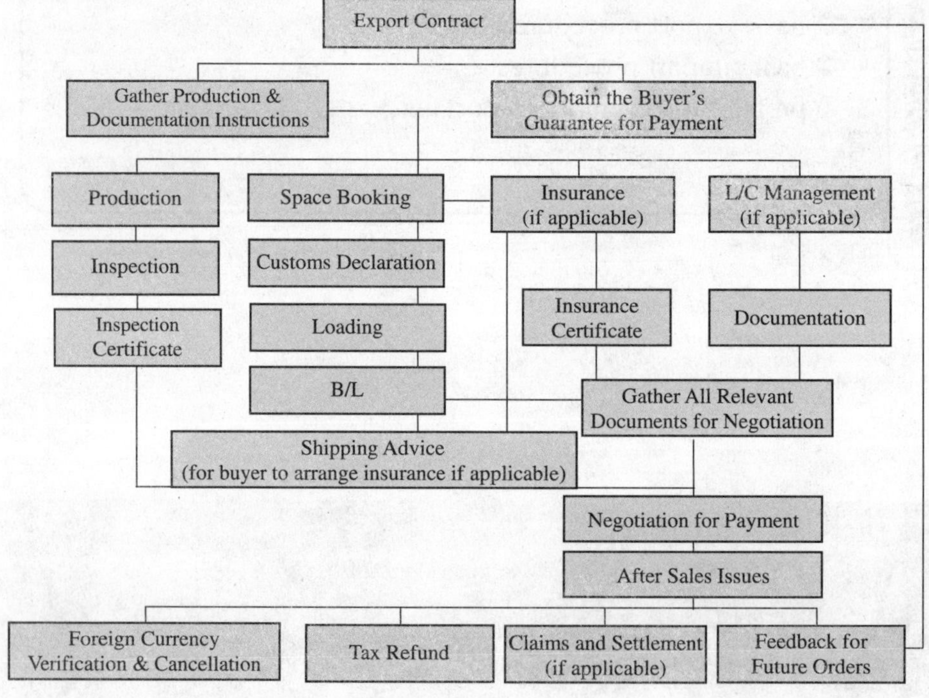

The above flow chart shows that the exporter will have to do a lot of work to perform the export contract which mainly deals with the coordination of the goods,

L/C, shipment and payment. This can be divided into stages of preparation, production, shipping, documentation and after sales issues.

10.1.1 Preparation

Preparation mainly involves further tying the buyer to the deal and collecting all necessary information from the buyer for the smooth production of goods and the preparation of the documents according to what the buyer exactly requires.

10.1.1.1 Obtaining the Buyer's Guarantee for Payment

The precondition for the seller to carry out his responsibilities of supplying the goods is for the buyer to guarantee the final payment. For transactions under T/T terms, the buyer should be required to pay the deposit; for D/P terms, the buyer should provide the details of the collecting bank, the account number and name; and for L/C terms, the buyer should be encouraged to establish the L/C within the time limit set in the contract, or if not applicable, within reasonable time span which will allow sufficient time for the seller to prepare the goods and documents before the expiry date of the L/C.

L/C management:

The seller normally reminds the buyer to establish an L/C by way of letter or electronic communications if:

➢The contract sets a shipment date as well as a deadline for the L/C establishment.

➢The buyer fails to open an L/C within the deadline as set in the contract while the seller does not want to go ahead to null and void the contract and claim for compensation according to the contract.

➢The seller is ready to ship the goods earlier than expected.

➢The buyer does not have good credit or the market situation is unstable.

After an L/C is received, the bank and the seller share the duties of checking it against *the Uniform Customs and Practice for Documentary Credits.*

An L/C should be irrevocable and the issuing bank should guarantee the payment. For L/Cs from certain countries, although stating "irrevocable", there are restrictive clauses or salvos about the payment responsibilities of the issuing bank. If the L/C states "valid only after the import license has been issued", "valid only upon notification after the import license has been issued", or "further details set out in a separate letter", the seller should not start any production or delivery of goods until such detailed clauses of the L/C have been validated with written notification.

In principle, the clauses in an L/C should comply with international trade policies and always be consistent with what is stipulated in the contract, which is the basis for the establishment of an L/C. However, in reality, it is not always the case because of all kinds of reasons such as negligence, faulty transmission of documents, different trading cultures, market changes or even the buyer's purposeful intention. Therefore, the seller needs to check the clauses regarding:

➢The amount and currency, which should allow margins in case the goods are over-delivered.

➢The goods' quality, specifications, quantity and packaging, especially when there are special conditions which are not workable or not acceptable.

➢The shipping date, expiry date and expiry place, to make sure there is a reasonable time span between the shipping date and the expiry date (normally 10—15 days) and the expiry place should normally be set in the exporter's country.

➢The type and number of documents and whether there are special or hidden conditions.

➢The bank fees, which other than particularly agreed upon, should be borne by the buyer for overseas banks, and on the seller for domestic banks.

Unacceptable clauses should be presented to the buyer for amendments as soon as possible since no production should take place until after the amended L/C has been received so as to avoid any losses. To make it convenient and save L/C amendment fees for the buyer, the seller should try to be well prepared and present to the buyer all items to be amended at one time. In practice, it is wise to require the buyer to fax the L/C clauses for preview before it is formally established.

10.1.1.2 Information Collection

The seller can always judge from the actions of the buyer, such as punctual deposit payment, or prompt L/C establishment to see whether the buyer is of good credit. Moreover the buyer's bank or shipping forwarder can always give reference on the buyer's credit too. With information about the buyer's credit, the seller is in a better position to decide how to solve problems during the trade.

In the meanwhile, further details of the product apart from those already listed in the contract or L/C should be collected from the buyer, which includes packing, bar code, artwork, shipping marks, pre-production samples, and the ways to fill out documents, etc.

10.1.2 Production

10.1.2.1 Quality Control and Production Management

All information about the product, either already listed in the contract or L/C, or obtained from the buyer in the preparation stage, should be passed on to the manufacturer in the form of an order, which carries all details of specifications (color, weight, size etc), quality, quantity, packing, shipping marks, delivery, together with payment terms for the manufacturer to commence manufacturing, counting, printing shipping marks, inspecting and certifying the goods.

The seller needs to verify according to the contract that the goods comply with all the specifications as required by the buyer.

The quality of products should be taken care of from the time the material is chosen to avoid quality problems from the very origin. Throughout the process of production, samples or pictures of the product, before mass production, during mass production, and after alteration, should all be presented to the buyer for confirmation in order to assure the final quality.

Margins of quantity should be allowed in case there are changes in storage capacity and possible replacement requirements in transportation.

Apart from meeting the requirements of the sales contract, the packaging should be able to protect the goods during transportation. Goods should be prepared within a time span to catch up with the date of shipment.

The seller should also guarantee the complete ownership of the goods which are to be sold to the buyer, that is, no any third party can claim any right to the goods, such as patent, copyright, etc.

10.1.2.2 Inspection and Certification

The inspection of the goods can be done by the seller, the customer, or a third-party. Inspection certificates should always be obtained if required by the contract or L/C.

All goods required by the law or regulations or contract to be inspected by China Import and Export Commodity Inspection Bureau should be presented to the Bureau for inspection when they are ready. Only after the goods are inspected with qualified inspection certificates issued by the Bureau will they be released by the customs. Application Form for Export Goods Inspection should be filled out for the goods requiring such inspection when applying at the Bureau. The application form normally covers product description, specification, quantity/weight, packaging, and place of origin, etc. The translated version, when required, should present exactly the same content. When submitting the application forms, other relevant documents such as the contract, copy of the L/C, invoice and packing list should be attached for the reference of the Bureau. The Bureau is responsible to inspect the goods within the shipment deadline. When there are mistakes or amendments of the L/C after the submission of the application, the seller needs to fill out a Change of Application Form stating the items needed to be changed and the reasons for the changes. For the goods that have passed the inspection, the Bureau issues an inspection certificate, which is the evidence to the customs for release. The seller needs to ship the goods within the expiry date as set out in the inspection certificate. An extension application should be submitted and a re-inspection will be imposed on the goods that failed to be shipped out before the expiry date.

For those goods without compulsory inspection requirements, random checks are performed by the inspection organizations in order to assure the quality of the export goods.

10.1.3 Shipping

While preparing the goods, the seller should also prepare for shipment, which includes shipping space booking, customs declaration and insurance arrangements.

10.1.3.1 Space Booking

Packing details should be obtained from the manufacturer well before the shipment for space booking, which includes the number of cartons, measurement and so on. The seller needs to charter a whole ship if the size of the consignment is big enough, which normally is the case with bulk cargo. The seller fills out a Booking Note carrying all the above details as well as shipment requirements from the contract or L/C. If the consignment is suitable after considering the shipping line's docks, berth and sailing date, the forwarder or shipping company issues a shipping order which shows that the transportation contract is set up and the consignment has been allocated to a certain ship on a certain sailing date together with details of where to send the customs declaration documents and where to send the goods so that the shipper can be prepared for the loading deadline. According to different loading instructions, the goods can be picked up from the factory, or they need to be transported to the forwarder's warehouse.

The shipping order is also an order for the captain to accept the goods. The captain or mate issues a mate's receipt after the shipment is loaded on board. The mate's receipt is a temporary receipt issued by the shipping company to the shipper as a proof that the consignment has been loaded onto the ship. The shipper will need to present this mate's receipt to the forwarder to pay for the freight and exchange for the B/L. Any special notes on the mate's receipt will be transferred onto the B/L. The B/L issued by a shipping company is called Ocean B/L, and those by a forwarder are called Cargo Receipt or House B/L.

In practice, the seller always gives written authorization and instructions to the forwarder for the whole process of shipping arrangements.

10.1.3.2 Customs Declaration

According to *the Customs Law of China*, all goods to be exported via ports, stations, or international airports must be declared to the customs for release. Currently in China, when declaring to the customs, apart from the Export Goods Declaration Form, the copy of the sales contract, invoice, packing list and commodity inspection certificate, Foreign Currency Verification and Cancellation Form and other relevant documents such as Vegetation Inspection Certificate are sometimes required to be presented to the customs. Goods need to be declared to the Customs Department by a qualified customs declaration clerk before they are loaded and shipped out. When declaring to the customs, the representative of the seller, normally the forwarder, presents an authorization letter from the seller and hands in the Verification and Cancellation Form, which are to be returned to the forwarder after the customs views and stamps them, and to be passed back to the seller for tax refund purposes when the seller pays the freight to the forwarder.

10.1.3.3 Insurance

For a CIF contract, the seller needs to insure the goods before the shipment. The applicant fills out the forms of insurance with all details including description, amount insured, transportation method, means of delivery, sailing date, type of insurance and so on. The insurance company will issue an insurance certificate as soon as they receive the application. One consignment of goods under different contract numbers or covered by different L/Cs should be insured separately under different policy numbers. There are insurance policies which generally cover all shipments from a particular company under one account.

For other trade terms like CFR, the seller needs to provide the shipping advice to the buyer as soon as it is available in order for the consignment to be insured without delay.

10.1.4 Documentation for Settlement of Payment

It is of great importance to prepare the documents well in time since most international transactions today deal with documents, when it comes to payment settlement or consignment ownership transfer.

10.1.4.1 Documentation and Negotiation

The preparation of documents for settlement of payment should start from the very moment of loading the ship or even before the production to assure safe and punctual receipt of payment. The documents, either required by L/C or the customer, mainly include commercial invoice, bill of exchange, B/L, insurance policy and supplementary documents such as inspection certificate, GSP Form A, certificate of origin, fumigation certificate, packing list, customs invoice (for Canada only), veterinary (health) certificate and so on.

The requirements for the documentation are: correct, complete, punctual, concise, and clean. The documents should match themselves as well as the L/C and the goods. All documents required should be presented. All columns in the documents should be filled in, such as the name of the original country, seal on the certificate of origin, descriptions and quantities. All documents should be presented to the bank before the expiry date. Time should be allowed for the negotiation bank to send the documents on to the issuing bank. Even before the goods are shipped out, the documents can always be presented to the negotiation bank for pre-check to allow time for corrections in case there are any discrepancies.

For T/T payment terms, the B/L, commercial invoice and packing list should be faxed and later on couriered to the buyer immediately for the prompt payment. For D/P terms, the documents required should be faxed to the buyer and couriered to the collecting bank without delay, not only for punctual payment, but also to allow the buyer sufficient time to clear the goods from the wharf with the B/L. For L/C terms, the whole set of documents required by the L/C need to be prepared and submitted to the bank for negotiation of payments within the set date of expiry as soon as the shipment has been effected.

The issuing bank will only be responsible for the payment after seeing that the whole set of documents is in full conformity with the L/C because, in credit operations, all parties concerned deal with documents and not with goods. Any discrepancies may cause refusal of payments. When receiving documents with discrepancies, the negotiation bank will normally:

➢Return the whole set of documents to the beneficiary for revisions within the expiry date if there are typos or missing documents;

➢Negotiate the payment with a letter of indemnity from the beneficiary, which states the reimbursement to the bank in case the payment is refused by the buyer's bank;

➢Communicate the issuing bank electronically with the discrepancies and pay or agree to pay after receiving the issuing bank's authorization, on the condition that the beneficiary agrees to do so and to pay for the costs. This is suitable when the amount is fairly big and the discrepancy is quite obvious;

➢Write to the issuing bank. This is suitable for smaller amount with obvious discrepancies and some confidence in the buyer's accepting this application. In this case, the negotiation bank lists all discrepancies on a notice to source the issuing bank's consent to pay;

➢Suggest that the seller change the payment term to D/P if there is a chance that the issuing bank may refuse the payment;

➢Pay as normal. Although there are discrepancies, however, judging from the negotiation bank's experience, the issuing bank would not turn it down;

➢Refuse to take in the application and return all documents to the beneficiary, when there are discrepancies not able to be corrected, such as late shipment, quality and specification not matching with the requirements, and so on, or the L/C's amendment clauses have not arrived though applied by the beneficiary beforehand with approval from the buyer in advance.

10.1.4.2 Settlement of Payment

There are three ways of foreign currency payment settlements for foreign trade in China: settlement on receipt, settlement on guarantee, and settlement on a set date.

(1) **Settlement on Receipt**

The negotiation bank sends the documents submitted by the seller to the payment bank (normally the issuing bank), and holds back the settlement of payment until the date it receives payment from the issuing bank.

(2) **Settlement on Guarantee**

The negotiation bank buys the bill of exchange and whole set of negotiation documents from the seller after checking to see that the documents contain no mistakes, less the interest to the approximate date of receiving the payment from the issuing bank, and remits the remaining amount of payment to the seller. The negotiation bank therefore becomes the owner of the bill of exchange with the whole set of documents and claims payment from the payment bank. This is to provide the seller with better cash flow.

(3) **Settlement on Set Date**

The negotiation bank sets out a fixed date of settlement according to an estimation of the payment date from the overseas payment bank.

10.1.5 After Sales Issues

10.1.5.1 Foreign Currency Verification and Cancellation

In China, the government keeps a close eye on the receipt of foreign currencies. The system of foreign currency verification and cancellation is designed to follow the foreign currency income of every export transaction to assure its safe inflow.

The export company, for the first time to apply for foreign currency verification and cancellation registration, should provide the ID and the representation confirmation certificate from the company, application letter, the authorization letter from the government department directly in charge, business license, the legal certificate of the identity of the enterprise, customs registration certificate and export contract to the Foreign Currency Administration Bureau for registration and obtain a permission certificate allowing for receiving forms of foreign currency verification and cancellation if the audit finds the company qualified.

The procedures for foreign currency verification and cancellation are:

➢Draw the form with the permission certificate before customs declaration;

➢Fill out the form with exactly the same information as on the Customs Declaration Application Form;

➢Register for export: for sight payment terms the foreign exchange should be verified and cancelled within 90 days; for term payments, the export contract should be submitted to the Foreign Currency Administration Bureau for registration;

➢Submit the form to the customs to be checked and stamped;

➢Receive the foreign currency payment and verify it with the proof of the bank's credit note against the registration in the Foreign Currency Administration Bureau to be cancelled.

Documents needed for these procedures are Foreign Currency Verification and Cancellation Form, Customs Declaration Form, credit note, and commercial invoice. The procedures can now be performed over the Internet other than the last step, which requires the broker (normally the forwarder) to go to the Bureau physically for it.

10.1.5.2 Tax Refund

In China, enterprises exporting goods can claim tax refund at different rates according to the variety of products.

The tax department will impose the tax first before it is refunded.

The exporter can apply to the tax department with relevant evidence after the customs declaration and conclusion of sales every month.

10.1.5.3 Claims and Settlement

In the process of implementing a sales contract, the party who has suffered loss because of the fault of the other party, can file claims accordingly.

In international trade, the most common compensation claim happens when the seller fails to provide the goods as required in the contract.

When handling claims, the seller should pay special attention to the following:

➢Check the legality of the documents the buyer has supplied carefully including those certificates issued by special inspection organizations in case they are fraudulent;

➢Inspections should be done in order to allocate responsibilities of different parties.

➢Decide a reasonable amount and reimbursement method according to the degree of loss.

The other way around, the seller can also claim for compensation from the buyer if the buyer delays opening the L/C or raises clauses which are too difficult to fulfil because of sudden drop of commodity price after the contract is signed, thus unwilling to have the goods, or the buyer purposely delays providing loading instructions under FOB trade term, thus causing the delay in shipment. The seller can also file claims with the insurance company, forwarder or other parties responsible for the claim.

While claiming for compensation, the seller can also insist that the buyer carry out his obligations as set in the contract, declare the contract null and void, and hold on to the goods in order to control the situation in case the buyer delays taking delivery of the goods and refuses to pay for the goods.

10.1.5.4 Feedback and Future Orders

A claim well handled can sometimes guarantee continuous orders in the future. For example, the seller's agreeing to provide certain extra quantity of goods in future orders to make up for the buyer's losses in previous shipments will secure the customer with continuous benefits and reliable good service.

With or without problems in one deal, the seller should always contact the buyer for feedback on the goods, such as the sales and recommendations on quality or design. This is not only the basic courtesy to the buyer, but also a shortcut to offer more adapted or new samples to the buyer to obtain future orders.

10. 2 Import Procedures

The performance of an import contract generally includes the following procedures: establishing the L/C, or paying the deposit, chartering or booking shipping space, organizing shipping, arranging insurance, paying against the documents, declaring to the customs for the importing goods, inspection, taking delivery, and claim if any, etc. The following flow chart shows the procedures of performing an import contract:

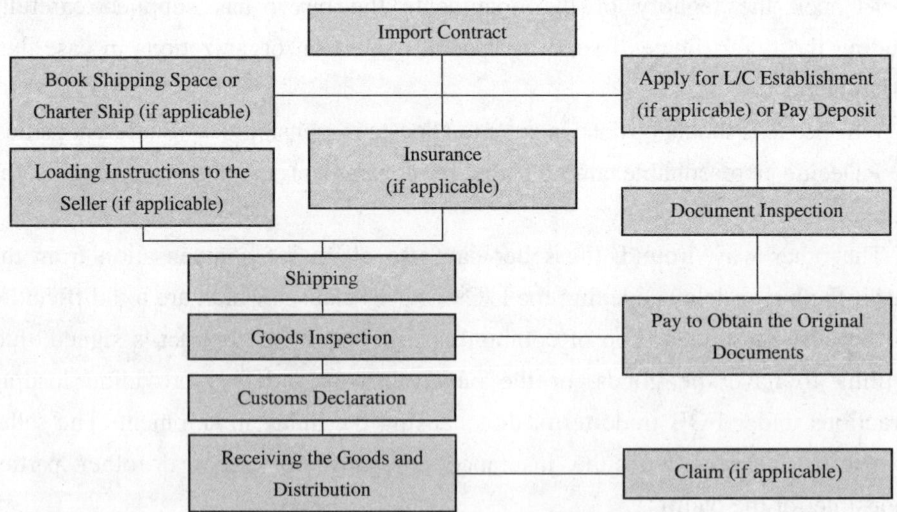

10.2.1 Establish the L/C

For an import contract under L/C payment terms, the buyer must fill out an application form at the bank to open an L/C according to the contract.

When filling out the application form for an L/C, the buyer should be cautious about the following:

➢The type of the L/C: Do not open transferable L/C unless the secondary beneficiary is reliable;

➢The amount of L/C: Do not use the words "about" or "approximately" in connection with the amount of the credit or the quantity or the unit price stated in the credit unless necessary because according to *UPC600*, these words are to be construed as allowing a tolerance not to exceed 10% more or 10% less than the amount;

➢The drawee / payer of the draft should be the issuing bank or other banks appointed in the L/C, not the applicant of the L/C, or otherwise, the draft will be considered as an additional paper not included in the negotiation documents;

➢Whether the draft should be sight or term needs to be followed strictly according to the contract;

➢Normally a whole set of clean ocean B/L blank endorsed made out to order is required. Other means of transportation, such as container shipment, air freight, railway transportation, or post, are only acceptable under FCA, CIP, or CPT terms with required transportation documents;

➢The issuing organization, form, content and certifying issues should be stated clearly for other required documents such as C/O, quality/weight inspection certificate, test certificate and so on;

➢Without special instructions partial and transshipment are to be considered as allowed even if against the contract;

➢The L/C is not valid without a set expiry date and place for the submission of negotiation documents;

➢The L/C should require an import license number on the commercial invoice for customs inspection since China exercises strict control over foreign currency.

10.2.2 Arrange Shipping

Under a FOB contract, the buyer should arrange a ship to pick up the goods at the seller's port. The seller will notify the buyer some time before the delivery the approximate time of shipment. The buyer will then book the space and notify the seller of the ship name and shipping date, so that the seller can be prepared for the loading. In the mean time, in order to avoid the situation where the ship and goods wait for each other, close contact should be made with the seller to make sure that the goods are to be ready at the right date. If the quality is important or quantities are large, sometimes the buyer will send representatives abroad to check. After the ship is loaded, the seller should notify the buyer in time for arranging insurance and taking the delivery.

The buyer sometimes authorizes the seller to arrange the ship locally and pays for the freight for FOB transactions.

Under the terms of CFR, FOB, FCA or CPT, the buyer is responsible for arranging the insurance. People's Insurance Company of China, the compulsory insurer for China's imports and exports, has set forms for all types of insurance. Upon receipt of the shipping advice from the seller, the buyer should provide the insurance company with the ship name, B/L number, sailing date, name and description, quantity, shipping port, destination port, etc. for the insurance application. The insurance company will then be responsible for the goods automatically and should pay for the losses that occur within the set conditions.

10.2.3 Check the Documents for Payment

Under sight L/C payment terms, the bank will pay the seller's bank at the sight of the bill of exchange and the set of documents if the buyer does not bring up objections within 3 working days after the documents are presented.

The buyer then needs to buy the foreign currency from the bank at the rate of the day and the bank will issue a credit note as the evidence for the currency exchange. In practice, the bank (normally the issuing bank) would contact the applicant of the L/C within 7 working days for decisions if discrepancies are found in the documents, and the decisions are normally to:

➢refuse the payment;

➢pay partially for those which comply;

➢hold on payment until the goods have arrived and passed inspection;
➢pay against the letter of indemnity from the seller or the negotiation bank;
➢require amendments from the seller; or
➢pay while reserving the right to claim for compensation.

10.2.4 Inspection

When the ship carrying the goods reaches the port, the shipping company will issue a Notice of Readiness to Discharge according to the address on the B/L to the consignee or its agent, who is normally the forwarder and whose address and contact should be listed in the contract or L/C.

The consignee or the agent checks the goods while unloading at the port and the shipping company and the Harbour Bureau should be contacted if short delivery or damages are found.

In case of short delivery, a "short delivery notice" should be filled out and handed to the freight forwarder to sign without delay with a written declaration to state the right to claim for compensation.

If damages are found during the unloading process, the goods should be stored in the warehouse appointed by the customs and wait for the insurance company to decide the compensation before further actions are taken.

For those goods requiring compulsory inspections, the whole set of documents including the contract, invoice, B/L, packing list and Import Goods Arrival Notice should be submitted to the Commodity Inspection Bureau at the port of unloading or the destination to apply for inspections. The goods are not allowed to be released, put into production, sold or used until they have passed the checks.

If damages are found in these inspections, the certificate issued by the bureau can be kept as the evidence for claims. The goods required by the contract, noted as damaged, short or abnormal, or indemnity which will expire soon, are subject to inspection at the port.

The United Nations Convention on Contracts for the International Sale of Goods stipulates that after the seller has supplied the goods, a reasonable period of time should be provided for the buyer to inspect the goods before being considered as accepted. The buyer has the right to claim for compensation or even refuse to accept the goods if the inspections find the goods not complying with the contract. The buyer should always inspect the goods within the time limit set in the contract for claims.

10.2.5 Customs Declaration

After the arrival and inspection of the goods, the importer or its authorized agent, normally the freight forwarder or professional customs broker should fill out and submit the Import Goods Declaration Form to the customs together with invoices, B/L, insurance policies, and inspection certificate for goods with compulsory inspection requirements.

The customs will check the goods against the application documents to see whether they match. The check is normally done in the warehouse or at a location within the customs' domain of supervision. With application, bulk, large or dangerous products may be checked alongside the ship.

10.2.6 Taking Delivery of the Goods

After the goods are cleared and collected, they need to be passed on to the customers. If the customers are not within the domain of discharging port, freight forwarders will be contacted to transfer the goods further to reach those customers. The import tax and duties/tariff and the cost of land freight are to be paid by the importer first before being reimbursed by the customers later on.

10.2.7 Claims

The buyer will sometimes lodge a claim because of quality, quantity, or packaging problems. There are three main parties which the buyer can claim against and the responsibilities should be divided clearly and the claim should be lodged without delay.

(1) **The Seller**

The following cases can all be claimed against the seller:

➢Short delivery;

➢Quality and specification not as per contract;

➢Faulty packaging causing damages to the goods;

➢Delayed or refused delivery;

➢Wrong delivery causing extra storage and transportation costs to the buyer.

(2) **The Carrier**

When the following happens, the carrier is the one to blame and should be responsible for the compensation:

➤Shortage in quantity as per the B/L;

➤A clean B/L with damaged goods and it can be traced that is caused by the shipping company;

➤The damages done to the goods for which the shipping company shall be held responsible according to the contract.

The time limit to claim from the carrier is one year after the goods arriving at the destination port.

(3) **The Insurance Company**

When lodging a claim with the insurer, the importer should prepare all necessary documents including insurance policy, transportation documents, invoice, inspection certificate, shortage or damage certificate, etc. and a loss notification should also be issued. In the meanwhile, the insurer can also cover the reasonable costs that have occurred while the buyer takes actions to stop further damages to the goods.

The following situations can be claims with the insurance company:

➤Natural disaster;

➤Accidents or other happenings causing the damage to goods and within the coverage of insurance;

➤The shipping company does not compensate or the compensation amount is not big enough to cover the loss and within the domain of the insurance.

The time limit for compensation claims to the insurer is two years after the goods being unloaded from the ship.

When claiming for compensation, the following needs to be taken into consideration:

Evidence

The documents needed to accompany the claims are: claim breakdown list, inspection certificate issued by the Commodity Inspection Bureau, invoice, packing list, copy of B/L. Other than these, different claims should attach different evidence of certificates. When claiming against the seller, the documents should include exact reasons and evidence for it. In case of an FOB or CFR contract, one copy of the insurance policy should also be attached; when claiming against the shipping company, the inspection report from the captain or officer from the Harbour Bureau or the shortage/ damage report from the captain should be attached. When claiming against the insurer, the joint inspection report by the insurer and the buyer should also be attached.

Amount

The amount for compensation can include not only the value of the goods but also the costs involved, such as the inspection fee, unloading fee, bank process fee, storage fee, damage control costs as well as potential interests from the goods.

Expiry date

A compensation claim should be lodged within the expiry date. If the inspection is going to take longer, an extension can be requested from the other party.

10.3 Major Import and Export Documents

(1) **Booking Note**

The Booking Note (B/N) is the application form from the shipper to the carrier to book space for the consignment. Once the B/N is signed and one copy returned to the shipper, the shipping contract is established.

(2) **Shipping Order**

The shipping company or its agent issues this Shipping Order to the shipper once their booking is taken up. This document has three functions: first it is the notice to let the shipper know when and which boat the consignment should be loaded; secondly it is one of the documents the shipper needs to submit to the customs to apply for the release of the goods; thirdly it is an order for the captain to take up this consignment.

(3) **Mate's Receipt**

The mate's receipt is an acknowledgement that the ship owner has received the goods in the condition stated therein, but usually has no further legal relevance. It is usually a preliminary document only, which is later given up in return for the bill of lading.

(4) **Bill of Lading**

The bill of lading is the most important document as it represents the ownership of the consignment.

There are many types of B/Ls and what the L/C requires should be strictly followed. Normally an L/C requires the B/L to be complete, clean, shipped one signed by the captain or forwarder with blank endorsement made out to order.

The consignee is the one who receives the goods and the B/L. Under L/C terms or negotiable payment terms, nearly all B/Ls are made out "To Order", or "To Order of Shipper". This kind of B/L will have to be back endorsed for its circulation.

Sometimes the B/L can also be made out "To Order of XXX Bank", which is normally the issuing bank.

The description of the goods on the B/L can be a general word without details. However it should not contradict to what is stated on the L/C.

The freight. Under CIF or CFR terms, the B/L should state "Freight Prepaid" and under FOB, the B/L should then state "Freight to Collect". Other than specified in the L/C, no details of the freight need to be listed.

The destination port and number of items. The destination port and number of items on the B/L should be the same as on the shipping marks. If there are shortages that happen during the loading, the shipping mark can be added with "EX" to show there are items missing. For example, "EX Nos.1-100".

The number of B/Ls. The bank takes the whole set of B/Ls including one or more original copies. If the B/L has more than one original, then they bear equal effect. However as soon as one of them is used to claim the goods, the other originals become invalid. Therefore, the contract or L/C requirement of a full set or complete set of B/Ls refers to all originals singed by the carrier.

The one who signs the B/L. If the L/C requires a sea freight B/L, the bank accepts the carrier or the agent of the carrier or the captain or deputy captain's signature on the B/L.

Other terms of shipment. The buyer sometimes will list the transportation clauses in an L/C because of the law, or to make sure of the prompt arrival of the goods or other reasons. The seller should combine the shipping situation, law and policies for the sake of flexibility. If the clauses are too difficult or unreasonable, the seller should ask the buyer for an amendment of the L/C.

(5) **Bill of Exchange / Draft**

Under L/C payment terms, the drawn clauses of a bill of exchange should always be stated as per the particular L/C issued by the particular bank, and the payer should always be filled out strictly according to the L/C requirement. The payee is normally the negotiation bank. The bill of exchange normally comes in two copies with equal power. However, one of them will be deemed invalid automatically as soon as the other one has been paid off. Documents required by the L/C to accompany the bill of exchange will differ accordingly.

(6) **Commercial Invoice**

There are many types of invoices among which the commercial invoice is the most common one. Other than this, there are also customs invoices, consular invoices and manufacturer's invoices.

Commercial invoice is the invoice issued by the seller stating the goods and the description, quantity, price and so on, as the main document for settling payment, as well as one of the necessary documents for the customs declaration and taxation.

There is no unified format for commercial invoices in China. However they should include the same main items which are: invoice number, date of issue, quantity, packaging, unit price, total price, and payment terms.

When filling out an invoice, one should be cautious about the following:

➢The consignee: under L/C payment terms, other than specifically required by the L/C, it should be the applicant of the L/C.

➢The description: specification, quantity, unit price and packaging for the goods, if it is under L/C terms, should comply with the L/C without any changes. If the L/C does not give details for these, it is necessary to add some wordings according to the contract. However it should not contradict the L/C, in case it is criticized by the overseas bank and turned down for payment.

➢If the customer requires that the invoice contains ship name, origin of production, manufacturer's name, import license number and so on, it can be done.

➢If the unit price in the L/C and contract contains commission, then the invoice should indicate commission instead of discount. If the L/C or contract states cash discount, the invoice should list exactly as stated, and no discount or trade discount wordings should appear in the invoice.

➢Under L/C terms, the total amount of the invoice should not exceed the maximum amount of the L/C, or the issuing bank can turn down such payment according to the conventions of banks.

➢If the L/C requires the optional charges, port congestion charges or additional premium to be covered by the buyer, and allows it to be taken out from the L/C, the amount can be added onto the invoice and claimed from the issuing bank together with the payment for the goods. However, if the L/C does not state this, while the contract says so, the amount cannot be claimed from the L/C. Unless the buyer agrees and notifies the bank to add these payments, these additional fees should be claimed separately with separate documents.

➢Since there are different laws, policies and conventions in different countries, some L/Cs require the notes "we hereby certify that the content in this invoice is true and without mistakes" to be stated on the invoice, which is called a "certified invoice"; or "payment has been received", which is called a "receipt invoice" or other certifying wordings for the seller's nationality, origin of production and so on. So far as they do not contradict the policies and laws of the importing country, they can be done according to the requirement. When issuing certified invoices, the wording of "E. & O.E." (errors and omissions excepted) should be deleted.

(7) **Manufacturer's Invoice**

The manufacturer's invoice is issued by the manufacturer of the exported goods stating the price in local currency and as a proof of the domestic market price. This is to serve the customs for evaluation, taxation calculation and anti-dumping taxation imposition. If this document is required by the L/C, it should be treated the same as a customs invoice.

(8) **Insurance Policy**

➢The insured should be the beneficiary on the L/C if there are no special instructions and the policy should have blank endorsement to allow transferring of the policy.

➢The type of insurance and the insured sum should comply with that of the L/C. In surface of the documents for CIF and CIP terms, when the insurance premium can be confirmed, the policy should state the minimum insured value, which is 110% of the CIF or CIP value. Otherwise the bank will have to decide on the higher one between 110% of the negotiable value and 110% of the invoice value. The currency in the policy should be the same as required by the L/C.

➢The issuing date of the insurance policy should be reasonable. Unless it states on the insurance policy that the insurance starts from the date the consignment is loading or shipping or under supervision, the bank will refuse to accept insurance policies which are later than the shipping or loading or supervision of the goods.

(9) **Certificate of Origin**

This is a certificate which certifies the original country of manufacturing or producing the goods. Those countries who do not take a customs invoice or consular invoice will require a certificate of origin, so as to ascertain the tax rate for the goods. Some countries do not allow goods to be imported from certain countries and therefore the certificate of origin is also required as evidence. The certificate of origin is normally issued by local notary public or commercial and industrial bodies. In China it is issued by *China Import and Export Goods Inspection Bureau* or *China Council for the Promotion of International Trade.*

(10) **Generalized System of Preferences Documents (GSP)**

The General System of Preferences Documents, abbreviated as GSP, is the certificate to show the customs as the evidence for reduced tariff. GSP Certificate of Origin Form A is suitable for general products and it is filled out by the seller and verified by *China Import and Export Goods Inspection Bureau.* Sellers should submit the GSP forms automatically in order to be benefited from the reduced tariff.

(11) **Packing List and Weight Memo**

These two documents are to make up for what is not sufficiently stated in a commercial invoice, and to make it convenient for the buyer and the customs to check the goods when the consignment arrives at the port.

The packing list gives a breakdown of each commodity in the shipment and the weight memo states the gross and net weight of each item of goods.

(12) **Inspection Certificate**

All kinds of inspection certificates are to prove the quality, quantity, weight and hygiene conditions of the commodities. These certificates are normally issued by *China Import and Export Goods Inspection Bureau*, or by certified inspection companies and if there are no special requirements in the contract or L/C, the export company or manufacturer can also issue such certificates accordingly. It is important that the description and test result of the items on the certificate should match what is required in the contract or L/C. There are requirements for the validity of the inspection certificate. For general products, it is 60 days. For fresh fruit and vegetables, it is 2-3 weeks. The goods are to be shipped within the expiry date. Otherwise they need to be re-inspected.

The above mentioned are the most common documents. According to the *UCP*, when an L/C requires documents other than transportation documents, insurance policies and commercial invoices, the L/C should specify the issuer and content of the documents required. If the L/C does not contain this specification, the bank will accept the submission of documents so long as the documents' expression has contained relevant information for the goods or service as related to what is said on the commercial invoice, or when the L/C does not require a commercial invoice, the expression can match the goods or service that is described in the L/C. Therefore when preparing the above documents, it should always be done strictly in conformity with the L/C.

With the modernization of the world, all countries are now simplifying their procedures for international trade. Forms are getting more standardized, unnecessary steps removed, and electronic ways are being used in the documentation preparation, which is sure to bring huge improvements in trade information exchange and data dealing, which will eventually bring about the further development of international trade.

10. 4 Vocabulary Check

artwork (印刷物上的)图片
authenticity 确实；确实性
authorize *v.* 授权
allocate *v.* 分派；分配
audit *n.* 审计；审核
blank endorsement 空白背书
bulk cargo 散装货
certify *v.* 证明；保证
compulsory 强制性的
courier 信使；送快件的人
coordination 协作；配合
compensation 赔偿
comply with 遵守；照办
construe *v.* 解释；推论
credit note 贷记通知单
diffluent 易溶解的
discharge 卸货
fraudulent 欺骗的
impose *v.* 强迫；强制
indemnity *n.* 赔偿；补偿
legality 合法性；法律性
less *prep.* 减去
margin 幅度；差额
mate's receipt 大副收据
null and void 无效的
negligence *n.* 疏忽；忽视
ordinal 顺序的
packing list 装箱单
notification *n.* 通知
patent 专利
punctual 按时的
precondition 先决条件；前提
restrictive 限制的
regulate *v.* 调整
retrieve *v.* 重新得到
reimbursement *n.* 偿还；付还
salvo 保留条款
treasury 国库；金库
typo 输入错误
validate *v.* 法律上有效；确认
verify *v.* 确认；查对
stock credit note 出仓单
weight list 重量单

10.5 Notes and Key Terms

1) **seller, buyer, importer, exporter:** 卖方，买方，进口人，出口人。《中华人民共和国对外贸易法》第十二条规定，对外贸易经营者可以接受他人的委托，在经营范围内代为办理对外贸易业务。通常在国际贸易中，由于某些公司不具有进出口权，因而虽然与外方签订了进出口合同，但是无法自己直接进行贸易，而必须通过进出口公司来代理。所以，在实际业务操作中，买卖方和进出口方往往可能不是同一家。但是，在本书中，为了方便理解，假想买卖双方均为具有进出口权的公司，因此，在本文中，可以将它们相应等同看待。

2) **foreign currency verification and cancellation:** 外汇核销，是国家加强出口收汇管理，确保国家外汇收入，防止外汇流失，指定外汇管理部门对出口企业贸易下的外汇收入情况进行监督检查的一种制度。

3) **tax refund:** 退税，指出口产品退(免)税，其基本含义是指对出口产品退还其在国内生产和流通环节实际缴纳的产品税、增值税、营业税和特别消费税。出口产品退税制度是一个国家税收的重要组成部分。出口退税主要是通过退还出口产品的国内已纳税款来平衡国内产品的税收负担，使本国产品以不含税成本进入国际市场，与国外产品在同等条件下进行竞争，从而增强竞争能力，扩大出口创汇。

4) **Booking Note (B/N):** 托运单，托单。租船或订舱的依据。

5) **carrier**：承运人。指专门经营水上、铁路、公路、航空等货物运输业务的交通运输部门，如船公司、铁路或公路运输公司、航空公司等。他们一般都拥有大量的运输工具，面向社会提供运输服务。

6) **ship broker:** 租船代理，又称租船经纪人，简称船代，指以船舶为商业活动对象而进行船舶租赁业务的人，主要业务是在市场上为船东寻找货运对象，促成租赁交易，以从中赚取佣金。

7) **freight forwarder:** 货运代理，简称货代，指接受货主的委托，代表货主办理有关货物报关、交接、仓储、调拨、检验、包装、转运、订舱等业务的人。主要有订舱揽货代理、货物装卸代理、转运代理、理货代理、储存代理、集装箱代理等。

8) **shipping agent:** 船务代理，是船代和货代的总称。

9) **GSP Form A:** 普惠制原产地证明书(申报和证明联合)格式A，是受惠国的原产品出口到给惠国时享受减、免关税优惠待遇的法律凭证。

GSP (Generalized System of Preferences)普惠制，即普遍优惠制，是一种关税制度，是发达国家(给惠国)对从发展中国家(受惠国)进口某些适合的产品时给予减免或免税的优惠待遇。我国是发展中国家，目前已有英国、法国、德国、意大利、荷兰、卢森堡、比利时、爱尔兰、丹麦、希腊、葡萄牙、西班牙、日本、挪威、新西兰、澳大利亚、瑞士、瑞典、芬兰、奥地利、加拿大和波兰等 22 个国家对我国实行普惠制。

10) **Certificate of Origin (C/O)**：产地证。C/O 和 GSP Form A 都是产地证，清关文件之一，不同之处在于，前者是产品产地的有效证明文件，而后者则是享受普惠制减、免税待遇的有效证件。根据国家商检局制定的普惠制签证管理办法及其实施细则规定，有进出口经营权的国内企业，三资企业，国外企业、商社常驻中国代表机构，对外承接来料加工、来图来样加工、来件装配和补偿贸易业务的企业，经营旅游商品的销售部门，参加国际经济、文化交流及拍卖等活动需出售展品、样品等的有关单位均可向当地商检机构申请办理普惠制原产地证书的签证。另外，Form A 是互惠的，是主动的。在进口清关时出示该证，货物可享受最惠国税率征税，(在普惠制协约国内)是无条件地享受的，所以是主动的。C/O 属一般原产地证，仅证明产地，是被动的。

11) **Foreign Currency Verification and Cancellation Form:** 外汇核销单，指由国家外汇管理局制发、出口单位和受托行及解付行填写、海关凭以受理报关、外汇管理部门凭以核销收汇的有顺序编号的凭证(核销单附有存根)。

10.6 Follow-up Practice

10.6.1 Review and Discussion Questions

1) Please describe briefly the procedures of performing a CIF export contract under L/C payment terms.
2) Please describe briefly the procedures of performing a FOB import contract under L/C payment terms.
3) Why is it important for the exporter to check the L/C against the sales contract carefully after receipt of the L/C?
4) When the L/C is to be amended, what are the points for attention?
5) What will the negotiation bank normally do when it receives documents with discrepancies?
6) What are the main negotiation documents for L/C payment and what are the general requirements for making out these documents?

10.6.2 Complete the following sentences with appropriate terms or words.

1) In international trade, ____________________________ check the L/C.

2) The application for amendments of an L/C should be submitted via ________________.

3) The shipper exchanges for the original B/L from the shipping company or its agent with ________________.

4) The payee of an L/C is normally ________________.

5) For a CFR contract, the seller needs to provide ________________ to the buyer as soon as it is available in order for the consignment to be insured without delay.

6) In export transactions, a Form A is issued by ________________.

7) In export transactions, without special instructions from an L/C, a C/O can be issued by ________________, ________________, or ________________.

8) For man-made damages to the goods during the shipment, the buyer can claim for compensation from ________________.

9) If an L/C sets 30 November 2007 as the expiry date without instructions on the latest shipment date, ________________ should be considered the latest date for shipment.

10) If an L/C amendment notification includes multiple items of amendments, the seller should either ________________ or ________________.

10.6.3 Decide whether the following statements are true or false.

1) In import and export trade, the basic obligation for the seller is only to provide the buyer with the goods which comply with the requirements in the contract. (   )

2) The mate's receipt is a temporary receipt issued by the shipping company to the shipper as a proof that the consignment has been loaded onto the ship. (   )

3) For T/T payment terms, the B/L, commercial invoice and packing list should be sent to the buyer through the bank for payment. (   )

4) If the seller fails to make shipment within the time of validity of the inspection certificate, he can request that the validity of the inspection certificate be extended automatically. (   )

5) The importer may refuse to pay if there are discrepancies in the negotiation documents. (   )

6) In credit operations, the bank deals with documents and not with goods. Any discrepancies may cause refusal of payments. (   )

7) If an L/C states the latest shipment date of 30 April, and expiry date of 15 May. An exporter ships the goods on the 12 April, and submits the documents complying with L/C requirements for negotiation on the 6th May. The bank should pay out according to *the Uniform Customs and Practice for Documentary Credits.* (   )

8) A clean B/L shows that the goods on board are in good condition. ( )
9) The expiry date in an L/C is the date for the seller to receive payment. ( )
10) For unacceptable clauses in an L/C, the seller should contact the issuing bank directly for amendments. ( )

10.6.4 Case Study

A Chinese exporter received an irrevocable sight L/C from the importer. The L/C required that the latest shipment date was 15th March 2007. Because of lack of shipping space, the exporter could not ship the goods on time so the exporter asked the importer to extend the shipment date to the 20th April 2007 and to extend the expiry date of the L/C accordingly. The importer replied to accept the changes with a phone call. The exporter then arranged the shipment on the 18th April and submitted the documents for negotiation on the 20th April, but was rejected by the bank. Is the bank right in so doing? Why?

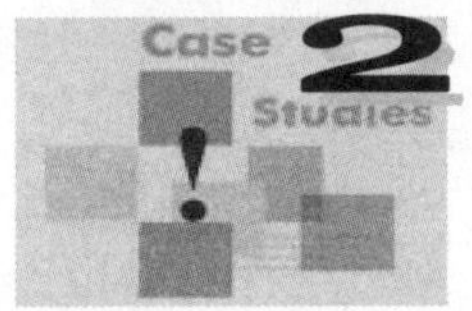

An import contract is signed in July under FOB terms setting out August as the shipment month. However because of lack of ships, the importer fails to obtain shipping space. What should the importer do?

1. http://www.mofcom.gov.cn 中国商务部网站
2. http://www.cnexp.net 外贸精英网
3. http://www.customs.gov.cn 中国海关网
4. http://www.info.china.alibaba.com 阿里巴巴网

Appendix I

United Nations Convention on Contracts for the International Sale of Goods

THE STATES PARTIES TO THIS CONVENTION,

BEARING IN MIND the broad objectives in the resolutions adopted by the sixth special session of the General Assembly of the United Nations on the establishment of a New International Economic Order,

CONSIDERING that the development of international trade on the basis of equality and mutual benefit is an important element in promoting friendly relations among States,

BEING OF THE OPINION that the adoption of uniform rules which govern contracts for the international sale of goods and take into account the different social, economic and legal systems would contribute to the removal of legal barriers in international trade and promote the development of international trade,

HAVE DECREED as follows:

PART I SPHERE OF APPLICATION AND GENERAL PROVISIONS

Chapter I SPHERE OF APPLICATION

Article 1

(1) This Convention applies to contracts of sale of goods between parties whose places of business are in different States:
    (a) when the States are Contracting States; or
    (b) when the rules of private international law lead to the application of the law of a Contracting State.

(2) The fact that the parties have their places of business in different States is to be disregarded whenever this fact does not appear either from the contract or from any dealings between, or from information disclosed by, the parties at any time before or at the conclusion of the contract.

(3) Neither the nationality of the parties nor the civil or commercial character of the parties or of the contract is to be taken into consideration in determining the application of this Convention.

Article 2

This Convention does not apply to sales:

(a) of goods bought for personal, family or household use, unless the seller, at any time before or at the conclusion of the contract, neither knew nor ought to have known that the goods were bought for any such use;

(b) by auction;

(c) on execution or otherwise by authority of law;

(d) of stocks, shares, investment securities, negotiable instruments or money;

(e) of ships, vessels, hovercraft or aircraft;

(f) of electricity.

Article 3

(1) Contracts for the supply of goods to be manufactured or produced are to be considered sales unless the party who orders the goods undertakes to supply a substantial part of the materials necessary for such manufacture or production.

(2) This Convention does not apply to contracts in which the preponderant part of the obligations of the party who furnishes the goods consists in the supply of labour or other services.

Article 4

This Convention governs only the formation of the contract of sale and the rights and obligations of the seller and the buyer arising from such a contract. In particular, except as otherwise expressly provided in this Convention, it is not concerned with:

(a) the validity of the contract or of any of its provisions or of any usage;

(b) the effect which the contract may have on the property in the goods sold.

Article 5

This Convention does not apply to the liability of the seller for death or personal injury caused by the goods to any person.

Article 6

The parties may exclude the application of this Convention or, subject to article 12, derogate from or vary the effect of any of its provisions.

Chapter II GENERAL PROVISIONS

Article 7

(1) In the interpretation of this Convention, regard is to be had to its international character and to the need to promote uniformity in its application and the observance of good faith in international trade.

(2) Questions concerning matters governed by this Convention which are not expressly settled in it are to be settled in conformity with the general principles on which it is based or, in the absence of such principles, in conformity with the law applicable by virtue of the rules of private international law.

Article 8

(1) For the purposes of this Convention statements made by and other conduct of a party are to be interpreted according to his intent where the other party knew or could not have been unaware what that intent was.

(2) If the preceding paragraph is not applicable, statements made by and other conduct of a party are to be interpreted according to the understanding that a reasonable person of the same kind as the other party would have had in the same circumstances.

(3) In determining the intent of a party or the understanding a reasonable person would have had, due consideration is to be given to all relevant circumstances of the case including the negotiations, any practices which the parties have established between themselves, usages and any subsequent conduct of the parties.

Article 9

(1) The parties are bound by any usage to which they have agreed and by any practices which they have established between themselves.

(2) The parties are considered, unless otherwise agreed, to have impliedly made applicable to their contract or its formation a usage of which the parties knew or ought to have known and which in international trade is widely known to, and regularly observed by, parties to contracts of the type involved in the particular trade concerned.

Article 10

For the purposes of this Convention:

(1) if a party has more than one place of business, the place of business is that which has the closest relationship to the contract and its performance, having regard to the circumstances known to or contemplated by the parties at any time before or at the conclusion of the contract;

(2) if a party does not have a place of business, reference is to be made to his habitual residence.

Article 11

A contract of sale need not be concluded in or evidenced by writing and is not subject to any other requirement as to form. It may be proved by any means, including witnesses.

Article 12

Any provision of article 11, article 29 or Part II of this Convention that allows a contract of sale or its modification or termination by agreement or any offer, acceptance or other indication of intention to be made in any form other than in writing does not apply where any party has his place of business in a Contracting State which has made a declaration under article 96 of this Convention. The parties may not derogate from or vary the effect or this article.

Article 13

For the purposes of this Convention "writing" includes telegram and telex.

PART II FORMATION OF THE CONTRACT

Article 14

(1) A proposal for concluding a contract addressed to one or more specific persons constitutes an offer if it is sufficiently definite and indicates the intention of the offeror to be bound in case of acceptance. A proposal is sufficiently definite if it indicates the goods and expressly or implicitly fixes or makes provision for determining the quantity and the price.

(2) A proposal other than one addressed to one or more specific persons is to be considered merely as an invitation to make offers, unless the contrary is clearly indicated by the person making the proposal.

Article 15

(1) An offer becomes effective when it reaches the offeree.

(2) An offer, even if it is irrevocable, may be withdrawn if the withdrawal reaches the offeree before or at the same time as the offer.

Article 16

(1) Until a contract is concluded an offer may be revoked if the revocation reaches the offeree before he has dispatched an acceptance.

(2) However, an offer cannot be revoked:

(a) if it indicates, whether by stating a fixed time for acceptance or otherwise, that it is irrevocable; or

(b) if it was reasonable for the offeree to rely on the offer as being irrevocable and the offeree has acted in reliance on the offer.

Article 17

An offer, even if it is irrevocable, is terminated when a rejection reaches the offeror.

Article 18

(1) A statement made by or other conduct of the offeree indicating assent to an offer is an acceptance. Silence or inactivity does not in itself amount to acceptance.

(2) An acceptance of an offer becomes effective at the moment the indication of assent reaches the offeror. An acceptance is not effective if the indication of assent does not reach the offeror within the time he has fixed or, if no time is fixed, within a reasonable time, due account being taken of the circumstances of the transaction, including the rapidity of the means of communication employed by the offeror. An oral offer must be accepted immediately unless the circumstances indicate otherwise.

(3) However, if, by virtue of the offer or as a result of practices which the parties have established between themselves or of usage, the offeree may indicate assent by performing an act, such as one relating to the dispatch of the goods or payment of the price, without notice to the offeror, the acceptance is effective at the moment the act is performed, provided that the act is performed within the period of time laid down in the preceding paragraph.

Article 19

(1) A reply to an offer which purports to be an acceptance but contains additions, limitations or other modifications is a rejection of the offer and constitutes a counter-offer.

(2) However, a reply to an offer which purports to be an acceptance but contains additional or different terms which do not materially alter the terms of the offer constitutes an acceptance, unless the offeror, without undue delay, objects orally to the discrepancy or dispatches a notice to that effect. If he does not so object, the terms of the contract are the terms of the offer with the modifications contained in the acceptance.

(3) Additional or different terms relating, among other things, to the price, payment, quality and quantity of the goods, place and time of delivery, extent of one party's liability to the other or the settlement of disputes are considered to alter the terms of the offer materially.

Article 20

(1) A period of time for acceptance fixed by the offeror in a telegram or a letter begins to run from the moment the telegram is handed in for dispatch or from the

date shown on the letter or, if no such date is shown, from the date shown on the envelope. A period of time for acceptance fixed by the offeror by telephone, telex or other means of instantaneous communication, begins to run from the moment that the offer reaches the offeree.

(2) Official holidays or non-business days occurring during the period for acceptance are included in calculating the period. However, if a notice of acceptance cannot be delivered at the address of the offeror on the last day of the period because that day falls on an official holiday or a non-business day at the place of business of the offeror, the period is extended until the first business day which follows.

Article 21

(1) A late acceptance is nevertheless effective as an acceptance if without delay the offeror orally so informs the offeree or dispatches a notice to that effect.

(2) If a letter or other writing containing a late acceptance shows that it has been sent in such circumstances that if its transmission had been normal it would have reached the offeror in due time, the late acceptance is effective as an acceptance unless, without delay, the offeror orally informs the offeree that he considers his offer as having lapsed or dispatches a notice to that effect.

Article 22

An acceptance may be withdrawn if the withdrawal reaches the offeror before or at the same time as the acceptance would have become effective.

Article 23

A contract is concluded at the moment when an acceptance of an offer becomes effective in accordance with the provisions of this Convention.

Article 24

For the purposes of this Part of the Convention, an offer, declaration of acceptance or any other indication of intention "reaches" the addressee when it is made orally to him or delivered by any other means to him personally, to his place of business or mailing address or, if he does not have a place of business or mailing address, to his habitual residence.

PART III SALE OF GOODS

Chapter I GENERAL PROVISIONS

Article 25

A breach of contract committed by one of the parties is fundamental if it results in such detriment to the other party as substantially to deprive him of what he is entitled to expect under the contract, unless the party in breach did not foresee and a reasonable person of the same kind in the same circumstances would not have foreseen such a result.

Article 26

A declaration of avoidance of the contract is effective only if made by notice to the other party.

Article 27

Unless otherwise expressly provided in this Part of the Convention, if any notice, request or other communication is given or made by a party in accordance with this Part and by means appropriate in the circumstances, a delay or error in the transmission of the communication or its failure to arrive does not deprive that party of the right to rely on the communication.

Article 28

If, in accordance with the provisions of this Convention, one party is entitled to require performance of any obligation by the other party, a court is not bound to enter a judgement for specific performance unless the court would do so under its own law in respect of similar contracts of sale not governed by this Convention.

Article 29

(1) A contract may be modified or terminated by the mere agreement of the parties.

(2) A contract in writing which contains a provision requiring any modification or termination by agreement to be in writing may not be otherwise modified or terminated by agreement. However, a party may be precluded by his conduct from asserting such a provision to the extent that the other party has relied on that conduct.

Chapter II OBLIGATIONS OF THE SELLER

Article 30

The seller must deliver the goods, hand over any documents relating to them and transfer the property in the goods, as required by the contract and this Convention.

Section I Delivery of the goods and handing over of documents

Article 31

If the seller is not bound to deliver the goods at any other particular place, his obligation to deliver consists:

(a) if the contract of sale involves carriage of the goods - in handing the goods over to the first carrier for transmission to the buyer;

(b) if, in cases not within the preceding subparagraph, the contract relates to specific goods, or unidentified goods to be drawn from a specific stock or to be manufactured or produced, and at the time of the conclusion of the contract the parties knew that the goods were at, or were to be manufactured or produced at, a particular place—in placing the goods at the buyer's disposal at that place;

(c) in other cases—in placing the goods at the buyer's disposal at the place where the seller had his place of business at the time of the conclusion of the contract.

Article 32

(1) If the seller, in accordance with the contract or this Convention, hands the goods over to a carrier and if the goods are not clearly identified to the contract by markings on the goods, by shipping documents or otherwise, the seller must give the buyer notice of the consignment specifying the goods.

(2) If the seller is bound to arrange for carriage of the goods, he must make such contracts as are necessary for carriage to the place fixed by means of transportation appropriate in the circumstances and according to the usual terms for such transportation.

(3) If the seller is not bound to effect insurance in respect of the carriage of the goods, he must, at the buyer's request, provide him with all available information necessary to enable him to effect such insurance.

Article 33

The seller must deliver the goods:

(a) if a date is fixed by or determinable from the contract, on that date;

(b) if a period of time is fixed by or determinable from the contract, at any time within that period unless circumstances indicate that the buyer is to choose a date; or

(c) in any other case, within a reasonable time after the conclusion of the contract.

Article 34

If the seller is bound to hand over documents relating to the goods, he must hand them over at the time and place and in the form required by the contract. If the seller has handed over documents before that time, he may, up to that time, cure any lack of conformity in the documents, if the exercise of this right does not cause the buyer unreasonable inconvenience or unreasonable expense. However, the buyer retains any right to claim damages as provided for in this Convention.

Section II　Conformity of the goods and third party claims

Article 35

(1) The seller must deliver goods which are of the quantity, quality and description

required by the contract and which are contained or packaged in the manner required by the contract.

(2) Except where the parties have agreed otherwise, the goods do not conform with the contract unless they:

(a) are fit for the purposes for which goods of the same description would ordinarily be used;

(b) are fit for any particular purpose expressly or impliedly made known to the seller at the time of the conclusion of the contract, except where the circumstances show that the buyer did not rely, or that it was unreasonable for him to rely, on the seller's skill and judgement;

(c) possess the qualities of goods which the seller has held out to the buyer as a sample or model;

(d) are contained or packaged in the manner usual for such goods or, where there is no such manner, in a manner adequate to preserve and protect the goods.

(3) The seller is not liable under subparagraphs (a) to (d) of the preceding paragraph for any lack of conformity of the goods if at the time of the conclusion of the contract the buyer knew or could not have been unaware of such lack of conformity.

Article 36

(1) The seller is liable in accordance with the contract and this Convention for any lack of conformity which exists at the time when the risk passes to the buyer, even though the lack of conformity becomes apparent only after that time.

(2) The seller is also liable for any lack of conformity which occurs after the time indicated in the preceding paragraph and which is due to a breach of any of his obligations, including a breach of any guarantee that for a period of time the goods will remain fit for their ordinary purpose or for some particular purpose or will retain specified qualities or characteristics.

Article 37

If the seller has delivered goods before the date for delivery, he may, up to that date, deliver any missing part or make up any deficiency in the quantity of the goods delivered, or deliver goods in replacement of any non-conforming goods delivered or remedy any lack of conformity in the goods delivered, provided that the exercise of this right does not cause the buyer unreasonable inconvenience or unreasonable expense. However, the buyer retains any right to claim damages as provided for in this Convention.

Article 38

(1) The buyer must examine the goods, or cause them to be examined, within as short a period as is practicable in the circumstances.

(2) If the contract involves carriage of the goods, examination may be deferred until after the goods have arrived at their destination.

(3) If the goods are redirected in transit or redispatched by the buyer without a reasonable opportunity for examination by him and at the time of the conclusion of the contract the seller knew or ought to have known of the possibility of such redirection or redispatch, examination may be deferred until after the goods have arrived at the new destination.

Article 39

(1) The buyer loses the right to rely on a lack of conformity of the goods if he does not give notice to the seller specifying the nature of the lack of conformity within a reasonable time after he has discovered it or ought to have discovered it.

(2) In any event, the buyer loses the right to rely on a lack of conformity of the goods if he does not give the seller notice thereof at the latest within a period of two years from the date on which the goods were actually handed over to the buyer, unless this time-limit is inconsistent with a contractual period of guarantee.

Article 40

The seller is not entitled to rely on the provisions of articles 38 and 39 if the lack of conformity relates to facts of which he knew or could not have been unaware and which he did not disclose to the buyer.

Article 41

The seller must deliver goods which are free from any right or claim of a third party, unless the buyer agreed to take the goods subject to that right or claim. However, if such right or claim is based on industrial property or other intellectual property, the seller's obligation is governed by article 42.

Article 42

(1) The seller must deliver goods which are free from any right or claim of a third party based on industrial property or other intellectual property, of which at the time of the conclusion of the contract the seller knew or could not have been unaware, provided that the right or claim is based on industrial property or other intellectual property:

(a) under the law of the State where the goods will be resold or otherwise used, if it was contemplated by the parties at the time of the conclusion of the contract that the goods would be resold or otherwise used in that State; or

(b) in any other case, under the law of the State where the buyer has his place of business.

(2) The obligation of the seller under the preceding paragraph does not extend to cases where:

(a) at the time of the conclusion of the contract the buyer knew or could not have been unaware of the right or claim; or

(b) the right or claim results from the seller's compliance with technical drawings, designs, formulae or other such specifications furnished by the buyer.

Article 43

(1) The buyer loses the right to rely on the provisions of article 41 or article 42 if he does not give notice to the seller specifying the nature of the right or claim of the third party within a reasonable time after he has become aware or ought to have become aware of the right or claim.

(2) The seller is not entitled to rely on the provisions of the preceding paragraph if he knew of the right or claim of the third party and the nature of it.

Article 44

Notwithstanding the provisions of paragraph (1) of article 39 and paragraph (1) of article 43, the buyer may reduce the price in accordance with article 50 or claim damages, except for loss of profit, if he has a reasonable excuse for his failure to give the required notice.

Section III Remedies for breach of contract by the seller

Article 45

(1) If the seller fails to perform any of his obligations under the contract or this convention, the buyer may:

(a) exercise the rights provided in articles 46 to 52;

(b) claim damages as provided in articles 74 to 77.

(2) The buyer is not deprived of any right he may have to claim damages by exercising his right to other remedies.

(3) No period of grace may be granted to the seller by a court or arbitral tribunal when the buyer resorts to a remedy for breach of contract.

Article 46

(1) The buyer may require performance by the seller of his obligations unless the

buyer has resorted to a remedy which is inconsistent with this requirement.

(2) If the goods do not conform with the contract, the buyer may require delivery of substitute goods only if the lack of conformity constitutes a fundamental breach of contract and a request for substitute goods is made either in conjunction with notice given under article 39 or within a reasonable time thereafter.

(3) If the goods do not conform with the contract, the buyer may require the seller to remedy the lack of conformity by repair, unless this is unreasonable having regard to all the circumstances. A request for repair must be made either in conjunction with notice given under article 39 or within a reasonable time thereafter.

Article 47

(1) The buyer may fix an additional period of time of reasonable length for performance by the seller of his obligations.

(2) Unless the buyer has received notice from the seller that he will not perform within the period so fixed, the buyer may not, during that period, resort to any remedy for breach of contract. However, the buyer is not deprived thereby of any right he may have to claim damages for delay in performance.

Article 48

(1) Subject to article 49, the seller may, even after the date for delivery, remedy at his own expense any failure to perform his obligations, if he can do so without unreasonable delay and without causing the buyer unreasonable inconvenience or uncertainty of reimbursement by the seller of expenses advanced by the buyer. However, the buyer retains any right to claim damages as provided for in this Convention.

(2) If the seller requests the buyer to make known whether he will accept performance and the buyer does not comply with the request within a reasonable time, the seller may perform within the time indicated in his request. The buyer may not, during that period of time, resort to any remedy which is inconsistent with performance by the seller.

(3) A notice by the seller that he will perform within a specified period of time is assumed to include a request, under the preceding paragraph, that the buyer make known his decision.

(4) A request or notice by the seller under paragraph (2) or (3) of this article is not effective unless received by the buyer.

Article 49

(1) The buyer may declare the contract avoided:

(a) if the failure by the seller to perform any of his obligations under the contract or this Convention amounts to a fundamental breach of contract; or

(b) in case of non-delivery, if the seller does not deliver the goods within the additional period of time fixed by the buyer in accordance with paragraph (1) of article 47 or declares that he will not deliver within the period so fixed.

(2) However, in cases where the seller has delivered the goods, the buyer loses the right to declare the contract avoided unless he does so:

(a) in respect of late delivery, within a reasonable time after he has become aware that delivery has been made;

(b) in respect of any breach other than late delivery, within a reasonable time:

(i) after he knew or ought to have known of the breach;

(ii) after the expiration of any additional period of time fixed by the buyer in accordance with paragraph (1) of article 47, or after the seller has declared that he will not perform his obligations within such an additional period; or

(iii) after the expiration of any additional period of time indicated by the seller in accordance with paragraph (2) of article 48, or after the buyer has declared that he will not accept performance.

Article 50

If the goods do not conform with the contract and whether or not the price has already been paid, the buyer may reduce the price in the same proportion as the value that the goods actually delivered had at the time of the delivery bears to the value that conforming goods would have had at that time. However, if the seller remedies any failure to perform his obligations in accordance with article 37 or article 48 or if the buyer refuses to accept performance by the seller in accordance with those articles, the buyer may not reduce the price.

Article 51

(1) If the seller delivers only a part of the goods or if only a part of the goods delivered is in conformity with the contract, articles 46 to 50 apply in respect of the part which is missing or which does not conform.

(2) The buyer may declare the contract avoided in its entirety only if the failure to make delivery completely or in conformity with the contract amounts to a fundamental breach of the contract.

Article 52

(1) If the seller delivers the goods before the date fixed, the buyer may take delivery or refuse to take delivery.

(2) If the seller delivers a quantity of goods greater than that provided for in the contract, the buyer may take delivery or refuse to take delivery of the excess quantity. If the buyer takes delivery of all or part of the excess quantity, he must pay for it at the contract rate.

Chapter III OBLIGATIONS OF THE BUYER

Article 53

The buyer must pay the price for the goods and take delivery of them as required by the contract and this Convention.

Section I Payment of the price

Article 54

The buyer's obligation to pay the price includes taking such steps and complying with such formalities as may be required under the contract or any laws and regulations to enable payment to be made.

Article 55

Where a contract has been validly concluded but does not expressly or implicitly fix or make provision for determining the price, the parties are considered, in the absence of any indication to the contrary, to have impliedly made reference to the price generally charged at the time of the conclusion of the contract for such goods sold under comparable circumstances in the trade concerned.

Article 56

If the price is fixed according to the weight of the goods, in case of doubt it is to be determined by the net weight.

Article 57

(1) If the buyer is not bound to pay the price at any other particular place, he must pay it to the seller:

(a) at the seller's place of business; or

(b) if the payment is to be made against the handing over of the goods or of documents, at the place where the handing over takes place.

(2) The seller must bear any increases in the expenses incidental to payment which is caused by a change in his place of business subsequent to the conclusion of the contract.

Article 58

(1) If the buyer is not bound to pay the price at any other specific time, he must pay it when the seller places either the goods or documents controlling their disposition at the buyer's disposal in accordance with the contract and this Convention. The seller may make such payment a condition for handing over the goods or documents.

(2) If the contract involves carriage of the goods, the seller may dispatch the goods on terms whereby the goods, or documents controlling their disposition, will not be handed over to the buyer except against payment of the price.

(3) The buyer is not bound to pay the price until he has had an opportunity to examine the goods, unless the procedures for delivery or payment agreed upon by the parties are inconsistent with his having such an opportunity.

Article 59

The buyer must pay the price on the date fixed by or determinable from the contract and this Convention without the need for any request or compliance with any formality on the part of the seller.

Section II Taking delivery

Article 60

The buyer's obligation to take delivery consists:

(1) in doing all the acts which could reasonably be expected of him in order to enable the seller to make delivery; and

(2) in taking over the goods.

Section III Remedies for breach of contract by the buyer

Article 61

(1) If the buyer fails to perform any of his obligations under the contract or this Convention, the seller may:

(a) exercise the rights provided in articles 62 to 65;

(b) claim damages as provided in articles 74 to 77.

(2) The seller is not deprived of any right he may have to claim damages by exercising his right to other remedies.

(3) No period of grace may be granted to the buyer by a court or arbitral tribunal when the seller resorts to a remedy for breach of contract.

Article 62

The seller may require the buyer to pay the price, take delivery or perform his other obligations, unless the seller has resorted to a remedy which is inconsistent with this requirement.

Article 63

(1) The seller may fix an additional period of time of reasonable length for performance by the buyer of his obligations.

(2) Unless the seller has received notice from the buyer that he will not perform within the period so fixed, the seller may not, during that period, resort to any remedy for breach of contract. However, the seller is not deprived thereby of any right he may have to claim damages for delay in performance.

Article 64

(1) The seller may declare the contract avoided:

(a) if the failure by the buyer to perform any of his obligations under the contract or this Convention amounts to a fundamental breach of contract; or

(b) if the buyer does not, within the additional period of time fixed by the seller in accordance with paragraph (1) of article 63, perform his obligation to pay the price or take delivery of the goods, or if he declares that he will not do so within the period so fixed.

(2) However, in cases where the buyer has paid the price, the seller loses the right to declare the contract avoided unless he does so:

(a) in respect of late performance by the buyer, before the seller has become aware that performance has been rendered; or

(b) in respect of any breach other than late performance by the buyer, within a reasonable time:

(i) after the seller knew or ought to have known of the breach; or

(ii) after the expiration of any additional period of time fixed by the seller in accordance with paragraph (1) of article 63, or after the buyer has declared that he will not perform his obligations within such an additional period.

Article 65

(1) If under the contract the buyer is to specify the form, measurement or other features of the goods and he fails to make such specification either on the date agreed upon or within a reasonable time after receipt of a request from the seller, the seller may, without prejudice to any other rights he may have, make the specification himself in accordance with the requirements of the buyer that may be known to him.

(2) If the seller makes the specification himself, he must inform the buyer of the

details thereof and must fix a reasonable time within which the buyer may make a different specification. If, after receipt of such a communication, the buyer fails to do so within the time so fixed, the specification made by the seller is binding.

Chapter IV PASSING OF RISK

Article 66

Loss of or damage to the goods after the risk has passed to the buyer does not discharge him from his obligation to pay the price, unless the loss or damage is due to an act or omission of the seller.

Article 67

(1) If the contract of sale involves carriage of the goods and the seller is not bound to hand them over at a particular place, the risk passes to the buyer when the goods are handed over to the first carrier for transmission to the buyer in accordance with the contract of sale. If the seller is bound to hand the goods over to a carrier at a particular place, the risk does not pass to the buyer until the goods are handed over to the carrier at that place. The fact that the seller is authorized to retain documents controlling the disposition of the goods does not affect the passage of the risk.

(2) Nevertheless, the risk does not pass to the buyer until the goods are clearly identified to the contract, whether by markings on the goods, by shipping documents, by notice given to the buyer or otherwise.

Article 68

The risk in respect of goods sold in transit passes to the buyer from the time of the conclusion of the contract. However, if the circumstances so indicate, the risk is assumed by the buyer from the time the goods were handed over to the carrier who issued the documents embodying the contract of carriage. Nevertheless, if at the time of the conclusion of the contract of sale the seller knew or ought to have known that the goods had been lost or damaged and did not disclose this to the buyer, the loss or damage is at the risk of the seller.

Article 69

(1) In cases not within articles 67 and 68, the risk passes to the buyer when he takes over the goods or, if he does not do so in due time, from the time when the goods are placed at his disposal and he commits a breach of contract by failing to take delivery.

(2) However, if the buyer is bound to take over the goods at a place other than a

place of business of the seller, the risk passes when delivery is due and the buyer is aware of the fact that the goods are placed at his disposal at that place.

(3) If the contract relates to goods not then identified, the goods are considered not to be placed at the disposal of the buyer until they are clearly identified to the contract.

Article 70

If the seller has committed a fundamental breach of contract, articles 67, 68 and 69 do not impair the remedies available to the buyer on account of the breach.

Chapter V PROVISIONS COMMON TO THE OBLIGATIONS OF THE SELLER AND OF THE BUYER

Section I Anticipatory breach and installment contracts

Article 71

(1) A party may suspend the performance of his obligations if, after the conclusion of the contract, it becomes apparent that the other party will not perform a substantial part of his obligations as a result of:

(a) a serious deficiency in his ability to perform or in his creditworthiness; or

(b) his conduct in preparing to perform or in performing the contract.

(2) If the seller has already dispatched the goods before the grounds described in the preceding paragraph become evident, he may prevent the handing over of the goods to the buyer even though the buyer holds a document which entitles him to obtain them. The present paragraph relates only to the rights in the goods as between the buyer and the seller.

(3) A party suspending performance, whether before or after dispatch of the goods, must immediately give notice of the suspension to the other party and must continue with performance if the other party provides adequate assurance of his performance.

Article 72

(1) If prior to the date for performance of the contract it is clear that one of the parties will commit a fundamental breach of contract, the other party may declare the contract avoided.

(2) If time allows, the party intending to declare the contract avoided must give reasonable notice to the other party in order to permit him to provide adequate assurance of his performance.

(3) The requirements of the preceding paragraph do not apply if the other party has

declared that he will not perform his obligations.

Article 73

(1) In the case of a contract for delivery of goods by installments, if the failure of one party to perform any of his obligations in respect of any installment constitutes a fundamental breach of contract with respect to that installment, the other party may declare the contract avoided with respect to that installment.

(2) If one party's failure to perform any of his obligations in respect of any installment gives the other party good grounds to conclude that a fundamental breach of contract will occur with respect to future installments, he may declare the contract avoided for the future, provided that he does so within a reasonable time.

(3) A buyer who declares the contract avoided in respect of any delivery may, at the same time, declare it avoided in respect of deliveries already made or of future deliveries if, by reason of their interdependence, those deliveries could not be used for the purpose contemplated by the parties at the time of the conclusion of the contract.

Section II Damages

Article 74

Damages for breach of contract by one party consist of a sum equal to the loss, including loss of profit, suffered by the other party as a consequence of the breach. Such damages may not exceed the loss which the party in breach foresaw or ought to have foreseen at the time of the conclusion of the contract, in the light of the facts and matters of which he then knew or ought to have known, as a possible consequence of the breach of contract.

Article 75

If the contract is avoided and if, in a reasonable manner and within a reasonable time after avoidance, the buyer has bought goods in replacement or the seller has resold the goods, the party claiming damages may recover the difference between the contract price and the price in the substitute transaction as well as any further damages recoverable under article 74.

Article 76

(1) If the contract is avoided and there is a current price for the goods, the party claiming damages may, if he has not made a purchase or resale under article 75, recover the difference between the price fixed by the contract and the current price at the time of avoidance as well as any further damages recoverable under

article 74. If, however, the party claiming damages has avoided the contract after taking over the goods, the current price at the time of such taking over shall be applied instead of the current price at the time of avoidance.

(2) For the purposes of the preceding paragraph, the current price is the price prevailing at the place where delivery of the goods should have been made or, if there is no current price at that place, the price at such other place as serves as a reasonable substitute, making due allowance for differences in the cost of transporting the goods.

Article 77

A party who relies on a breach of contract must take such measures as are reasonable in the circumstances to mitigate the loss, including loss of profit, resulting from the breach. If he fails to take such measures, the party in breach may claim a reduction in the damages in the amount by which the loss should have been mitigated.

Section III Interest

Article 78

If a party fails to pay the price or any other sum that is in arrears, the other party is entitled to interest on it, without prejudice to any claim for damages recoverable under article 74.

Section IV Exemptions

Article 79

(1) A party is not liable for a failure to perform any of his obligations if he proves that the failure was due to an impediment beyond his control and that he could not reasonably be expected to have taken the impediment into account at the time of the conclusion of the contract or to have avoided or overcome it or its consequences.

(2) If the party's failure is due to the failure by a third person whom he has engaged to perform the whole or a part of the contract, that party is exempt from liability only if:

(a) he is exempt under the preceding paragraph; and

(b) the person whom he has so engaged would be so exempt if the provisions of that paragraph were applied to him.

(3) The exemption provided by this article has effect for the period during which the impediment exists.

(4) The party who fails to perform must give notice to the other party of the impediment and its effect on his ability to perform. If the notice is not received

by the other party within a reasonable time after the party who fails to perform knew or ought to have known of the impediment, he is liable for damages resulting from such non-receipt.

(5) Nothing in this article prevents either party from exercising any right other than to claim damages under this Convention.

Article 80

A party may not rely on a failure of the other party to perform, to the extent that such failure was caused by the first party's act or omission.

Section V Effects of avoidance

Article 81

(1) Avoidance of the contract releases both parties from their obligations under it, subject to any damages which may be due. Avoidance does not affect any provision of the contract for the settlement of disputes or any other provision of the contract governing the rights and obligations of the parties consequent upon the avoidance of the contract.

(2) A party who has performed the contract either wholly or in part may claim restitution from the other party of whatever the first party has supplied or paid under the contract. If both parties are bound to make restitution, they must do so concurrently.

Article 82

(1) The buyer loses the right to declare the contract avoided or to require the seller to deliver substitute goods if it is impossible for him to make restitution of the goods substantially in the condition in which he received them.

(2) The preceding paragraph does not apply:

(a) if the impossibility of making restitution of the goods or of making restitution of the goods substantially in the condition in which the buyer received them is not due to his act or omission;

(b) if the goods or part of the goods have perished or deteriorated as a result of the examination provided for in article 38; or

(c) if the goods or part of the goods have been sold in the normal course of business or have been consumed or transformed by the buyer in the course of normal use before he discovered or ought to have discovered the lack of conformity.

Article 83

A buyer who has lost the right to declare the contract avoided or to require the seller to deliver substitute goods in accordance with article 82 retains all other remedies under the contract and this Convention.

Article 84

(1) If the seller is bound to refund the price, he must also pay interest on it, from the date on which the price was paid.

(2) The buyer must account to the seller for all benefits which he has derived from the goods or part of them:

(a) if he must make restitution of the goods or part of them; or

(b) if it is impossible for him to make restitution of all or part of the goods or to make restitution of all or part of the goods substantially in the condition in which he received them, but he has nevertheless declared the contract avoided or required the seller to deliver substitute goods.

Section VI Preservation of the goods

Article 85

If the buyer is in delay in taking delivery of the goods or, where payment of the price and delivery of the goods are to be made concurrently, if he fails to pay the price, and the seller is either in possession of the goods or otherwise able to control their disposition, the seller must take such steps as are reasonable in the circumstances to preserve them. He is entitled to retain them until he has been reimbursed his reasonable expenses by the buyer.

Article 86

(1) If the buyer has received the goods and intends to exercise any right under the contract or this Convention to reject them, he must take such steps to preserve them as are reasonable in the circumstances. He is entitled to retain them until he has been reimbursed his reasonable expenses by the seller.

(2) If goods dispatched to the buyer have been placed at his disposal at their destination and he exercises the right to reject them, he must take possession of them on behalf of the seller, provided that this can be done without payment of the price and without unreasonable inconvenience or unreasonable expense. This provision does not apply if the seller or a person authorized to take charge of the goods on his behalf is present at the destination. If the buyer takes possession of the goods under this paragraph, his rights and obligations are governed by the preceding paragraph.

Article 87

A party who is bound to take steps to preserve the goods may deposit them in a warehouse of a third person at the expense of the other party provided that the expense incurred is not unreasonable.

Article 88

(1) A party who is bound to preserve the goods in accordance with article 85 or 86 may sell them by any appropriate means if there has been an unreasonable delay by the other party in taking possession of the goods or in taking them back or in paying the price or the cost of preservation, provided that reasonable notice of the intention to sell has been given to the other party.

(2) If the goods are subject to rapid deterioration or their preservation would involve unreasonable expense, a party who is bound to preserve the goods in accordance with article 85 or 86 must take reasonable measures to sell them. To the extent possible he must give notice to the other party of his intention to sell.

(3) A party selling the goods has the right to retain out of the proceeds of sale an amount equal to the reasonable expenses of preserving the goods and of selling them. He must account to the other party for the balance.

PART IV FINAL PROVISIONS

Article 89

The Secretary-General of the United Nations is hereby designated as the depositary for this Convention.

Article 90

This Convention does not prevail over any international agreement which has already been or may be entered into and which contains provisions concerning the matters governed by this Convention, provided that the parties have their places of business in States parties to such agreement.

Article 91

(1) This Convention is open for signature at the concluding meeting of the United Nations Conference on Contracts for the International Sale of Goods and will remain open for signature by all States at the Headquarters of the United Nations, New York until 30 September 1981.

(2) This Convention is subject to ratification, acceptance or approval by the signatory States.

(3) This Convention is open for accession by all States which are not signatory States as from the date it is open for signature.

(4) Instruments of ratification, acceptance, approval and accession are to be deposited with the Secretary-General of the United Nations.

Article 92

(1) A Contracting State may declare at the time of signature, ratification, acceptance, approval or accession that it will not be bound by Part II of this Convention or that it will not be bound by Part III of this Convention.

(2) A Contracting State which makes a declaration in accordance with the preceding paragraph in respect of Part II or Part III of this Convention is not to be considered a Contracting State within paragraph (1) of article 1 of this Convention in respect of matters governed by the Part to which the declaration applies.

Article 93

(1) If a Contracting State has two or more territorial units in which, according to its constitution, different systems of law are applicable in relation to the matters dealt with in this Convention, it may, at the time of signature, ratification, acceptance, approval or accession, declare that this Convention is to extend to all its territorial units or only to one or more of them, and may amend its declaration by submitting another declaration at any time.

(2) These declarations are to be notified to the depositary and are to state expressly the territorial units to which the Convention extends.

(3) If, by virtue of a declaration under this article, this Convention extends to one or more but not all of the territorial units of a Contracting State, and if the place of business of a party is located in that State, this place of business, for the purposes of this Convention, is considered not to be in a Contracting State, unless it is in a territorial unit to which the Convention extends.

(4) If a Contracting State makes no declaration under paragraph (1) of this article, the Convention is to extend to all territorial units of that State.

Article 94

(1) Two or more Contracting States which have the same or closely related legal rules on matters governed by this Convention may at any time declare that the Convention is not to apply to contracts of sale or to their formation where the parties have their places of business in those States. Such declarations may be made jointly or by reciprocal unilateral declarations.

(2) A Contracting State which has the same or closely related legal rules on matters governed by this Convention as one or more non-Contracting States may at any time declare that the Convention is not to apply to contracts of sale or to their

formation where the parties have their places of business in those States.

(3) If a State which is the object of a declaration under the preceding paragraph subsequently becomes a Contracting State, the declaration made will, as from the date on which the Convention enters into force in respect of the new Contracting State, have the effect of a declaration made under paragraph (1), provided that the new Contracting State joins in such declaration or makes a reciprocal unilateral declaration.

Article 95

Any State may declare at the time of the deposit of its instrument of ratification, acceptance, approval or accession that it will not be bound by subparagraph (1)(b) of article 1 of this Convention.

Article 96

A Contracting State whose legislation requires contracts of sale to be concluded in or evidenced by writing may at any time make a declaration in accordance with article 12 that any provision of article 11, article 29, or Part II of this Convention, that allows a contract of sale or its modification or termination by agreement or any offer, acceptance, or other indication of intention to be made in any form other than in writing, does not apply where any party has his place of business in that State.

Article 97

(1) Declarations made under this Convention at the time of signature are subject to confirmation upon ratification, acceptance or approval.

(2) Declarations and confirmations of declarations are to be in writing and be formally notified to the depositary.

(3) A declaration takes effect simultaneously with the entry into force of this Convention in respect of the State concerned. However, a declaration of which the depositary receives formal notification after such entry into force takes effect on the first day of the month following the expiration of six months after the date of its receipt by the depositary. Reciprocal unilateral declarations under article 94 take effect on the first day of the month following the expiration of six months after the receipt of the latest declaration by the depositary.

(4) Any State which makes a declaration under this Convention may withdraw it at any time by a formal notification in writing addressed to the depositary. Such withdrawal is to take effect on the first day of the month following the expiration of six months after the date of the receipt of the notification by the depositary.

(5) A withdrawal of a declaration made under article 94 renders inoperative, as from

the date on which the withdrawal takes effect, any reciprocal declaration made by another State under that article.

Article 98

No reservations are permitted except those expressly authorized in this Convention.

Article 99

(1) This Convention enters into force, subject to the provisions of paragraph (6) of this article, on the first day of the month following the expiration of twelve months after the date of deposit of the tenth instrument of ratification, acceptance, approval or accession, including an instrument which contains a declaration made under article 92.

(2) When a State ratifies, accepts, approves or accedes to this Convention after the deposit of the tenth instrument of ratification, acceptance, approval or accession, this Convention, with the exception of the Part excluded, enters into force in respect of that State, subject to the provisions of paragraph (6) of this article, on the first day of the month following the expiration of twelve months after the date of the deposit of its instrument of ratification, acceptance, approval or accession.

(3) A State which ratifies, accepts, approves or accedes to this Convention and is a party to either or both the Convention relating to a Uniform Law on the Formation of Contracts for the International Sale of Goods done at The Hague on 1 July 1964 (1964 Hague Formation Convention) and the Convention relating to a Uniform Law on the International Sale of Goods done at The Hague on 1 July 1964 (1964 Hague Sales Convention) shall at the same time denounce, as the case may be, either or both the 1964 Hague Sales Convention and the 1964 Hague Formation Convention by notifying the Government of the Netherlands to that effect.

(4) A State party to the 1964 Hague Sales Convention which ratifies, accepts, approves or accedes to the present Convention and declares or has declared under article 52 that it will not be bound by Part II of this Convention shall at the time of ratification, acceptance, approval or accession denounce the 1964 Hague Sales Convention by notifying the Government of the Netherlands to that effect.

(5) A State party to the 1964 Hague Formation Convention which ratifies, accepts, approves or accedes to the present Convention and declares or has declared under article 92 that it will not be bound by Part III of this Convention shall at the time of ratification, acceptance, approval or accession denounce the 1964 Hague Formation Convention by notifying the Government of the Netherlands to that effect.

(6) For the purpose of this article, ratifications, acceptances, approvals and accessions

in respect of this Convention by States parties to the 1964 Hague Formation Convention or to the 1964 Hague Sales Convention shall not be effective until such denunciations as may be required on the part of those States in respect of the latter two Conventions have themselves become effective. The depositary of this Convention shall consult with the Government of the Netherlands, as the depositary of the 1964 Conventions, so as to ensure necessary co-ordination in this respect.

Article 100

(1) This Convention applies to the formation of a contract only when the proposal for concluding the contract is made on or after the date when the Convention enters into force in respect of the Contracting States referred to in subparagraph (1)(a) or the Contracting State referred to in subparagraph (1)(b) of article 1.

(2) This Convention applies only to contracts concluded on or after the date when the Convention enters into force in respect of the Contracting States referred to in subparagraph (1)(a) or the Contracting State referred to in subparagraph (1)(b) of article 1.

Article 101

(1) A Contracting State may denounce this Convention, or Part II or Part III of the Convention, by a formal notification in writing addressed to the depositary.

(2) The denunciation takes effect on the first day of the month following the expiration of twelve months after the notification is received by the depositary. Where a longer period for the denunciation to take effect is specified in the notification, the denunciation takes effect upon the expiration of such longer period after the notification is received by the depositary.

DONE at Vienna, this day of eleventh day of April, one thousand nine hundred and eighty, in a single original, of which the Arabic, Chinese, English, French, Russian and Spanish texts are equally authentic.

IN WITNESS WHEREOF the undersigned plenipotentiaries, being duly authorized by their respective Governments, have signed this Convention.

Appendix II

INCOTERMS 2000:
ICC Official Rules for the Interpretation of Trade Terms

(Excerpts)

FOB—Free On Board (...named port of shipment)

"Free on Board" means that the seller delivers when the goods pass the ship's rail at the named port of shipment. This means that the buyer has to bear all costs and risks of loss of or damage to the goods from that point. The FOB term requires the seller to clear the goods for export. This term can be used only for sea or inland waterway transport. If the parties do not intend to deliver the goods across the ship's rail, the FCA term should be used.

A. THE SELLER'S OBLIGATIONS

B. THE BUYER'S OBLIGATIONS

A1 Provision of goods in conformity with the contract

The seller must provide the goods and the commercial invoice, or its equivalent electronic message, in conformity with the contract of sale and any other evidence of conformity which may be required by the contract.

B1 Payment of the price

The buyer must pay the price as provided in the contract of sale.

A2 Licences, authorisations and formalities

The seller must obtain at his own risk and expense any export licence or other official authorisation and carry out, where applicable, all customs formalities necessary for the export of the goods.

B2 Licences, authorisations and formalities

The buyer must obtain at his own risk and expense any import licence or other official authorisation and carry out, where applicable, all customs formalities for the import of the goods and, where necessary, for their transit through any country.

A3 Contracts of carriage and insurance

a) Contract of carriage

No obligation

b) Contract of insurance

No obligation

B3 Contracts of carriage and insurance

a) Contract of carriage

The buyer must contract at his own expense for the carriage of the goods from the named port of shipment.

b) Contract of insurance

No obligation

A4 Delivery

The seller must deliver the goods on the date or within the agreed period at the named port of shipment and in the manner customary at the port on board the vessel nominated by the buyer.

B4 Taking delivery

The buyer must take delivery of the goods when they have been delivered in accordance with A4.

A5 Transfer of risks

The seller must, subject to the provisions of B5, bear all risks of loss of or damage to the goods until such time as they have passed the ship's rail at the named port of shipment.

B5 Transfer of risks

The buyer must bear all risks of loss of or damage to the goods

- from the time they have passed the ship's rail at the named port of shipment; and
- from the agreed date or the expiry date of the agreed period for delivery which arise because he fails to give notice in accordance with B7, or because the vessel nominated by him fails to arrive on time, or is unable to take the goods, or closes for cargo earlier than the time notified in accordance with B7, provided, however, that the goods have been duly appropriated to the contract, that is to say, clearly set aside or otherwise identified as the contract goods.

A6 Division of costs

The seller must, subject to the provisions of B6, pay

- all costs relating to the goods until such time as they have passed the ship's rail at the named port of shipment; and

- where applicable, the costs of customs formalities necessary for export as well as all duties, taxes and other charges payable upon export.

B6 Division of costs

The buyer must pay

- all costs relating to the goods from the time they have passed the ship's rail at the named port of shipment; and
- any additional costs incurred, either because the vessel nominated by him fails to arrive on time, or is unable to take the goods, or closes for cargo earlier than the time notified in accordance with B7, or because the buyer has failed to give appropriate notice in accordance with B7, provided, however, that the goods have been duly appropriated to the contract, that is to say, clearly set aside or otherwise identified as the contract goods; and
- where applicable, all duties, taxes and other charges as well as the costs of carrying out customs formalities payable upon import of the goods and for their transit through any country.

A7 Notice to the buyer

The seller must give the buyer sufficient notice that the goods have been delivered in accordance with A4.

B7 Notice to the seller

The buyer must give the seller sufficient notice of the vessel name, loading point and required delivery time.

A8 Proof of delivery, transport document or equivalent electronic message

The seller must provide the buyer at the seller's expense with the usual proof of delivery in accordance with A4.

Unless the document referred to in the preceding paragraph is the transport document, the seller must render the buyer, at the latter's request, risk and expense, every assistance in obtaining a transport document for the contract of carriage (for example, a negotiable bill of lading, a non-negotiable sea waybill, an inland waterway document, or a multimodal transport document).

Where the seller and the buyer have agreed to communicate electronically, the document referred to in the preceding paragraph may be replaced by an equivalent electronic data interchange (EDI) message.

B8 Proof of delivery, transport document or equivalent electronic message

The buyer must accept the proof of delivery in accordance with A8.

A9 Checking - packaging - marking

The seller must pay the costs of those checking operations (such as checking quality, measuring, weighing, counting) which are necessary for the purpose of delivering the goods in accordance with A4.
The seller must provide at his own expense packaging (unless it is usual for the particular trade to ship the goods of the contract description unpacked) which is required for the transport of the goods, to the extent that the circumstances relating to the transport (for example modalities, destination) are made known to the seller before the contract of sale is concluded. Packaging is to be marked appropriately.

B9 Inspection of goods

The buyer must pay the costs of any pre-shipment inspection except when such inspection is mandated by the authorities of the country of export.

A10 Other obligations

The seller must render the buyer at the latter's request, risk and expense, every assistance in obtaining any documents or equivalent electronic messages (other than those mentioned in A8) issued or transmitted in the country of shipment and/or of origin which the buyer may require for the import of the goods and, where necessary, for their transit through any country.
The seller must provide the buyer, upon request, with the necessary information for procuring insurance.

B10 Other obligations

The buyer must pay all costs and charges incurred in obtaining the documents or equivalent electronic messages mentioned in A10 and reimburse those incurred by the seller in rendering his assistance in accordance therewith.

CFR—Cost and Freight (...named port of destination)

"Cost and Freight" means that the seller delivers when the goods pass the ship's rail in the port of shipment.
The seller must pay the costs and freight necessary to bring the goods to the named port of destination BUT the risk of loss of or damage to the goods, as well as any additional costs due to events occurring after the time of delivery, are transferred from the seller to the buyer.
The CFR term requires the seller to clear the goods for export. This term can be used only for sea and inland waterway transport. If the parties do not intend to deliver the

goods across the ship's rail, the CPT term should be used.

A. THE SELLER'S OBLIGATIONS
B. THE BUYER'S OBLIGATIONS

A1 Provision of goods in conformity with the contract

The seller must provide the goods and the commercial invoice, or its equivalent electronic message, in conformity with the contract of sale and any other evidence of conformity which may be required by the contract.

B1 Payment of the price

The buyer must pay the price as provided in the contract of sale.

A2 Licences, authorisations and formalities

The seller must obtain at his own risk and expense any export licence or other official authorisation and carry out, where applicable, all customs formalities necessary for the export of the goods.

B2 Licences, authorisations and formalities

The buyer must obtain at his own risk and expense any import licence or other official authorisation and carry out, where applicable, all customs formalities for the import of the goods and for their transit through any country.

A3 Contracts of carriage and insurance

a) Contract of carriage

The seller must contract on usual terms at his own expense for the carriage of the goods to the named port of destination by the usual route in a seagoing vessel (or inland waterway vessel as the case may be) of the type normally used for the transport of goods of the contract description.

b) Contract of insurance

No obligation

B3 Contracts of carriage and insurance

a) Contract of carriage

No obligation

b) Contract of insurance

No obligation

A4 Delivery

The seller must deliver the goods on board the vessel at the port of shipment on the date or within the agreed period.

B4 Taking delivery

The buyer must accept delivery of the goods when they have been delivered in accordance with A4 and receive them from the carrier at the named port of destination.

A5 Transfer of risks

The seller must, subject to the provisions of B5, bear all risks of loss of or damage to the goods until such time as they have passed the ship's rail at the port of shipment.

B5 Transfer of risks

The buyer must bear all risks of loss of or damage to the goods from the time they have passed the ship's rail at the port of shipment.

The buyer must, should he fail to give notice in accordance with B7, bear all risks of loss of or damage to the goods from the agreed date or the expiry date of the period fixed for shipment provided, however, that the goods have been duly appropriated to the contract, that is to say, clearly set aside or otherwise identified as the contract goods.

A6 Division of costs

- The seller must, subject to the provisions of B6, pay
- all costs relating to the goods until such time as they have been delivered in accordance with A4; and
- the freight and all other costs resulting from A3 a), including the costs of loading the goods on board and any charges for unloading at the agreed port of discharge which were for the seller's account under the contract of carriage; and
- where applicable, the costs of customs formalities necessary for export as well as all duties, taxes and other charges payable upon export, and for their transit through any country if they were for the seller's account under the contract of carriage.

B6 Division of costs

The buyer must, subject to the provisions of A3 a), pay

- all costs relating to the goods from the time they have been delivered in accordance with A4; and
- all costs and charges relating to the goods whilst in transit until their arrival at the port of destination, unless such costs and charges were for the seller's account under the contract of carriage; and
- unloading costs including lighterage and wharfage charges, unless such costs

and charges were for the seller's account under the contract of carriage; and

- all additional costs incurred if he fails to give notice in accordance with B7, for the goods from the agreed date or the expiry date of the period fixed for shipment, provided, however, that the goods have been duly appropriated to the contract, that is to say, clearly set aside or otherwise identified as the contract goods; and
- where applicable, all duties, taxes and other charges as well as the costs of carrying out customs formalities payable upon import of the goods and, where necessary, for their transit through any country unless included within the cost of the contract of carriage.

A7 Notice to the buyer

The seller must give the buyer sufficient notice that the goods have been delivered in accordance with A4 as well as any other notice required in order to allow the buyer to take measures which are normally necessary to enable him to take the goods.

B7 Notice to the seller

The buyer must, whenever he is entitled to determine the time for shipping the goods and/or the port of destination, give the seller sufficient notice thereof.

A8 Proof of delivery, transport document or equivalent electronic message

The seller must at his own expense provide the buyer without delay with the usual transport document for the agreed port of destination.

This document (for example a negotiable bill of lading, a non-negotiable sea waybill or an inland waterway document) must cover the contract goods, be dated within the period agreed for shipment, enable the buyer to claim the goods from the carrier at the port of destination and, unless otherwise agreed, enable the buyer to sell the goods in transit by the transfer of the document to a subsequent buyer (the negotiable bill of lading) or by notification to the carrier.

When such a transport document is issued in several originals, a full set of originals must be presented to the buyer.

Where the seller and the buyer have agreed to communicate electronically, the document referred to in the preceding paragraphs may be replaced by an equivalent electronic data interchange (EDI) message.

B8 Proof of delivery, transport document or equivalent electronic message

The buyer must accept the transport document in accordance with A8 if it is in conformity with the contract.

A9 Checking - packaging - marking

The seller must pay the costs of those checking operations (such as checking quality, measuring, weighing, counting) which are necessary for the purpose of delivering the goods in accordance with A4.

The seller must provide at his own expense packaging (unless it is usual for the particular trade to ship the goods of the contract description unpacked) which is required for the transport of the goods arranged by him. Packaging is to be marked appropriately.

B9 Inspection of goods

The buyer must pay the costs of any pre-shipment inspection except when such inspection is mandated by the authorities of the country of export.

A10 Other obligations

The seller must render the buyer at the latter's request, risk and expense, every assistance in obtaining any documents or equivalent electronic messages (other than those mentioned in A8) issued or transmitted in the country of shipment and/or of origin which the buyer may require for the import of the goods and, where necessary, for their transit through any country.

The seller must provide the buyer, upon request, with the necessary information for procuring insurance.

B10 Other obligations

The buyer must pay all costs and charges incurred in obtaining the documents or equivalent electronic messages mentioned in A10 and reimburse those incurred by the seller in rendering his assistance in accordance therewith.

CIF—Cost, Insurance and Freight (...named port of destination)

"Cost, Insurance and Freight" means that the seller delivers when the goods pass the ship's rail in the port of shipment.

The seller must pay the costs and freight necessary to bring the goods to the named port of destination BUT the risk of loss of or damage to the goods, as well as any additional costs due to events occurring after the time of delivery, are transferred from the seller to the buyer.

CIF the seller also has to procure marine insurance against the buyer's risk of loss of or damage to the goods during the carriage.

Consequently, the seller contracts for insurance and pays the insurance premium.

The buyer should note that under the CIF term the seller is required to obtain insurance only on minimum cover. Should the buyer wish to have the protection of greater cover, he would either need to agree as much expressly with the seller or to make his own extra insurance arrangements.

The CIF term requires the seller to clear the goods for export. This term can be used only for sea and inland waterway transport. If the parties do not intend to deliver the goods across the ship's rail, the CIP term should be used.

A. THE SELLER'S OBLIGATIONS

B. THE BUYER'S OBLIGATIONS

A1 Provision of goods in conformity with the contract

The seller must provide the goods and the commercial invoice, or its equivalent electronic message, in conformity with the contract of sale and any other evidence of conformity which may be required by the contract.

B1 Payment of the price

The buyer must pay the price as provided in the contract of sale.

A2 Licences, authorisations and formalities

The seller must obtain at his own risk and expense any export licence or other official authorisation and carry out, where applicable, all customs formalities necessary for the export of the goods.

B2 Licences, authorisations and formalities

The buyer must obtain at his own risk and expense any import licence or other official authorisation and carry out, where applicable, all customs formalities for the import of the goods and for their transit through any country.

A3 Contracts of carriage and insurance

a) Contract of carriage

The seller must contract on usual terms at his own expense for the carriage of the goods to the named port of destination by the usual route in a seagoing vessel (or inland waterway vessel as the case may be) of the type normally used for the transport of goods of the contract description.

b) Contract of insurance

No obligation

B3 Contracts of carriage and insurance

a) Contract of carriage

No obligation

b) Contract of insurance

No obligation

A4 Delivery

The seller must deliver the goods on board the vessel at the port of shipment on the date or within the agreed period.

B4 Taking delivery

The buyer must accept delivery of the goods when they have been delivered in accordance with A4 and receive them from the carrier at the named port of destination.

A5 Transfer of risks

The seller must, subject to the provisions of B5, bear all risks of loss of or damage to the goods until such time as they have passed the ship's rail at the port of shipment.

B5 Transfer of risks

The buyer must bear all risks of loss of or damage to the goods from the time they have passed the ship's rail at the port of shipment.

The buyer must, should he fail to give notice in accordance with B7, bear all risks of loss of or damage to the goods from the agreed date or the expiry date of the period fixed for shipment provided, however, that the goods have been duly appropriated to the contract, that is to say, clearly set aside or otherwise identified as the contract goods.

A6 Division of costs

The seller must, subject to the provisions of B6, pay

- all costs relating to the goods until such time as they have been delivered in accordance with A4; and
- the freight and all other costs resulting from A3 a), including the costs of loading the goods on board; and
- the costs of insurance resulting from A3 b); and
- any charges for unloading at the agreed port of discharge which were for the seller's account under the contract of carriage; and
- where applicable, the costs of customs formalities necessary for export as well as all duties, taxes and other charges payable upon export, and for their transit through any country if they were for the seller's account under the contract of carriage.

B6 Division of costs

The buyer must, subject to the provisions of A3, pay

- all costs relating to the goods from the time they have been delivered in accordance with A4; and
- all costs and charges relating to the goods whilst in transit until their arrival at the port of destination, unless such costs and charges were for the seller's account under the contract of carriage; and
- unloading costs including lighterage and wharfage charges, unless such costs and charges were for the seller's account under the contract of carriage; and
- all additional costs incurred if he fails to give notice in accordance with B7, for the goods from the agreed date or the expiry date of the period fixed for shipment, provided, however, that the goods have been duly appropriated to the contract, that is to say, clearly set aside or otherwise identified as the contract goods; and
- where applicable, all duties, taxes and other charges as well as the costs of carrying out customs formalities payable upon import of the goods and, where necessary, for their transit through any country unless included within the cost of the contract of carriage.

A7 Notice to the buyer

The seller must give the buyer sufficient notice that the goods have been delivered in accordance with A4 as well as any other notice required in order to allow the buyer to take measures which are normally necessary to enable him to take the goods.

B7 Notice to the seller

The buyer must, whenever he is entitled to determine the time for shipping the goods and/or the port of destination, give the seller sufficient notice thereof.

A8 Proof of delivery, transport document or equivalent electronic message

The seller must, at his own expense, provide the buyer without delay with the usual transport document for the agreed port of destination.

This document (for example a negotiable bill of lading, a non-negotiable sea waybill or an inland waterway document) must cover the contract goods, be dated within the period agreed for shipment, enable the buyer to claim the goods from the carrier at the port of destination and, unless otherwise agreed, enable the buyer to sell the goods in transit by the transfer of the document to a subsequent buyer (the negotiable bill of lading) or by notification to the carrier.

When such a transport document is issued in several originals, a full set of originals must be presented to the buyer. Where the seller and the buyer have agreed to communicate electronically, the document referred to in the preceding paragraphs may be replaced by an equivalent electronic data interchange (EDI) message.

B8 Proof of delivery, transport document or equivalent electronic message

The buyer must accept the transport document in accordance with A8 if it is in conformity with the contract.

A9 Checking - packaging - marking

The seller must pay the costs of those checking operations (such as checking quality, measuring, weighing, counting) which are necessary for the purpose of delivering the goods in accordance with A4.

The seller must provide at his own expense packaging (unless it is usual for the particular trade to ship the goods of the contract description unpacked) which is required for the transport of the goods arranged by him. Packaging is to be marked appropriately.

B9 Inspection of goods

The buyer must pay the costs of any pre-shipment inspection except when such inspection is mandated by the authorities of the country of export.

A10 Other obligations

The seller must render the buyer at the latter's request, risk and expense, every assistance in obtaining any documents or equivalent electronic messages (other than those mentioned in A8) issued or transmitted in the country of shipment and/or of origin which the buyer may require for the import of the goods and, where necessary, for their transit through any country.

The seller must provide the buyer, upon request, with the necessary information for procuring any additional insurance.

B10 Other obligations

The buyer must pay all costs and charges incurred in obtaining the documents or equivalent electronic messages mentioned in A10 and reimburse those incurred by the seller in rendering his assistance in accordance therewith.

The buyer must provide the seller, upon request, with the necessary information for procuring insurance.

FCA—Free Carrier (...named place)

"Free Carrier" means that the seller delivers the goods, cleared for export, to the carrier nominated by the buyer at the named place. It should be noted that the chosen place of delivery has an impact on the obligations of loading and unloading the goods at that place. If delivery occurs at the seller's premises, the seller is responsible for loading. If delivery occurs at any other place, the seller is not responsible for unloading.

This term may be used irrespective of the mode of transport, including multimodal transport.

"Carrier" means any person who, in a contract of carriage, undertakes to perform or to procure the performance of transport by rail, road, air, sea, inland waterway or by a combination of such modes.

If the buyer nominates a person other than a carrier to receive the goods, the seller is deemed to have fulfilled his obligation to deliver the goods when they are delivered to that person.

A. THE SELLER'S OBLIGATIONS

B. THE BUYER'S OBLIGATIONS

A1 Provision of goods in conformity with the contract

The seller must provide the goods and the commercial invoice, or its equivalent electronic message, in conformity with the contract of sale and any other evidence of conformity which may be required by the contract.

B1 Payment of the price

The buyer must pay the price as provided in the contract of sale.

A2 Payment of the price

The buyer must pay the price as provided in the contract of sale.

B2 Licences, authorisations and formalities

The buyer must obtain at his own risk and expense any import licence or other official authorisation and carry out, where applicable, all customs formalities for the import of the goods and for their transit through any country.

A3 Contracts of carriage and insurance

a) Contract of carriage

No obligation. However, if requested by the buyer or if it is commercial practice and the buyer does not give an instruction to the contrary in due time, the seller may contract for carriage on usual terms at the buyer's risk and expense. In either case, the seller may decline to make the contract and, if he does, shall promptly notify the buyer accordingly.

b) Contract of insurance

No obligation

B3 Contracts of carriage and insurance

a) Contract of carriage

The buyer must contract at his own expense for the carriage of the goods from the named place, except when the contract of carriage is made by the seller as provided for in A3 a).

b) Contract of insurance

No obligation

A4 Delivery

The seller must deliver the goods to the carrier or another person nominated by the buyer, or chosen by the seller in accordance with A3 a), at the named place on the date or within the period agreed for delivery. Delivery is completed;

a) If the named place is the seller's premises, when the goods have been loaded on the means of transport provided by the carrier nominated by the buyer or another person acting on his behalf.

b) If the named place is anywhere other than a), when the goods are placed at the disposal of the carrier or another person nominated by the buyer, or chosen by the seller in accordance with A3 a) on the seller's means of transport not unloaded.

If no specific point has been agreed within the named place, and if there are several points available, the seller may select the point at the place of delivery which best suits his purpose.

Failing precise instructions from the buyer, the seller may deliver the goods for carriage in such a manner as the transport mode and/or the quantity and/or nature of the goods may require.

B4 Taking delivery

The buyer must take delivery of the goods when they have been delivered in accordance with A4.

A5 Transfer of risks

The seller must, subject to the provisions of B5, bear all risks of loss of or damage to the goods until such time as they have been delivered in accordance with A4.

B5 Transfer of risks

The buyer must bear all risks of loss of or damage to the goods

- from the time they have been delivered in accordance with A4;and
- from the agreed date or the expiry date of any agreed period for delivery which arise either because he fails to nominate the carrier or another person in accordance with A4, or because the carrier or the party nominated by the buyer fails to take the goods into his charge at the agreed time, or because the buyer fails to give appropriate notice in accordance with B7, provided, however, that the goods have been duly appropriated to the contract, that is to say, clearly set aside or otherwise identified as the contract goods.

A6 Division of costs

The seller must, subject to the provisions of B6, pay

- all costs relating to the goods until such time as they have been delivered in accordance with A4; and
- where applicable, the costs of customs formalities as well as all duties, taxes, and other charges payable upon export.

B6 Division of costs

The buyer must pay

- all costs relating to the goods from the time they have been delivered in accordance with A4; and
- any additional costs incurred, either because he fails to nominate the carrier or another person in accordance with A4 or because the party nominated by the buyer fails to take the goods into his charge at the agreed time, or because he has failed to give appropriate notice in accordance with B7, provided, however, that the goods have been duly appropriated to the contract, that is to say, clearly set aside or otherwise identified as the contract goods; and
- where applicable, all duties, taxes and other charges as well as the costs of carrying out customs formalities payable upon import of the goods and for their transit through any country.

A7 Notice to the buyer

The seller must give the buyer sufficient notice that the goods have been delivered in accordance with A4. Should the carrier fail to take delivery in accordance with A4 at the time agreed, the seller must notify the buyer accordingly.

B7 Notice to the seller

The buyer must give the seller sufficient notice of the name of the party designated in A4 and, where necessary, specify the mode of transport, as well as the date or period for delivering the goods to him and, as the case may be, the point within the place where the goods should be delivered to that party.

A8 Proof of delivery, transport document or equivalent electronic message

The seller must provide the buyer at the seller's expense with the usual proof of delivery of the goods in accordance with A4.

Unless the document referred to in the preceding paragraph is the transport document, the seller must render the buyer at the latter's request, risk and expense, every assistance in obtaining a transport document for the contract of carriage (for example a negotiable bill of lading, a non-negotiable sea waybill, an inland waterway document, an air waybill, a railway consignment note, a road consignment note, or a multimodal transport document).

When the seller and the buyer have agreed to communicate electronically, the document referred to in the preceding paragraph may be replaced by an equivalent electronic data interchange (EDI) message.

B8 Proof of delivery, transport document or equivalent electronic message

The buyer must accept the proof of delivery in accordance with A8.

A9 Checking - packaging - marking

The seller must pay the costs of those checking operations (such as checking quality, measuring, weighing, counting) which are necessary for the purpose of delivering the goods in accordance with A4.

The seller must provide at his own expense packaging (unless it is usual for the particular trade to send the goods of the contract description unpacked) which is required for the transport of the goods, to the extent that the circumstances relating to the transport (for example modalities, destination) are made known to the seller before the contract of sale is concluded. Packaging is to be marked appropriately.

B9 Inspection of goods

The buyer must pay the costs of any pre-shipment inspection except when such inspection is mandated by the authorities of the country of export.

A10 Other obligations

The seller must render the buyer at the latter's request, risk and expense, every assistance in obtaining any documents or equivalent electronic messages (other than those mentioned in A8) issued or transmitted in the country of delivery and/or of origin which the buyer may require for the import of the goods and, where necessary, for their transit through any country.

The seller must provide the buyer, upon request, with the necessary information for procuring insurance.

B10 Other obligations

The buyer must pay all costs and charges incurred in obtaining the documents or equivalent electronic messages mentioned in A10 and reimburse those incurred by the seller in rendering his assistance in accordance therewith and in contracting for carriage in accordance with A3 a).

The buyer must give the seller appropriate instructions whenever the seller's assistance in contracting for carriage is required in accordance with A3 a).

CPT—Carriage Paid To (...named place of destination)

"Carriage paid to..." means that the seller delivers the goods to the carrier nominated by him but the seller must in addition pay the cost of carriage necessary to bring the goods to the named destination. This means that the buyer bears all risks and any other costs occurring after the goods have been so delivered.

"Carrier" means any person who, in a contract of carriage, undertakes to perform or to procure the performance of transport, by rail, road, air, sea, inland waterway or by a combination of such modes. If subsequent carriers are used for the carriage to the agreed destination, the risk passes when the goods have been delivered to the first carrier.

The CPT term requires the seller to clear the goods for export. This term may be used irrespective of the mode of transport including multimodal transport.

A. THE SELLER'S OBLIGATIONS

B. THE BUYER'S OBLIGATIONS

A1 Provision of goods in conformity with the contract

The seller must provide the goods and the commercial invoice, or its equivalent electronic message, in conformity with the contract of sale and any other evidence of conformity which may be required by the contract.

B1 Payment of the price

The buyer must pay the price as provided in the contract of sale.

A2 Licences, authorisations and formalities

The seller must obtain at his own risk and expense any export licence or other official authorisation and carry out, where applicable, all customs formalities necessary for the export of the goods.

B2 Licences, authorisations and formalities

The buyer must obtain at his own risk and expense any import licence or other official authorisation and carry out, where applicable, all customs formalities for the import of the goods and for their transit through any country.

A3 Contracts of carriage and insurance

a) Contract of carriage

The seller must contract on usual terms at his own expense for the carriage of the goods to the agreed point at the named place of destination by a usual route and in a customary manner. If a point is not agreed or is not determined by practice, the seller may select the point at the named place of destination which best suits his purpose.

b) Contract of insurance

No obligation

B3 Contracts of carriage and insurance

a) Contract of carriage

No obligation

b) Contract of insurance

No obligation

A4 Delivery

The seller must deliver the goods to the carrier contracted in accordance with A3 or, if there are subsequent carriers to the first carrier, for transport to the agreed point at the named place on the date or within the agreed period.

B4 Taking delivery

The buyer must accept delivery of the goods when they have been delivered in accordance with A4 and receive them from the carrier at the named place.

A5 Transfer of risks

The seller must, subject to the provisions of B5, bear all risks of loss of or damage to the goods until such time as they have been delivered in accordance with A4.

B5 Transfer of risks

The buyer must bear all risks of loss of or damage to the goods from the time they have been delivered in accordance with A4.

The buyer must, should he fail to give notice in accordance with B7, bear all risks of the goods from the agreed date or the expiry date of the period fixed for delivery provided, however, that the goods have been duly appropriated to the contract, that is to say, clearly set aside or otherwise identified as the contract goods.

A6 Division of costs

The seller must, subject to the provisions of B6, pay

- all costs relating to the goods until such time as they have been delivered in accordance with A4 as well as the freight and all other costs resulting from A3 a), including the costs of loading the goods and any charges for unloading at the place of destination which were for the seller's account under the contract of carriage; and
- where applicable, the costs of customs formalities necessary for export as well as all duties, taxes or other charges payable upon export, and for their transit through any country if they were for the seller's account under the contract of carriage

B6 Division of costs

The buyer must, subject to the provisions of A3 a), pay

- all costs relating to the goods from the time they have been delivered in accordance with A4; and
- all costs and charges relating to the goods whilst in transit until their arrival at the agreed place of destination, unless such costs and charges were for the seller's account under the contract of carriage; and
- unloading costs unless such costs and charges were for the seller's account under the contract of carriage; and
- all additional costs incurred if he fails to give notice in accordance with B7, for the goods from the agreed date or the expiry date of the period fixed for dispatch, provided, however, that the goods have been duly appropriated to the contract, that is to say, clearly set aside or otherwise identified as the contract goods; and
- where applicable, all duties, taxes and other charges as well as the costs of carrying out customs formalities payable upon import of the goods and for their transit through any country unless included within the cost of the contract of carriage.

A7 Notice to the buyer

The seller must give the buyer sufficient notice that the goods have been delivered in accordance with A4 as well as any other notice required in order to allow the buyer to take measures which are normally necessary to enable him to take the goods.

B7 Notice to the seller

The buyer must, whenever he is entitled to determine the time for dispatching the goods and/or the destination, give the seller sufficient notice thereof.

A8 Proof of delivery, transport document or equivalent electronic message

The seller must provide the buyer at the seller's expense, if customary, with the usual transport document or documents (for example a negotiable bill of lading, a non-negotiable sea waybill, an inland waterway document, an air waybill, a railway consignment note, a road consignment note, or a multimodal transport document) for the transport contracted in accordance with A3.

Where the seller and the buyer have agreed to communicate electronically, the document referred to in the preceding paragraph may be replaced by an equivalent electronic data interchange (EDI) message.

B8 Proof of delivery, transport document or equivalent electronic message

The buyer must accept the transport document in accordance with A8 if it is in conformity with the contract.

A9 Checking - packaging - marking

The seller must pay the costs of those checking operations (such as checking quality, measuring, weighing, counting) which are necessary for the purpose of delivering the goods in accordance with A4.

The seller must provide at his own expense packaging (unless it is usual for the particular trade to send the goods of the contract description unpacked) which is required for the transport of the goods arranged by him. Packaging is to be marked appropriately.

B9 Inspection of goods

The buyer must pay the costs of any pre-shipment inspection except when such inspection is mandated by the authorities of the country of export.

A10 Other obligations

The seller must render the buyer at the latter's request, risk and expense, every assistance in obtaining any documents or equivalent electronic messages (other than those mentioned in A8) issued or transmitted in the country of dispatch and/or of origin which the buyer may require for the import of the goods and for their transit through any country.

The seller must provide the buyer, upon request, with the necessary information for procuring insurance.

B10 Other obligations

The buyer must pay all costs and charges incurred in obtaining the documents or equivalent electronic messages mentioned in A10 and reimburse those incurred by the seller in rendering his assistance in accordance therewith.

CIP—Carriage and Insurance Paid To (...named place of destination)

"Carriage and Insurance paid to..."means that the seller delivers the goods to the carrier nominated by him but the seller must in addition pay the cost of carriage necessary to bring the goods to the named destination. This means that the buyer bears all risks and any additional costs occurring after the goods have been so delivered. However, in CIP the seller also has to procure insurance against the buyer's risk of loss of or damage to the goods during the carriage.

Consequently, the seller contracts for insurance and pays the insurance premium.

The buyer should note that under the CIP term the seller is required to obtain insurance only on minimum cover. Should the buyer wish to have the protection of greater cover, he would either need to agree as much expressly with the seller or to make his own extra insurance arrangements.

"Carrier" means any person who, in a contract of carriage, undertakes to perform or to procure the performance of transport, by rail, road, air, sea, inland waterway or by a combination of such modes.

If subsequent carriers are used for the carriage to the agreed destination, the risk passes when the goods have been delivered to the first carrier.

The CIP term requires the seller to clear the goods for export.

This term may be used irrespective of the mode of transport including multimodal transport.

A. THE SELLER'S OBLIGATIONS

B. THE BUYER'S OBLIGATIONS

A1 Provision of goods in conformity with the contract

The seller must provide the goods and the commercial invoice, or its equivalent electronic message, in conformity with the contract of sale and any other evidence of conformity which may be required by the contract.

B1 Payment of the price

The buyer must pay the price as provided in the contract of sale.

A2 Licences, authorisations and formalities

The seller must obtain at his own risk and expense any export licence or other official authorisation and carry out, where applicable, all customs formalities necessary for the export of the goods.

B2 Licences, authorisations and formalities

The buyer must obtain at his own risk and expense any import licence or other official authorisation and carry out, where applicable, all customs formalities for the import of the goods and for their transit through any country.

A3 Contracts of carriage and insurance

a) Contract of carriage

The seller must contract on usual terms at his own expense for the carriage of the goods to the agreed point at the named place of destination by a usual route and in a customary manner. If a point is not agreed or is not determined by practice, the seller may select the point at the named place of destination which best suits his purpose.

b) Contract of insurance

The seller must obtain at his own expense cargo insurance as agreed in the contract, such that the buyer, or any other person having an insurable interest in the goods, shall be entitled to claim directly from the insurer and provide the buyer with the insurance policy or other evidence of insurance cover.

The insurance shall be contracted with underwriters or an insurance company of good repute and, failing express agreement to the contrary, be in accordance with minimum cover of the Institute Cargo Clauses (Institute of London Underwriters) or any similar set of clauses. The duration of insurance cover shall be in accordance with B5 and B4.

When required by the buyer, the seller shall provide at the buyer's expense war, strikes, riots and civil commotion risk insurances if procurable. The minimum insurance shall cover the price provided in the contract plus ten per cent (i.e. 110 %) and shall be provided in the currency of the contract.

B3 Contracts of carriage and insurance

a) Contract of carriage

No obligation

b) Contract of insurance

No obligation

A4 Delivery

The seller must deliver the goods to the carrier contracted in accordance with A3 or, if there are subsequent carriers to the first carrier, for transport to the agreed point at the named place on the date or within the agreed period.

B4 Taking delivery

The buyer must accept delivery of the goods when they have been delivered in accordance with A4 and receive them from the carrier at the named place.

A5 Transfer of risks

The seller must, subject to the provisions of B5, bear all risks of loss of or damage to the goods until such time as they have been delivered in accordance with A4.

B5 Transfer of risks

The buyer must bear all risks of loss of or damage to the goods from the time they have been delivered in accordance with A4.

The buyer must, should he fail to give notice in accordance with B7, bear all risks of the goods from the agreed date or the expiry date of the period fixed for delivery provided, however, that the goods have been duly appropriated to the contract, that is to say, clearly set aside or otherwise identified as the contract goods.

A6 Division of costs

The seller must, subject to the provisions of B6, pay

- all costs r, elating to the goods until such time as they have been delivered in accordance with A4 as well as the freight and all other costs resulting from A3 a), including the costs of loading the goods and any charges for unloading at the place of destination which were for the seller's account under the contract of carriage; and
- the costs of insurance resulting from A3 b); and
- where applicable, the costs of customs formalities necessary for export as well as all duties, taxes or other charges payable upon export, and for their transit through any country if they were for the seller's account under the contract of carriage.

B6 Division of costs

The buyer must, subject to the provisions of A3 a), pay

- all costs relating to the goods from the time they have been delivered in accordance with A4; and
- all costs and charges relating to the goods whilst in transit until their arrival at the agreed place of destination, unless such costs and charges were for the seller's account under the contract of carriage; and
- unloading costs unless such costs and charges were for the seller's account under the contract of carriage; and
- all additional costs incurred if he fails to give notice in accordance with B7, for the goods from the agreed date or the expiry date of the period fixed for dispatch, provided, however, that the goods have been duly appropriated to the contract, that is to say, clearly set aside or otherwise identified as the contract goods; and
- where applicable, all duties, taxes and other charges as well as the costs of carrying out customs formalities payable upon import of the goods and for their transit through any country unless included within the cost of the contract of carriage.

A7 Notice to the buyer

The seller must give the buyer sufficient notice that the goods have been delivered in accordance with A4 as well as any other notice required in order to allow the buyer to take measures which are normally necessary to enable him to take the goods.

B7 Notice to the seller

The buyer must, whenever he is entitled to determine the time for dispatching the goods and/or the destination, give the seller sufficient notice thereof.

A8 Proof of delivery, transport document or equivalent electronic message

The seller must provide the buyer at the seller's expense, if customary, with the usual transport document or documents (for example a negotiable bill of lading, a non-negotiable sea waybill, an inland waterway document, an air waybill, a railway consignment note, a road consignment note, or a multimodal transport document) for the transport contracted in accordance with A3.

Where the seller and the buyer have agreed to communicate electronically, the document referred to in the preceding paragraph may be replaced by an equivalent electronic data interchange (EDI) message

B8 Proof of delivery, transport document or equivalent electronic message

The buyer must accept the transport document in accordance with A8 if it is in conformity with the contract.

A9 Checking - packaging - marking

The seller must pay the costs of those checking operations (such as checking quality, measuring, weighing, counting) which are necessary for the purpose of delivering the goods in accordance with A4.

The seller must provide at his own expense packaging (unless it is usual for the particular trade to send the goods of the contract description unpacked) which is required for the transport of the goods arranged by him. Packaging is to be marked appropriately.

B9 Inspection of goods

The buyer must pay the costs of any pre-shipment inspection except when such inspection is mandated by the authorities of the country of export.

A10 Other obligations

The seller must render the buyer at the latter's request, risk and expense, every assistance in obtaining any documents or equivalent electronic messages (other than those mentioned in A8) issued or transmitted in the country of dispatch and/or of origin which the buyer may require for the import of the goods and for their transit through any country.

The seller must provide the buyer, upon request, with the necessary information for procuring any additional insurance.

B10 Other obligations

The buyer must pay all costs and charges incurred in obtaining the documents or equivalent electronic messages mentioned in A10 and reimburse those incurred by the seller in rendering his assistance in accordance therewith.

The buyer must provide the seller, upon request, with the necessary information for procuring any additional insurance.

Appendix III

Uniform Customs and Practice for Documentary Credits

ICC Publication No. 600　Effective July 1, 2007

Article 1　Application of UCP

The Uniform Customs and Practice for Documentary Credits, 2007 Revision, ICC Publication no. 600 ("UCP") are rules that apply to any documentary credit ("credit") (including, to the extent to which they may be applicable, any standby letter of credit) when the text of the credit expressly indicates that it is subject to these rules. They are binding on all parties thereto unless expressly modified or excluded by the credit.

Article 2　Definitions

For the purpose of these rules:

Advising bank means the bank that advises the credit at the request of the issuing bank.

Applicant means the party on whose request the credit is issued.

Banking day means a day on which a bank is regularly open at the place at which an act subject to these rules is to be performed.

Beneficiary means the party in whose favour a credit is issued.

Complying presentation means a presentation that is in accordance with the terms and conditions of the credit, the applicable provisions of these rules and international standard banking practice.

Confirmation means a definite undertaking of the confirming bank, in addition to that of the issuing bank, to honour or negotiate a complying presentation.

Confirming bank means the bank that adds its confirmation to a credit upon the issuing bank's authorization or request.

Credit means any arrangement, however named or described, that is irrevocable and thereby constitutes a definite undertaking of the issuing bank to honour a complying presentation.

Honour means:

a. to pay at sight if the credit is available by sight payment.

b. to incur a deferred payment undertaking and pay at maturity if the credit is available by deferred payment.

c. to accept a bill of exchange ("draft") drawn by the beneficiary and pay at maturity if the credit is available by acceptance.

Issuing bank means the bank that issues a credit at the request of an applicant or on its own behalf.

Negotiation means the purchase by the nominated bank of drafts (drawn on a bank other than the nominated bank) and/or documents under a complying presentation, by advancing or agreeing to advance funds to the beneficiary on or before the banking day on which reimbursement is due to to be paid the nominated bank.

Nominated bank means the bank with which the credit is available or any bank in the case of a credit available with any bank.

Presentation means either the delivery of documents under a credit to the issuing bank or nominated bank or the documents so delivered.

Presenter means a beneficiary, bank or other party that makes a presentation.

Article 3 Interpretations

For the purpose of these rules:

Where applicable, words in the singular include the plural and in the plural include the singular.

A credit is irrevocable even if there is no indication to that effect.

A document may be signed by handwriting, facsimile signature, perforated signature, stamp, symbol or any other mechanical or electronic method of authentication.

A requirement for a document to be legalized, visaed, certified or similar will be satisfied by any signature, mark, stamp or label on the document which appears to satisfy that requirement.

Branches of a bank in different countries are considered to be separate banks.

Terms such as "first class", "well known", "qualified", "independent", "official", "competent" or "local" used to describe the issuer of a document allow any issuer except the beneficiary to issue that document.

Unless required to be used in a document, words such as "prompt", "immediately" or "as soon as possible" will be disregarded.

The expression "on or about" or similar will be interpreted as a stipulation that an event is to occur during a period of five calendar days before until five calendar days after the specified date, both start and end dates included.

The words "to", "until", "till", "from" and "between" when used to determine a period of shipment include the date or dates mentioned, and the words "before" and "after" exclude the date mentioned.

The words "from" and "after" when used to determine a maturity date exclude the date mentioned.

The terms "first half" and "second half" of a month shall be construed respectively as the 1st to the 15th and the 16th to the last day of the month, all dates inclusive.

The terms "beginning", "middle" and "end" of a month shall be construed respectively as the 1st to the 10th, the 11th to the 20th and the 21st to the last day of the month, all dates inclusive.

Article 4　Credits v. Contracts

a. A credit by its nature is a separate transaction from the sale or other contract on which it may be based. Banks are in no way concerned with or bound by such contract, even if any reference whatsoever to it is included in the credit. Consequently, the undertaking of a bank to honour, to negotiate or to fulfil any other obligation under the credit is not subject to claims or defences by the applicant resulting from its relationships with the issuing bank or the beneficiary. A beneficiary can in no case avail itself of the contractual relationships existing between banks or between the applicant and the issuing bank.

b. An issuing bank should discourage any attempt by the applicant to include, as an integral part of the credit, copies of the underlying contract, proforma invoice and the like.

Article 5　Documents v. Goods, Services or Performance

Banks deal with documents and not with goods, services or performance to which the documents may relate.

Article 6　Availability, Expiry Date and Place for Presentation

a. A credit must state the bank with which it is available or whether it is available with any bank. A credit available with a nominated bank is also available with the issuing bank.

b. A credit must state whether it is available by sight payment, deferred payment, acceptance or negotiation.

c. A credit must not be issued available by a draft drawn on the applicant.

d. i. A credit must state an expiry date for presentation. An expiry date stated for honour or negotiation will be deemed to be an expiry date for presentation.

   ii. The place of the bank with which the credit is available is the place for presentation. The place for presentation under a credit available with any bank is that of any bank. A place for presentation other than that of the issuing bank is in addition to the place of the issuing bank.

e. Except as provided in sub-article 29 (a), a presentation by or on behalf of the beneficiary must be made on or before the expiry date.

Article 7 Issuing Bank Undertaking

a. Provided that the stipulated documents are presented to the nominated bank or to the issuing bank and that they constitute a complying presentation, the issuing bank must honour if the credit is available by:

i. sight payment, deferred payment or acceptance with the issuing bank;

ii. sight payment with a nominated bank and that nominated bank does not pay;

iii. deferred payment with a nominated bank and that nominated bank does not incur its deferred payment undertaking or, having incurred its deferred payment undertaking, does not pay at maturity;

iv. acceptance with a nominated bank and that nominated bank does not accept a draft drawn on it or, having accepted a draft drawn on it, does not pay at maturity;

v. negotiation with a nominated bank and that nominated bank does not negotiate.

b. An issuing bank is irrevocably bound to honour as of the time it issues the credit.

c. An issuing bank undertakes to reimburse a nominated bank that has honoured or negotiated a complying presentation and forwarded the documents to the issuing bank. Reimbursement for the amount of a complying presentation under a credit available by acceptance or deferred payment is due at maturity, whether or not the nominated bank prepaid or purchased before maturity. An issuing bank's undertaking to reimburse a nominated bank is independent of the issuing bank's undertaking to the beneficiary.

Article 8 Confirming Bank Undertaking

a. Provided that the stipulated documents are presented to the confirming bank or to any other nominated bank and that they constitute a complying presentation, the confirming bank must:

i. honour, if the credit is available by:

a) sight payment, deferred payment or acceptance with the confirming bank;

b) sight payment with another nominated bank and that nominated bank does not pay;

c) deferred payment with another nominated bank and that nominated bank does not incur its deferred payment undertaking or, having incurred its deferred payment undertaking, does not pay at maturity;

d) acceptance with another nominated bank and that nominated bank does not accept a draft drawn on it or, having accepted a draft drawn on it, does not pay at maturity;

e) negotiation with another nominated bank and that nominated bank does not negotiate.

ii. negotiate, without recourse, if the credit is available by negotiation with the confirming bank.

b. A confirming bank is irrevocably bound to honour or negotiate as of the time it adds its confirmation to the credit.

c. A confirming bank undertakes to reimburse another nominated bank that has honoured or negotiated a complying presentation and forwarded the documents to the confirming bank. Reimbursement for the amount of a complying presentation under a credit available by acceptance or deferred payment is due at maturity, whether or not another nominated bank prepaid or purchased before maturity. A confirming bank's undertaking to reimburse another nominated bank is independent of the confirming bank's undertaking to the beneficiary.

d. If a bank is authorized or requested by the issuing bank to confirm a credit but is not prepared to do so, it must inform the issuing bank without delay and may advise the credit without confirmation.

Article 9 Advising of Credits and Amendments

a. A credit and any amendment may be advised to a beneficiary through an advising bank. An advising bank that is not a confirming bank advises the credit and any amendment without any undertaking to honour or negotiate.

b. By advising the credit or amendment, the advising bank signifies that it has satisfied itself as to the apparent authenticity of the credit or amendment and that the advice accurately reflects the terms and conditions of the credit or amendment received.

c. An advising bank may utilize the services of another bank ("second advising bank") to advise the credit and any amendment to the beneficiary. By advising the credit or amendment, the second advising bank signifies that it has satisfied itself as to the apparent authenticity of the advice it has received and that the advice accurately reflects the terms and conditions of the credit or amendment received.

d. A bank utilizing the services of an advising bank or second advising bank to advise a credit must use the same bank to advise any amendment thereto.

e. If a bank is requested to advise a credit or amendment but elects not to do so, it must so inform, without delay, the bank from which the credit, amendment or advice has been received.

f. If a bank is requested to advise a credit or amendment but cannot satisfy itself as to the apparent authenticity of the credit, the amendment or the advice, it must so inform, without delay, the bank from which the instructions appear to have been received. If the advising bank or second advising bank elects nonetheless to advise the credit or amendment, it must inform the beneficiary or second advising bank that it has not been able to satisfy itself as to the apparent authenticity of the credit, the amendment or the advice.

Article 10 Amendments

a. Except as otherwise provided by article 38, a credit can neither be amended nor cancelled without the agreement of the issuing bank, the confirming bank, if any, and the beneficiary.

b. An issuing bank is irrevocably bound by an amendment as of the time it issues the amendment. A confirming bank may extend its confirmation to an amendment and will be irrevocably bound as of the time it advises the amendment. A confirming bank may, however, choose to advise an amendment without extending its confirmation and, if so, it must inform the issuing bank without delay and inform the beneficiary in its advice.

c. The terms and conditions of the original credit (or a credit incorporating previously accepted amendments) will remain in force for the beneficiary until the beneficiary communicates its acceptance of the amendment to the bank that advised such amendment. The beneficiary should give notification of acceptance or rejection of an amendment. If the beneficiary fails to give such notification, a presentation that complies with the credit and to any not yet accepted amendment will be deemed to be notification of acceptance by the beneficiary of such amendment. As of that moment the credit will be amended.

d. A bank that advises an amendment should inform the bank from which it received the amendment of any notification of acceptance or rejection.

e. Partial acceptance of an amendment is not allowed and will be deemed to be notification of rejection of the amendment.

f. A provision in an amendment to the effect that the amendment shall enter into force unless rejected by the beneficiary within a certain time shall be disregarded.

Article 11 Teletransmitted and Pre-Advised Credits and Amendments

a. An authenticated teletransmission of a credit or amendment will be deemed to be the operative credit or amendment, and any subsequent mail confirmation shall be disregarded.

If a teletransmission states "full details to follow" (or words of similar effect), or states that the mail confirmation is to be the operative credit or amendment, then the teletransmission will not be deemed to be the operative credit or amendment. The issuing bank must then issue the operative credit or amendment without delay in terms not inconsistent with the teletransmission.

b. A preliminary advice of the issuance of a credit or amendment ("pre-advice") shall only be sent if the issuing bank is prepared to issue the operative credit or amendment. An issuing bank that sends a pre-advice is irrevocably committed to issue the operative credit or amendment, without delay, in terms not inconsistent with the pre-advice.

Article 12 Nomination

a. Unless a nominated bank is the confirming bank, an authorization to honour or negotiate does not impose any obligation on that nominated bank to honour or negotiate, except when expressly agreed to by that nominated bank and so communicated to the beneficiary.

b. By nominating a bank to accept a draft or incur a deferred payment undertaking, an issuing bank authorizes that nominated bank to prepay or purchase a draft accepted or a deferred payment undertaking incurred by that nominated bank.

c. Receipt or examination and forwarding of documents by a nominated bank that is not a confirming bank does not make that nominated bank liable to honour or negotiate, nor does it constitute honour or negotiation.

Article 13 Bank-to-Bank Reimbursement Arrangements

a. If a credit states that reimbursement is to be obtained by a nominated bank ("claiming bank") claiming on another party ("reimbursing bank"), the credit must state if the reimbursement is subject to the ICC rules for bank-to-bank reimbursements in effect on the date of issuance of the credit.

b. If a credit does not state that reimbursement is subject to the ICC rules for bank-to-bank reimbursements, the following apply:

i. An issuing bank must provide a reimbursing bank with a reimbursement authorization that conforms with the availability stated in the credit. The reimbursement authorization should not be subject to an expiry date.

ii. A claiming bank shall not be required to supply a reimbursing bank with a certificate of compliance with the terms and conditions of the credit.

iii. An issuing bank will be responsible for any loss of interest, together with any expenses incurred, if reimbursement is not provided on first demand by a reimbursing bank in accordance with the terms and conditions of the credit.

iv. A reimbursing bank's charges are for the account of the issuing bank. However, if the charges are for the account of the beneficiary, it is the responsibility of an issuing bank to so indicate in the credit and in the reimbursement authorization. If a reimbursing bank's charges are for the account of the beneficiary, they shall be deducted from the amount due to a claiming bank when reimbursement is made. If no reimbursement is made, the reimbursing bank's charges remain the obligation of the issuing bank.

c. An issuing bank is not relieved of any of its obligations to provide reimbursement if reimbursement is not made by a reimbursing bank on first demand.

Article 14 Standard for Examination of Documents

a. A nominated bank acting on its nomination, a confirming bank, if any, and the issuing bank must examine a presentation to determine, on the basis of the documents alone, whether or not the documents appear on their face to constitute a complying presentation.

b. A nominated bank acting on its nomination, a confirming bank, if any, and the issuing bank shall each have a maximum of five banking days following the day of presentation to determine if a presentation is complying. This period is not curtailed or otherwise affected by the occurrence on or after the date of presentation of any expiry date or last day for presentation.

c. A presentation including one or more original transport documents subject to articles 19, 20, 21, 22, 23, 24 or 25 must be made by or on behalf of the beneficiary not later than 21 calendar days after the date of shipment as described in these rules, but in any event not later than the expiry date of the credit.

d. Data in a document, when read in context with the credit, the document itself and international standard banking practice, need not be identical to, but must not conflict with, data in that document, any other stipulated document or the credit.

e. In documents other than the commercial invoice, the description of the goods, services or performance, if stated, may be in general terms not conflicting with their description in the credit.

f. If a credit requires presentation of a document other than a transport document, insurance document or commercial invoice, without stipulating by whom the document is to be issued or its data content, banks will accept the document as presented if its content appears to fulfil the function of the required document and otherwise complies with sub-article 14 (d).

g. A document presented but not required by the credit will be disregarded and may be returned to the presenter.

h. If a credit contains a condition without stipulating the document to indicate compliance with the condition, banks will deem such condition as not stated and will disregard it.

i. A document may be dated prior to the issuance date of the credit, but must not be dated later than its date of presentation.

j. When the addresses of the beneficiary and the applicant appear in any stipulated document, they need not be the same as those stated in the credit or in any other stipulated document, but must be within the same country as the respective addresses mentioned in the credit. Contact details (telefax, telephone, email and the like) stated as part of the beneficiary's and the applicant's address will be disregarded. However, when the address and contact details of the applicant appear as part of the consignee or notify party details on a transport document subject to articles 19, 20, 21, 22, 23, 24 or 25, they must be as stated in the credit.

k. The shipper or consignor of the goods indicated on any document need not be the beneficiary of the credit.

l. A transport document may be issued by any party other than a carrier, owner, master or charterer provided that the transport document meets the requirements of articles 19, 20, 21, 22, 23 or 24 of these rules.

Article 15 Complying Presentation

a. When an issuing bank determines that a presentation is complying, it must honour.

b. When a confirming bank determines that a presentation is complying, it must honour or negotiate and forward the documents to the issuing bank.

c. When a nominated bank determines that a presentation is complying and honours or negotiates, it must forward the documents to the confirming bank or issuing bank.

Article 16 Discrepant Documents, Waiver and Notice

a. When a nominated bank acting on its nomination, a confirming bank, if any, or the issuing bank determines that a presentation does not comply, it may refuse to honour or negotiate.

b. When an issuing bank determines that a presentation does not comply, it may in its sole judgement approach the applicant for a waiver of the discrepancies. This does not, however, extend the period mentioned in sub-article 14 (b).

c. When a nominated bank acting on its nomination, a confirming bank, if any, or the issuing bank decides to refuse to honour or negotiate, it must give a single notice to that effect to the presenter.

The notice must state:

i. that the bank is refusing to honour or negotiate; and

ii. each discrepancy in respect of which the bank refuses to honour or negotiate; and

iii. a) that the bank is holding the documents pending further instructions from the presenter; or

b) that the issuing bank is holding the documents until it receives a waiver from the applicant and agrees to accept it, or receives further instructions from the presenter prior to agreeing to accept a waiver; or

c) that the bank is returning the documents; or

d) that the bank is acting in accordance with instructions previously received from the presenter.

d. The notice required in sub-article 16 (c) must be given by telecommunication or, if that is not possible, by other expeditious means no later than the close of the fifth banking day following the day of presentation.

e. A nominated bank acting on its nomination, a confirming bank, if any, or the issuing bank may, after providing notice required by sub-article 16 (c) (iii) (a) or (b), return the documents to the presenter at any time.

f. If an issuing bank or a confirming bank fails to act in accordance with the provisions of this article, it shall be precluded from claiming that the documents do not constitute a complying presentation.

g. When an issuing bank refuses to honour or a confirming bank refuses to honour or negotiate and has given notice to that effect in accordance with this article, it shall then be entitled to claim a refund, with interest, of any reimbursement made.

Article 17 Original Documents and Copies

a. At least one original of each document stipulated in the credit must be presented.

b. A bank shall treat as an original any document bearing an apparently original signature, mark, stamp, or label of the issuer of the document, unless the document itself indicates that it is not an original.

c. Unless a document indicates otherwise, a bank will also accept a document as original if it:

i. appears to be written, typed, perforated or stamped by the document issuer's hand; or

ii. appears to be on the document issuer's original stationery; or

iii. states that it is original, unless the statement appears not to apply to the document presented.

d. If a credit requires presentation of copies of documents, presentation of either originals or copies is permitted.

e. If a credit requires presentation of multiple documents by using terms such as "in duplicate", "in two fold" or "in two copies", this will be satisfied by the presentation of at least one original and the remaining number in copies, except when the document itself indicates otherwise.

Article 18 Commercial Invoice

a. A commercial invoice:

i. must appear to have been issued by the beneficiary (except as provided in article 38);

ii. must be made out in the name of the applicant (except as provided in sub-article 38 (g));

iii. must be made out in the same currency as the credit; and

iv. need not be signed.

b. A nominated bank acting on its nomination, a confirming bank, if any, or the issuing bank may accept a commercial invoice issued for an amount in excess of the amount permitted by the credit, and its decision will be binding upon all parties, provided the bank in question has not honoured or negotiated for an amount in excess of that permitted by the credit.

c. The description of the goods, services or performance in a commercial invoice must correspond with that appearing in the credit.

Article 19 Transport Document Covering at Least Two Different Modes of Transport

a. A transport document covering at least two different modes of transport (multimodal or combined transport document), however named, must appear to:

i. indicate the name of the carrier and be signed by:

- the carrier or a named agent for or on behalf of the carrier, or
- the master or a named agent for or on behalf of the master.

Any signature by the carrier, master or agent must be identified as that of the carrier, master or agent.

Any signature by an agent must indicate whether the agent has signed for or on behalf of the carrier or for or on behalf of the master.

ii. indicate that the goods have been dispatched, taken in charge or shipped on board at the place stated in the credit, by:

- pre-printed wording, or
- a stamp or notation indicating the date on which the goods have been dispatched, taken in charge or shipped on board.

The date of issuance of the transport document will be deemed to be the date of dispatch, taking in charge or shipped on board, and the date of shipment. However, if the transport document indicates, by stamp or notation, a date of dispatch, taking in charge or shipped on board, this date will be deemed to be the date of shipment.

iii. indicate the place of dispatch, taking in charge or shipment and the place of final destination stated in the credit, even if:

a) the transport document states, in addition, a different place of dispatch, taking in charge or shipment or place of final destination, or

b) the transport document contains the indication "intended" or similar qualification in relation to the vessel, port of loading or port of discharge.

iv. be the sole original transport document or, if issued in more than one original, be the full set as indicated on the transport document.

v. contain terms and conditions of carriage or make reference to another source containing the terms and conditions of carriage (short form or blank back transport document). Contents of terms and conditions of carriage will not be examined.

vi. contain no indication that it is subject to a charter party.

b. For the purpose of this article, transhipment means unloading from one means of conveyance and reloading to another means of conveyance (whether or not in different modes of transport) during the carriage from the place of dispatch, taking in charge or shipment to the place of final destination stated in the credit.

c. i. A transport document may indicate that the goods will or may be transhipped provided that the entire carriage is covered by one and the same transport document.

ii. A transport document indicating that transhipment will or may take place is acceptable, even if the credit prohibits transhipment.

Article 20 Bill of Lading

a. A bill of lading, however named, must appear to:

i. indicate the name of the carrier and be signed by:

- the carrier or a named agent for or on behalf of the carrier, or
- the master or a named agent for or on behalf of the master.

Any signature by the carrier, master or agent must be identified as that of the carrier, master or agent.

Any signature by an agent must indicate whether the agent has signed for or on behalf of the carrier or for or on behalf of the master.

ii. indicate that the goods have been shipped on board a named vessel at the port of loading stated in the credit by:

- pre-printed wording, or
- an on board notation indicating the date on which the goods have been shipped on board.

The date of issuance of the bill of lading will be deemed to be the date of shipment unless the bill of lading contains an on board notation indicating the date of shipment, in which case the date stated in the on board notation will be deemed to be the date of shipment.

If the bill of lading contains the indication "intended vessel" or similar qualification in relation to the name of the vessel, an on board notation indicating the date of shipment and the name of the actual vessel is required.

iii. indicate shipment from the port of loading to the port of discharge stated in the credit.

If the bill of lading does not indicate the port of loading stated in the credit as the port of loading, or if it contains the indication "intended" or similar qualification in relation to the port of loading, an on board notation indicating the port of loading as stated in the credit, the date of shipment and the name of the vessel is required. This provision applies even when loading on board or shipment on a named vessel is indicated by pre-printed wording on the bill of lading.

iv. be the sole original bill of lading or, if issued in more than one original, be the full set as indicated on the bill of lading.

v. contain terms and conditions of carriage or make reference to another source containing the terms and conditions of carriage (short form or blank back bill of lading). Contents of terms and conditions of carriage will not be examined.

vi. contain no indication that it is subject to a charter party.

b. For the purpose of this article, transhipment means unloading from one vessel and reloading to another vessel during the carriage from the port of loading to the port of discharge stated in the credit.

c. i. A bill of lading may indicate that the goods will or may be transhipped provided that the entire carriage is covered by one and the same bill of lading.

ii. A bill of lading indicating that transhipment will or may take place is acceptable, even if the credit prohibits transhipment, if the goods have been shipped in a container, trailer or LASH barge as evidenced by the bill of lading.

d. Clauses in a bill of lading stating that the carrier reserves the right to tranship will be disregarded.

Article 21 Non-Negotiable Sea Waybill

a. A non-negotiable sea waybill, however named, must appear to:

i. indicate the name of the carrier and be signed by:

- the carrier or a named agent for or on behalf of the carrier, or
- the master or a named agent for or on behalf of the master.

Any signature by the carrier, master or agent must be identified as that of the carrier, master or agent.

Any signature by an agent must indicate whether the agent has signed for or on behalf of the carrier or for or on behalf of the master.

ii. indicate that the goods have been shipped on board a named vessel at the port of loading stated in the credit by:

- pre-printed wording, or
- an on board notation indicating the date on which the goods have been shipped on board.

The date of issuance of the non-negotiable sea waybill will be deemed to be the date of shipment unless the non-negotiable sea waybill contains an on board notation indicating the date of shipment, in which case the date stated in the on board notation will be deemed to be the date of shipment.

If the non-negotiable sea waybill contains the indication "intended vessel" or similar qualification in relation to the name of the vessel, an on board notation indicating the date of shipment and the name of the actual vessel is required.

iii. indicate shipment from the port of loading to the port of discharge stated in the credit.

If the non-negotiable sea waybill does not indicate the port of loading stated in the credit as the port of loading, or if it contains the indication "intended" or similar qualification in relation to the port of loading, an on board notation indicating the port of loading as stated in the credit, the date of shipment and the name of the vessel is required. This provision applies even when loading on board or shipment on a named vessel is indicated by pre-printed wording on the non-negotiable sea waybill.

iv. be the sole original non-negotiable sea waybill or, if issued in more than one original, be the full set as indicated on the non-negotiable sea waybill.

v. contain terms and conditions of carriage or make reference to another source containing the terms and conditions of carriage (short form or blank back non-negotiable sea waybill). Contents of terms and conditions of carriage will not be examined.

vi. contain no indication that it is subject to a charter party.

b. For the purpose of this article, transhipment means unloading from one vessel and reloading to another vessel during the carriage from the port of loading to the port of discharge stated in the credit.

c. i. A non-negotiable sea waybill may indicate that the goods will or may be transhipped provided that the entire carriage is covered by one and the same non-negotiable sea waybill.

ii. A non-negotiable sea waybill indicating that transhipment will or may take place is acceptable, even if the credit prohibits transhipment, if the goods have been shipped in a container, trailer or LASH barge as evidenced by the non-negotiable sea waybill.

d. Clauses in a non-negotiable sea waybill stating that the carrier reserves the right to tranship will be disregarded.

Article 22 Charter Party Bill of Lading

a. A bill of lading, however named, containing an indication that it is subject to a charter party (charter party bill of lading), must appear to:

i. be signed by:

- the master or a named agent for or on behalf of the master, or
- the owner or a named agent for or on behalf of the owner, or
- the charterer or a named agent for or on behalf of the charterer.

Any signature by the master, owner, charterer or agent must be identified as that of the master, owner, charterer or agent.

Any signature by an agent must indicate whether the agent has signed for or on behalf of the master, owner or charterer.

An agent signing for or on behalf of the owner or charterer must indicate the name of the owner or charterer.

ii. indicate that the goods have been shipped on board a named vessel at the port of loading stated in the credit by:

- pre-printed wording, or
- an on board notation indicating the date on which the goods have been shipped on board.

The date of issuance of the charter party bill of lading will be deemed to be the date of shipment unless the charter party bill of lading contains an on board notation indicating the date of shipment, in which case the date stated in the on board notation will be deemed to be the date of shipment.

iii. indicate shipment from the port of loading to the port of discharge stated in the credit. The port of discharge may also be shown as a range of ports or a geographical area, as stated in the credit.

iv. be the sole original charter party bill of lading or, if issued in more than one original, be the full set as indicated on the charter party bill of lading.

b. A bank will not examine charter party contracts, even if they are required to be presented by the terms of the credit.

Article 23 Air Transport Document

a. An air transport document, however named, must appear to:

i. indicate the name of the carrier and be signed by:

- the carrier, or
- a named agent for or on behalf of the carrier.

Any signature by the carrier or agent must be identified as that of the carrier or agent.

Any signature by an agent must indicate that the agent has signed for or on behalf of the carrier.

ii. indicate that the goods have been accepted for carriage.

iii. indicate the date of issuance. This date will be deemed to be the date of shipment unless the air transport document contains a specific notation of the actual date of shipment, in which case the date stated in the notation will be deemed to be the date of shipment.

Any other information appearing on the air transport document relative to the flight number and date will not be considered in determining the date of shipment.

iv. indicate the airport of departure and the airport of destination stated in the credit.

v. be the original for consignor or shipper, even if the credit stipulates a full set of originals.

vi. contain terms and conditions of carriage or make reference to another source containing the terms and conditions of carriage. Contents of terms and conditions of carriage will not be examined.

b. For the purpose of this article, transhipment means unloading from one aircraft and reloading to another aircraft during the carriage from the airport of departure to the airport of destination stated in the credit.

c. i. An air transport document may indicate that the goods will or may be transhipped, provided that the entire carriage is covered by one and the same air transport document.

ii. An air transport document indicating that transhipment will or may take place is acceptable, even if the credit prohibits transhipment.

Article 24 Road, Rail or Inland Waterway Transport Documents

a. A road, rail or inland waterway transport document, however named, must appear to:

i. indicate the name of the carrier and:

- be signed by the carrier or a named agent for or on behalf of the carrier, or
- indicate receipt of the goods by signature, stamp or notation by the carrier or a named agent for or on behalf of the carrier.

Any signature, stamp or notation of receipt of the goods by the carrier or agent must be identified as that of the carrier or agent.

Any signature, stamp or notation of receipt of the goods by the agent must indicate that the agent has signed or acted for or on behalf of the carrier.

If a rail transport document does not identify the carrier, any signature or stamp of the railway company will be accepted as evidence of the document being signed by the carrier.

ii. indicate the date of shipment or the date the goods have been received for shipment, dispatch or carriage at the place stated in the credit. Unless the transport document contains a dated reception、stamp, an indication of the date of receipt or a date of shipment, the date of issuance of the transport document will be deemed to be the date of shipment.

iii. indicate the place of shipment and the place of destination stated in the credit.

b. i. A road transport document must appear to be the original for consignor or shipper or bear no marking indicating for whom the document has been prepared.

ii. A rail transport document marked “duplicate” will be accepted as an original.

iii. A rail or inland waterway transport document will be accepted as an original whether marked as an original or not.

c. In the absence of an indication on the transport document as to the number of originals issued, the number presented will be deemed to constitute a full set.

d. For the purpose of this article, transhipment means unloading from one means of conveyance and reloading to another means of conveyance, within the same mode of transport, during the carriage from the place of shipment, dispatch or carriage to the place of destination stated in the credit.

e. i. A road, rail or inland waterway transport document may indicate that the goods will or may be transhipped provided that the entire carriage is covered by one and the same transport document.

ii. A road, rail or inland waterway transport document indicating that transhipment will or may take place is acceptable, even if the credit prohibits transhipment.

Article 25 Courier Receipt, Post Receipt or Certificate of Posting

a. A courier receipt, however named, evidencing receipt of goods for transport, must appear to:

i. indicate the name of the courier service and be stamped or signed by the named courier service at the place from which the credit states the goods are to be shipped; and

ii. indicate a date of pick-up or of receipt or wording to this effect. This date will be deemed to be the date of shipment.

b. A requirement that courier charges are to be paid or prepaid may be satisfied by a transport document issued by a courier service evidencing that courier charges are for the account of a party other than the consignee.

c. A post receipt or certificate of posting, however named, evidencing receipt of goods for transport, must appear to be stamped or signed and dated at the place from which the credit states the goods are to be shipped. This date will be deemed to be the date of shipment.

Article 26 "On Deck", "Shipper's Load and Count", "Said by Shipper to Contain" and Charges Additional to Freight

a. A transport document must not indicate that the goods are or will be loaded on deck. A clause on a transport document stating that the goods may be loaded on deck is acceptable.

b. A transport document bearing a clause such as "shipper's load and count" and "said by shipper to contain" is acceptable.

c. A transport document may bear a reference, by stamp or otherwise, to charges additional to the freight.

Article 27 Clean Transport Document

A bank will only accept a clean transport document. A clean transport document is one bearing no clause or notation expressly declaring a defective condition of the goods or their packaging. The word "clean" need not appear on a transport document, even if a credit has a requirement for that transport document to be "clean on board".

Article 28 Insurance Document and Coverage

a. An insurance document, such as an insurance policy, an insurance certificate or a declaration under an open cover, must appear to be issued and signed by an insurance company, an underwriter or their agents or their proxies.

   Any signature by an agent or proxy must indicate whether the agent or proxy has signed for or on behalf of the insurance company or underwriter.

b. When the insurance document indicates that it has been issued in more than one original, all originals must be presented.

c. Cover notes will not be accepted.

d. An insurance policy is acceptable in lieu of an insurance certificate or a declaration under an open cover.

e. The date of the insurance document must be no later than the date of shipment, unless it appears from the insurance document that the cover is effective from a date not later than the date of shipment.

f. i. The insurance document must indicate the amount of insurance coverage and be in the same currency as the credit.

   ii. A requirement in the credit for insurance coverage to be for a percentage of the value of the goods, of the invoice value or similar is deemed to be the minimum amount of coverage required.

   If there is no indication in the credit of the insurance coverage required, the amount of insurance coverage must be at least 110% of the CIF or CIP value of the goods.

   When the CIF or CIP value cannot be determined from the documents, the amount of insurance coverage must be calculated on the basis of the amount for which honour or negotiation is requested or the gross value of the goods as shown on the invoice, whichever is greater.

   iii. The insurance document must indicate that risks are covered at least between the place of taking in charge or shipment and the place of discharge or final destination as stated in the credit.

g. A credit should state the type of insurance required and, if any, the additional risks to be covered. An insurance document will be accepted without regard to any risks that are not covered if the credit uses imprecise terms such as "usual risks" or "customary risks".

h. When a credit requires insurance against "all risks" and an insurance document is presented containing any "all risks" notation or clause, whether or not bearing the heading "all risks", the insurance document will be accepted without regard to any risks stated to be excluded.

i. An insurance document may contain reference to any exclusion clause.

j. An insurance document may indicate that the cover is subject to a franchise or excess (deductible).

Article 29 Extension of Expiry Date or Last Day for Presentation

a. If the expiry date of a credit or the last day for presentation falls on a day when the bank to which presentation is to be made is closed for reasons other than those referred to in article 36, the expiry date or the last day for presentation, as the case may be, will be extended to the first following banking day.

b. If presentation is made on the first following banking day, a nominated bank must provide the issuing bank or confirming bank with a statement on its covering schedule that the presentation was made within the time limits extended in accordance with sub-article 29 (a).

c. The latest date for shipment will not be extended as a result of sub-article 29 (a).

Article 30 Tolerance in Credit Amount, Quantity and Unit Prices

a. The words "about" or "approximately" used in connection with the amount of the credit or the quantity or the unit price stated in the credit are to be construed as allowing a tolerance not to exceed 10% more or 10% less than the amount, the quantity or the unit price to which they refer.

b. A tolerance not to exceed 5% more or 5% less than the quantity of the goods is allowed, provided the credit does not state the quantity in terms of a stipulated number of packing units or individual items and the total amount of the drawings does not exceed the amount of the credit.

c. Even when partial shipments are not allowed, a tolerance not to exceed 5% less than the amount of the credit is allowed, provided that the quantity of the goods, if stated in the credit, is shipped in full and a unit price, if stated in the credit, is not reduced or that sub-article 30 (b) is not applicable. This tolerance does not apply when the credit stipulates a specific tolerance or uses the expressions referred to in sub-article 30 (a).

Article 31 Partial Drawings or Shipments

a. Partial drawings or shipments are allowed.

b. A presentation consisting of more than one set of transport documents evidencing shipment commencing on the same means of conveyance and for the same journey, provided they indicate the same destination, will not be regarded as covering a partial shipment, even if they indicate different dates of shipment or different ports of loading, places of taking in charge or dispatch. If the presentation consists of more than one set of transport documents, the latest date of shipment as evidenced on any of the sets of transport documents will be regarded as the date of shipment.

A presentation consisting of one or more sets of transport documents evidencing shipment on more than one means of conveyance within the same mode of transport will be regarded as covering a partial shipment, even if the means of conveyance leave on the same day for the same destination.

c. A presentation consisting of more than one courier receipt, post receipt or certificate of posting will not be regarded as a partial shipment if the courier receipts, post receipts or certificates of posting appear to have been stamped or signed by the same courier or postal service at the same place and date and for the same destination.

Article 32 Installment Drawings or Shipments

If a drawing or shipment by installments within given periods is stipulated in the credit and any installment is not drawn or shipped within the period allowed for that installment, the credit ceases to be available for that and any subsequent installment.

Article 33 Hours of Presentation

A bank has no obligation to accept a presentation outside of its banking hours.

Article 34 Disclaimer on Effectiveness of Documents

A bank assumes no liability or responsibility for the form, sufficiency, accuracy, genuineness, falsification or legal effect of any document, or for the general or particular conditions stipulated in a document or superimposed thereon; nor does it assume any liability or responsibility for the description, quantity, weight, quality, condition, packing, delivery, value or existence of the goods, services or other performance represented by any document, or for the good faith or acts or omissions, solvency, performance or standing of the consignor, the carrier, the forwarder, the consignee or the insurer of the goods or any other person.

Article 35 Disclaimer on Transmission and Translation

A bank assumes no liability or responsibility for the consequences arising out of delay, loss in transit, mutilation or other errors arising in the transmission of any messages or delivery of letters or documents, when such messages, letters or documents are transmitted or sent according to the requirements stated in the credit, or when the bank may have taken the initiative in the choice of the delivery service in the absence of such instructions in the credit.

If a nominated bank determines that a presentation is complying and forwards the documents to the issuing bank or confirming bank, whether or not the nominated bank has honoured or negotiated, an issuing bank or confirming bank must honour or negotiate, or reimburse that nominated bank, even when the documents have been lost in transit between the nominated bank and the issuing bank or confirming bank, or between the confirming bank and the issuing bank.

A bank assumes no liability or responsibility for errors in translation or interpretation of technical terms and may transmit credit terms without translating them.

Article 36 Force Majeure

A bank assumes no liability or responsibility for the consequences arising out of the interruption of its business by Acts of God, riots, civil commotions, insurrections, wars, acts of terrorism, or by any strikes or lockouts or any other causes beyond its control.

A bank will not, upon resumption of its business, honour or negotiate under a credit that expired during such interruption of its business.

Article 37 Disclaimer for Acts of an Instructed Party

a. A bank utilizing the services of another bank for the purpose of giving effect to the instructions of the applicant does so for the account and at the risk of the applicant.

b. An issuing bank or advising bank assumes no liability or responsibility should the instructions it transmits to another bank not be carried out, even if it has taken the initiative in the choice of that other bank.

c. A bank instructing another bank to perform services is liable for any commissions, fees, costs or expenses ("charges") incurred by that bank in connection with its instructions.

If a credit states that charges are for the account of the beneficiary and charges cannot be collected or deducted from proceeds, the issuing bank remains liable for payment of charges.

A credit or amendment should not stipulate that the advising to a beneficiary is conditional upon the receipt by the advising bank or second advising bank of its charges.

d. The applicant shall be bound by and liable to indemnify a bank against all obligations and responsibilities imposed by foreign laws and usages.

Article 38 Transferable Credits

a. A bank is under no obligation to transfer a credit except to the extent and in the manner expressly consented to by that bank.

b. For the purpose of this article:

Transferable credit means a credit that specifically states it is "transferable". A transferable credit may be made available in whole or in part to another beneficiary ("second beneficiary") at the request of the beneficiary ("first beneficiary").

Transferring bank means a nominated bank that transfers the credit or, in a credit available with any bank, a bank that is specifically authorized by the issuing bank to transfer and that transfers the credit. An issuing bank may be a transferring bank.

Transferred credit means a credit that has been made available by the transferring bank to a second beneficiary.

c. Unless otherwise agreed at the time of transfer, all charges (such as commissions, fees, costs or expenses) incurred in respect of a transfer must be paid by the first beneficiary.

d. A credit may be transferred in part to more than one second beneficiary provided partial drawings or shipments are allowed.

A transferred credit cannot be transferred at the request of a second beneficiary to any subsequent beneficiary. The first beneficiary is not considered to be a subsequent beneficiary.

e. Any request for transfer must indicate if and under what conditions amendments may be advised to the second beneficiary. The transferred credit must clearly indicate those conditions.

f. If a credit is transferred to more than one second beneficiary, rejection of an amendment by one or more second beneficiary does not invalidate the acceptance by any other second beneficiary, with respect to which the transferred credit will be amended accordingly. For any second beneficiary that rejected the amendment, the transferred credit will remain unamended.

g. The transferred credit must accurately reflect the terms and conditions of the credit, including confirmation, if any, with the exception of:

— the amount of the credit,

— any unit price stated therein,

— the expiry date,

— the period for presentation, or

— the latest shipment date or given period for shipment,

— any or all of which may be reduced or curtailed.

The percentage for which insurance cover must be effected may be increased to provide the amount of cover stipulated in the credit or these articles.

The name of the first beneficiary may be substituted for that of the applicant in the credit.

If the name of the applicant is specifically required by the credit to appear in any document other than the invoice, such requirement must be reflected in the transferred credit.

h. The first beneficiary has the right to substitute its own invoice and draft, if any, for those of a second beneficiary for an amount not in excess of that stipulated in the credit, and upon such substitution the first beneficiary can draw under the credit for the difference, if any, between its invoice and the invoice of a second beneficiary.

i. If the first beneficiary is to present its own invoice and draft, if any, but fails to do so on first demand, or if the invoices presented by the first beneficiary create discrepancies that did not exist in the presentation made by the second beneficiary and the first beneficiary fails to correct them on first demand, the transferring bank has the right to present the documents as received from the second beneficiary to the issuing bank, without further responsibility to the first beneficiary.

j. The first beneficiary may, in its request for transfer, indicate that honour or negotiation is to be effected to a second beneficiary at the place to which the credit has been transferred, up to and including the expiry date of the credit. This is without prejudice to the right of the first beneficiary in accordance with sub-article 38 (h).

k. Presentation of documents by or on behalf of a second beneficiary must be made to the transferring bank.

Article 39 Assignment of Proceeds

The fact that a credit is not stated to be transferable shall not affect the right of the beneficiary to assign any proceeds to which it may be or may become entitled under the credit, in accordance with the provisions of applicable law. This article relates only to the assignment of proceeds and not to the assignment of the right to perform under the credit.

References

[1] Brenton Paul. *International Trade*. Oxford University Press, 1997.

[2] Goldsmith, Howard R. *Import/Export*. Prentice Hall, 1989.

[3] Michael R. Czinkota, Ilkka A. Ronkainen, Michael H. Moffett. *International Business* (4th Edition). Singapore: Harcourt Brace & Company Asia Pte Ltd, 1996.

[4] William G. Nickels, James M. McHugh, and Susan M. McHugh. *Understanding Business* (6th Edition). McGraw-Hill, 2002.

[5] Schmitthoff C M. *Export Trade, the law and practice of international trade*. London: Sweet & Maxwell, 2000.

[6] 程达军. 李延玉. 国际贸易实务. 北京：高等教育出版社，2006.

[7] 曹　菱. 外贸英语实务. 北京：外语教学与研究出版社，2000.

[8] 程怀儒. 国际贸易实务. 北京：人民教育出版社，2006.

[9] 刘法公. 国际贸易实务英语. 杭州：浙江大学出版社，2002.

[10] 黎孝先. 国际贸易实务. 北京：对外经济贸易大学出版社，2000.

[11] 国际商会中国国家委员会. 2000 年国际贸易术语解释通则. 上海：中信出版社，2000.

[12] 帅建林. 国际贸易实务(英文版). 成都：西南财经大学出版社，2005.

[13] 帅建林. 国际贸易惯例案例解析(中英文). 北京：对外经济贸易大学出版社，2006.

[14] 孙湘生, 易滟. 国际贸易实务. 北京：清华大学出版社，北京交通大学出版社，2005.

[15] 王沅沅. 国际贸易实务. 北京：高等教育出版社，2002.

[16] 吴百福. 进出口贸易实务教程(第 4 版). 上海：上海人民出版社，2003.

[17] 翁凤翔. 国际商贸实践. 杭州：浙江大学出版社，2004.

[18] 邹　勇. 国际商贸英语实务. 成都：西南财经大学出版社，2006.

[19] 张立玉，何康民. 国际贸易进出口实务. 武汉：武汉大学出版社，2004.

[20] 张素芳. 国际贸易理论与实务. 北京：对外经济贸易大学出版社，2003.

[21] 周耀宗，庄学艺编著. 进出口业务概要. 上海：上海外语教育出版社，2000.

[22] 祝 卫. 出口贸易模拟操作教程. 上海：上海人民出版社，1999.

[23] 姚曾荫. 国际贸易概论. 北京：人民出版社，1987.

[24] 杨丽华，董俊英. 贸易实务英语. 北京：首都经济贸易大学出版社，2000.

[25] 尹翔硕. 国际贸易教程(第二版). 上海：复旦大学出版社，2002.

[26] 薛荣久. 国际贸易. 成都：四川人民出版社，1995.